Sri
VENKATESWARA

Sri VENKATESWARA

Lord Balaji and His Holy Abode of Tirupathi

Shantha Nair

JAICO PUBLISHING HOUSE
Ahmedabad Bangalore Bhopal Bhubaneswar Chennai
Delhi Hyderabad Kolkata Lucknow Mumbai

Published by Jaico Publishing House
A-2 Jash Chambers, 7-A Sir Phirozshah Mehta Road
Fort, Mumbai - 400 001
jaicopub@jaicobooks.com
www.jaicobooks.com

© Shantha Nair

SRI VENKATESWARA
ISBN 978-81-8495-445-6

First Jaico Impression: 2013

No part of this book may be reproduced or utilized in
any form or by any means, electronic or
mechanical including photocopying, recording or by any
information storage and retrieval system,
without permission in writing from the publishers.

Printed by

Placed at the sacred feet of Lord Venkateswara
With utmost gratitude and pranams.

Acknowledgements

I am grateful to the Tirumala-Tirupathi Devasthanams (TTD). Much of the information given in this book was sourced from the TTD official website and also from books in the Central Library of the TTD. These are books either published by the TTD or published with financial aid provided by the TTD. I am also grateful to the authors of these books. I whole-heartedly thank the authors of several other books and articles and the hosts of many websites about Tirupathi and Tirumala for valuable information about Tirupathi, Tirumala and the temples and places of interest in and around Tirupathi.

I am grateful to my husband Sri K C N Nair for his continuous support, advice, help, guidance and cooperation. I take pride in mentioning the fact that I could obtain most of the material for writing this book because of the constant assistance and help of my son Uday Gowri Shankar. Since his infancy he has been brought up in Tirupathi and he earnestly feels, along with my husband and me, that our family owes its immense blessings to Lord Venkateswara. May the Lord guide him, protect him and bless him always. I am thankful to my daughter-in-law Roopa Shankar for her cooperation. My grandchildren Pranav Shankar and Gayatri Shankar who have also been brought up in Tirupathi since their infancy, I hope, would feel the same way as their father, my son, and be grateful for all the blessings of the Lord and become good human beings when they grow up. Last but not the least, I owe my gratitude to my late uncle Sri K N Chandrasekharan Nair for encouraging me, till his last breath, to write books.

Preface

The glory, sanctity and antiquity of the sacred Hill known as Tirumala and that of the Teerthas or the holy springs that are found there, the Temple located on top of it and most important, the Supreme power or energy that resides in the inner core of all beings, and that has manifested itself as Lord Venkateswara or Srinivasa, is beyond human understanding.

However, an attempt is made in this book to describe the sanctity, glory and antiquity of the Temple through the legendary tales found in the various Puranas and in the beliefs of the Bhakthas. The Deity, the Temple and the sacred Hill known as Tirumala attract millions of devotees. It is considered 'Kaliyuga Vaikunta' and the Deity the 'Kaliyuga Varada' who washes away all the sins of His devotees and grants material prosperity and a happy and peaceful life on Earth for all who sincerely pray to him. He uplifts the minds of those who take refuge in Him and liberates them from the sorrows of life. He blesses them with the experience of Sat-Chit-Ananda that is Existence-Consciousness-Bliss.

An effort is also made to explain the history of the sacred Hill, the Temple and Tirupathi and Tirumala regions. The structure of the Temple, the inscriptions found on the walls and the Sevas and festivals are also described.

A short sketch of the various activities of the Tirumala

Tirupathi Devasthanams that administers this Temple and that is taken mainly from the TTD official website is also presented here.

This book is a guide to the visiting pilgrim, both to first-time and regular devotees. I have compiled and summarised the information that I collected from various sources. Therefore any credit due goes to the authors of the sources from where the required information could be obtained and not to the author of this book. The book was written as a mark of gratitude to Lord Venkateswara for all His blessings. I place it at His feet. May the Lord forgive me for any errors. May the Lord bless all beings on Earth with material and spiritual well-being, happiness and peace.

— Dr. Shantha N Nair

Contents

1	Tirupathi and Tirumala	1
2	Sanctity, Glory and Antiquity of the Deity and Tirumala	42
3	Sanctity of the Teerthas of Tirumala	75
4	History of Tirupathi, Tirumala and the Temple	94
5	Important Contributions of Kings, Mahants, TTD and Other Devotees	118
6	History of Festivals, Vahana and Administration	157
7	The Structure of the Temple	180
8	The Deity, Sevas, Festivals and Darshan of the Lord	204
9	The Tirumala Tirupathi Devasthanams (TTD)	236

1
Tirupathi and Tirumala

TIRUPATHI

Location

Tirupathi is a temple town and a major pilgrimage centre located in Chittoor district of southern Andhra Pradesh. It lies between 13°N and 79°E at an average elevation of about 162 m (531 feet) above sea level. Tirupathi nestles in a large circular plain that is surrounded by a chain of hills that form part of the Eastern Ghats. It is at the foot of the Tirumala hills in the north of this chain.

By road, it is around 740 km from Hyderabad, the capital of Andhra Pradesh, 150 km from Chennai, the capital of Tamil Nadu, and 250 km from Bengaluru, the capital of Karnataka.

Climate

Tirupathi experiences a moderate monsoon. In summer, from April to June, the temperature varies from 39°C to 43°C and in winter, from November to March, the minimum temperature falls to between 10°C and 15°C.

History

In his book *Symposium on Tirupathi Venkateswara*, Dr. Jagannatha Rao writes that Tirupathi's original name may have been 'Tripathi'. According to him, 'Tiru' derives from 'Tri' a Sanskrit word. The *Venkatesha Ashtakshari Mantra*, a form of the *Gayatri mantra* dedicated specially to Lord Venkateswara states, *"Venkateshaya Vidmahe, Tripathi Nadhaya Dheemahi, Thannoah Srinivasa Prachodayath."* Here the Lord is referred to as the 'Lord of Tripathy', denoting the sacred Hill.

Tirupathi is the gateway to Tirumala—the abode of Lord Srinivasa or Venkateswara. The town owes its existence to the famous shrine dedicated to the Lord on the Tirumala hills. In Tamil, 'thiru' means 'the sacred'. It also denotes Goddess Lakshmi and 'pathi' means 'husband'. So Tirupathi means the sacred abode of Lord Narayana or Vishnu. In the English translation of a few Malayalam manuscripts found at Chandragiri in 1802, the town below the sacred Hill is referred to as 'Tripati' as well as 'Teeropaty'. Whether these were Anglicised names that originated during British rule, is not known. In the Mackenzie collections, manuscript translations and reports translated from Marathi by Baboo Rao in 1804, 'Tripathy' was the name given to this town.

Around 1500 years ago, there was no human habitation below the sacred Hill. There was just a huge forest that extended all around the Hill stretching up to the Bay of Bengal in the east and the River Pinakini or Penna in the north and extending for miles towards the west and south. Gradually, with the growing importance and popularity of the temple upon the sacred Tirumala Hill, a village came up at its foot. It gradually grew into a town and the town acquired the name of the hill. Even today, many devotees refer to Tirupathi town as Lower Tirupathi and Tirumala as Upper Tirupathi. Originally the town was near

Kotturu, that is, the present KT Road area. Later it was shifted to the vicinity of the Sri Govindarajaswami temple.

In addition to the renowned temple of Lord Venkateswara and shrines in and around Tirupathi, there are also several other temples here. Right from olden times, Chandragiri and Tiruchanoor (once Thiruchokkanur), have been places of importance in the vicinity of Tirupathi.

Tiruchanoor is a small village that is about 5 km southwest of Tirupathi. It is also known as Alamelu Mangapuram, where the temple for Sri Padmavathi Devi, the consort of Lord Venkateswara, is located. Inscriptions on the walls of the ancient temples of Tirupathi indicate the existence of an equally old temple here that was known as 'Ilan Koil'. It is said that there was an 'Ilan Koil' important to Saivites at Tiruchanoor before the 7th century, when Saivism thrived here. Most probably, the Saivite temple was replaced around the 7th century by the Vaishnavite 'Ilan Koil'. This temple was called either Thiruvengadathu Perumanadigal, Thiruvilan Koil Perumanadigal or Thirumantrasalai Perumanadigal. The inscriptions here reveal that it was built towards the end of the 8th century. Tiruchanoor was practically the last point on the old highway known as Vadakkuvazhi that connected the Tamil country of Thondaimandalam with the region towards the north of the Hills known as the land of the Vadugars.

Chandragiri lies to the southwest of Tirupathi. It came into prominence during the time of Saluva Mangideva, the great-grandfather of Saluva Narasimha, one of the generals who served under the command of Vira Kumara Kampanna in the second quarter of the 14th century. Later, it grew in importance when the Saluva and Vijayanagara kings built their forts and palaces here. It was the second capital of the Vijayanagara empire.

Modern Tirupathi

Although Chittoor is the district headquarters, most of the businesses and major government establishments are in Tirupathi. There are a few large and medium scale industries here—notable among them, the government-owned Railway Carriage Workshop, Amara Raja Power Systems and Lanco Industries. Tirupathi is one of the biggest hubs of education and centres of tourism and culture in Andhra Pradesh. It is also famous for its red wooden toys and copper and brass idols.

Tirupathi acquired special-grade Municipal Corporation status on 2nd March 2007. The Tirupathi Urban Development Authority (TUDA) expanded the town limits by about 1,380 km. TUDA looks after the development of Tirupathi. However, a major contributor to Tirupathi's progress and prosperity is the Tirumala-Tirupathi Devasthanams (TTD).

Tirupathi East and Tirupathi West are the two railway stations here. The Tirupathi East station has ten platforms. It is undergoing modernisation with the construction of three escalators. It is the fourth station in India to be recognised as world-class, next only to the Delhi, Mumbai and Secunderabad terminuses. The Renigunta junction is 10 km from Tirupathi. Most of the trains pass through Renigunta and Tirupathi East station is a major terminus.

Tirupathi is well-connected by road to all parts of the state and also the neighbouring states of Tamil Nadu and Karnataka. The town has a well-planned network of roads with a synchronised traffic control system. The Tirupathi Central Bus Station is the third-largest in Andhra Pradesh. It has more than 50 platforms. A number of private bus services and those operated by the Andhra Pradesh State Road Transport Corporation (APSRTC), connect Tirupathi to other cities and places in South India.

Tirupathi airport, located about 15 km from the city centre, is the third airport in Andhra Pradesh. At present, it is a domestic airport with regular flights operated by Indian Airlines to Hyderabad, New Delhi, Visakhapatnam, Chennai and Bengaluru. It is now being upgraded to an international airport.

Accommodation

There are a large number of private hotels here with boarding and lodging facilities besides the choultries and guest houses that are run by the TTD.

Demography

According to the 2011 provisional census report, the population of Tirupathi is 2,87,035 of which 1,45,977 are males and 1,41,058 are females, giving a sex ratio of 966 females per 1000 males. The average literacy rate is 87.55% (92.74% for males and 82.21% for females). The urban population is 4,59,985, of which 2,31,456 are males and 2,28,529 are females.

Telugu is the principal and official language here. There is a large floating pilgrim population, so associated services like travel and tourism are major sources of income for Tirupathi.

The TTD contributes significantly to the development of the city. Major roads like the Tirumala bypass and the railway subway near the East railway station were projects undertaken by the TTD jointly with TUDA.

Hospitals

Government and other Hospitals

The Ram Narayana Ruia Hospital (SVRR) is a government general hospital attached to the SV Medical College.

There is also a government-run maternity home and a children's hospital.

TTD Hospitals

- The Sri Venkateswara Institute of Medical Sciences (SVIMS) is a super-speciality hospital.
- The TTD Central Hospital is run by the TTD for its employees.
- The SV Ayurveda Hospital is attached to the Ayurveda College.
- BIRRD is an orthopaedic centre for the physically handicapped.
- The SV Health Centre is administered by the SV University for its employees.
- ESIS Hospital is meant for the health care of labour in industry.

Besides these, there are also a large number of private general and multi-speciality hospitals in Tirupathi.

Charitable Institutions

The TTD manages several old age homes and homes for the visually-impaired and mentally-challenged children in Tirupathi. It maintains an orphanage called Bala Mandir, a leprosy home and a school for hearing- and speech-impaired children. The BC and SC hostels are run by the government.

Educational Facilities

Tirupathi has several universities. The Sri Venkateswara University, Sri Padmavathi Mahila Vishva Vidyalaya (one of the two women's universities in the country), Rashtriya Sanskrit Vidyapeeth, Medical University, Vedic University and SV Agricultural University are some of them.

There are many schools offering classes from Nursery to Std.12, junior colleges, degree colleges, medical colleges, a number of colleges of engineering, management, computer applications, veterinary science, agriculture, Oriental studies, music, dentistry and law. These are managed by the concerned universities, the government, TTD and the private sector.

Temples in and Around Tirupathi

Sri Govindarajaswami Temple

According to legend, this shrine was consecrated by the great Vaishnava saint Sri Ramanujacharya around 1130 CE with the idol of Govindarajaswami in a reclining *yoga nidra* posture. Sri Govindaraja is believed to be the elder brother of Lord Venkateswara. It was built around 1628 by the Nayakars who were the successors of the Vijayanagara emperors. The innermost shrine is believed to have been constructed between the 14th and 15th centuries CE. This is a big temple, with a gopuram or tower rising seven storeys high. Several carvings depicting stories from the *Puranas* can be seen on the gopuram. The temple is located in the heart of Tirupathi town near the Tirupathi East railway station.

Inside the temple complex, there are many subsidiary shrines dedicated to Andal, Sri Parthasarathyswami, Sri Kalyana Venkateswara, Sri Salai Nachiyar Ammavaru, Sri Ramanuja, Sri Vyasaraya Anjaneya Swami and many others, including the Alwar saints. The idol of Lord Krishna as Parthasarathy or the charioteer of Arjuna, with His consorts Rukmini and Satyabhama, is said to have been the original deity of the temple and it was Sri Ramanuja who added the idol of Sri Govindaraja. Some parts of the inner shrine date back to the 9th and 10th centuries CE.

To the left of this temple, one can see the shrine of Goddess Mahalakshmi. Near the first gopuram, is the shrine for Vedantha Desika. Near the Vahana mandapam or pillared outdoor pavilion, one can see the memorial for the three Alwars namely,

Thirumallisai Alwar, Nammalwar and Kuratalwar, who were great devotees of Lord Vishnu. On the left of the second entrance is the idol of Lord Vishnu in His Kurmavatara (tortoise incarnation). There is a separate shrine for Sri Ramanuja on the left side of the second entrance.

The festivals celebrated in this temple are similar to those of the temple of Lord Venkateswara on Tirumala. The annual Brahmotsavam is held during May-June.

Sri Kodandaramaswami Temple

This temple with the deities of Sri Rama, Lakshmana and Sita, is also located in the heart of Tirupathi town. It is supposed to have been constructed by a Chola king in the 10th century CE and rebuilt in 1481 CE. The temple for Anjaneya Swami is located opposite.

The festivals conducted here are: the visit of Sri Rama to Tirupathi, Ugadi (the Telugu New Year day), Sri Rama Navami and the annual Brahmotsavam that is held during March-April.

Sri Kapileshwaraswami Temple

Excavated out of rock, this is a Shiva temple at the foot of the Tirumala Hills and lies 3 km north of Tirupathi. There is a separate shrine for Goddess Parvathi adjacent to the main shrine. It is believed that Sage Kapila had a *darshan* of Lord Shiva and His consort here and it is he who installed the *shivalinga.*

The deity here is named Kapileshwara and there is a waterfall called Kapila Teertha or Alwar Teertha. The water flows into the temple tank. Many subsidiary shrines, such as the shrines for Lord Venkateswara, Sri Venugopalaswami, Sri Lakshmi Narayana and Lord Ganesha are located inside the temple.

Pilgrims visit the shrine after taking a holy dip in the sacred tank and then proceed to Tirumala.

The festivals conducted here are: the annual Brahmotsavam,

Vinayaka Chathurthi, Mahashivaratri, Skanda Sashti, Karthika Deepam, Float Festival, Arudra Darshanam Utsavam, Navaratri and Kamakshi Devi Chandana Alankaram.

Gangamma Temple

Another temple in the city centre has a deity called Goddess Gangamma who is believed to be the sister of Lord Venkateswara.

The important festival conducted here is the Gangamma Jatra or Ganga Jatra celebrated for seven days in the month of May every year.

ISKCON Temple

This temple is located at the foot of the hills on land donated by the TTD. With towers of gold and white and interiors decorated with beautiful carvings, the ISKCON temple is a sight to behold. There are attractive carvings of Lord Narasimhaswami, Lord Varahaswami and Lord Krishna's *leelas* depicted in glass paintings on the windows. The ten avatars or incarnations of Lord Vishnu are depicted on the pillars. The ceilings are covered with beautiful artworks. In the sanctum, the idol of Lord Krishna with the *gopis* can be seen.

This temple has a lovely garden dotted with ponds, fountains and the idols of Lord Krishna. There is also a Goshala or cowshed. Sri Krishna Jayanthi is celebrated here in a grand manner.

Sri Padmavathi Temple

The shrine of Goddess Padmavathi, the consort of Lord Venkateswara, is at Tiruchanoor or Alamelu Mangapuram, about 3 km from Tirupathi. Padmavathi Devi is seated here in the *padmasana* or lotus pose holding lotuses in her front-facing hands.

The two hands in the rear are in *abhaya* and *varada hastas*.

It is believed that after Goddess Lakshmi left Vaikunta, she performed penance for 12 years in a temple tank here. Then in the 13th year of her penance, during the month of Karthika, on Panchami day, in the last fortnight of the star Uttarashada, Goddess Lakshmi emerged from a golden lotus. This is why the tank is known as Padma Sarovar and the Goddess is named Padmavathi.

It is said that a visit to the temple of Lord Venkateswara is complete only if the pilgrim visits the Sri Ammavari Temple at Tiruchanoor.

In the temple complex, there are shrines for Lord Krishna, Balarama, Sri Sundareshwara, and Sri Suryanarayana. The important festivals celebrated here include Padmavathi Parinayam, Dasara or Navaratri, Karthika Brahmotsavam, Float Festival, Vasanthotsavam and Ratha Sapthami.

Srivari Paduka Mandapam

It is located at the beginning of the footway to the Hill. It has been renovated recently. It bears the footprints of Lord Venkateswara along with the idol of the Lord. Devotees carry the Lord's sandals on their heads and circumambulate the main shrine before they climb the sacred Hill.

Lakshmi Narayana Temple

It is located at the foot of the Hill, at the point where the Sopana Marga or the pedestrian walkway to Tirumala starts.

Kalyana Venkateswaraswami Temple, Srinivasa Mangapuram

This village is about 12 km to the west of Tirupathi. The temple here houses Lord Venkateswara as Kalyana Venkateswara. It is believed that Lord Venkateswara stayed here after his wedding with Padmavathi Devi before proceeding to Tirumala.

The important festivals here are the annual Brahmotsavam and Sakshatkara Vaibhavam. Kalyanotsavam is also performed here by devotees.

Shiva Temple, Thondavada

This temple is about 10 km from Tirupathi. As the *shivalinga* here was installed by the sage Agasthya, the deity here is known as Agastheeshwara. The temple faces east and has three entrances enclosed by a big compound wall. There is a separate shrine for Goddess Parvathi adjacent to the main shrine of Lord Shiva. Parvathi is known here as Vallimatha. In the middle of the river that flows near the temple, there is a shrine for Lord Aiyappa.

Kalyana Venkateswaraswami Temple, Narayanavanam

This small village is located about 22 km to the southeast of Tirupathi. It is believed that Lord Srinivasa married Padmavathi Devi, daughter of Akasha Raju in this place. The temple has four small shrines for Sri Padmavathi, Andal, Sri Prayaga Madhavaswami and Sri Varadarajaswami. At the entrance in front of the sanctum is the small Garudalwar Sannidhi. In addition to these, there are five more temples attached to the main one. These are dedicated to Sri Parasareswara Swami, Sri Veerabhadra Swami, Sri Sakthi Vinayaka Swami, Sri Agastheeshwara Swami and Sri Avanakshamma.

The annual Brahmotsavam is conducted in the main Venkateswara temple here as well as in Veerabhadra Swami and Sri Avanakshamma temples. Navaratri celebrations are also held in the Avanakshamma temple. At the end of Sankranthi every year, Giri Pradakshinam, that is, circumambulation of the Hill, is held and the *utsava moorthis* of Sri Parasareswara Swami and Sri Champakavalli Ammavaru, Sri Agastheeshwaraswami and

Sri Marakathavalli Ammavaru are taken in procession. Other festivals include Andal Neerotsavam, Panguni Uttarotsavam, Varalakshmi Vrutham, Float Festival and Anivara Asthanam.

Vedanarayanaswami Temple, Nagalapuram

Located about 65 km southeast of Tirupathi, it is believed that Lord Narayana, in His *matsya* avatar, retrieved the *Vedas* after killing Somaka the *asura* here. This is an ancient stone temple probably built by the Cholas or Pallavas. Beautiful sculptures can be seen on the huge pillars in the Prakaram (circumambulatory and processional pathway) surrounding the sanctum. The idol of Lord Vishnu here is flanked by Sri Devi and Bhu Devi and the form of *matsya* or fish can be seen at its feet. The idol holds a *Sudarsana Chakra*. The temple has several subsidiary shrines devoted to Vedavathi Thayar (that faces the main sanctum and has a huge many-pillared mandapam), Kodandaramaswami, Lakshmi Varahaswami, Venugopalaswami, Lakshmi Narayana and Sri Hayagriva. There are also the sculptures of Vigneshwara and other gods, on the outer wall of the sanctum. There is a flagpost inside the main entrance.

Krishnadevaraya, the emperor of Vijayanagara, is said to have reconstructed the temple in the last years of his reign at the behest of his mother Nagamamba. It is said that this place was then known as Nagamambapuram. It is also said that as the work was begun when his reign was coming to an end, the emperor could not complete it.

The most important festivals in the main temple here are the annual Brahmotsavam, Soorya Puja and Float festival.

During the three days of the Soorya Puja, the sun's rays fall on the main deity from 6 to 6.15 pm On the first day, the sun's rays fall on the feet, the second day on the chest and the third day on the Lord's forehead. It is believed that during these days, the Sun god worships the deity.

Other Hindu festival days are also observed here, besides the periodical *sevas* or worship.

Prasanna Venkateswaraswami Temple, Appalaya Gunta

It is believed that Lord Venkateswara visited this place, about 15 km from Tirupathi, after his marriage with Goddess Padmavathi Devi and that He blessed Sri Siddeshwara along with other sages here. It also houses shrines for Anjaneya, Padmavathi Devi and Andal. The idol of Lord Venkateswara is in the *abhayahastha* pose here.

The imposing image of Anjaneya, the Wind god, is worshipped by devotees who pray for relief from chronic diseases.

The important festivals include the annual Brahmotsavam, Theppotsavam, Anivara Asthanam, Deepavali, Vaikunta Ekadasi and Dwadasi, Ratha Sapthami and Ugadi.

Sri Venugopalaswami Temple, Karvetinagaram

This town is about 58 km from Tirupathi and the main deity in the temple here is Lord Krishna along with His consorts Rukmini and Satyabhama. There is also a shrine here for Lord Rama accompanied by Sita Devi, Lakshmana and Anjaneya, the Parthasarathy, Avanakshamma and Renuka Parameshwari temples and Skanda Pushkarini.

The temple was once maintained by the Narayanavanam rulers.

The important festivals observed here include the annual Brahmotsavam, Utlotsavam, Vaikunta Ekadasi or Mukkoti Ekadasi, Ugadi, Gokulashtami, Teppotsavam and Sankranthi.

Sri Chennakeshavaswami Temple, Talappakka

It is located at a distance of about 100 km from Tirupathi. This is the birthplace of Sri Annamacharya who composed several *keerthanas* or Carnatic music compositions praising Lord

Venkateswara. According to legend, the temple is nearly a thousand years old.

There are two subsidiary shrines here—one for Siddheshwara Swami along with Kamakshi and the other for Chakrathalwar.

The important festivals held here are the annual Brahmotsavam, Annamacharya Jayanthi and Vardanthi Utsavam.

Venkateswaraswami Temple, Kalikiri

It is believed by some that this is the spot where the Lord first stepped on Earth. Situated on top of Kalikiri Hill near Puthalapattu, Chittoor, it is 75 km from Tirupathi.

Kashi Vishwanathaswami Temple, Buqqa Agraharam

This temple, on the outskirts of Nagari on the banks of Kusasthali River, is 56 km from Tirupathi. It houses the idols of Kashi Vishwanatha, His consort Goddess Annapurna, Kamakshi Devi and Prayaga Madhava Swami along with His consorts Sri Devi and Bhu Devi.

The important festivals held here are Mahasivaratri, Karthika Somavaram, Pradosham and Kala Bhairava Ashtami.

Sri Kariyamanikyaswami Temple (Perumalaswami Temple), Nagari

This temple is located at a distance of 51 km from Tirupathi. It is believed that Lord Vishnu liberated Gajendra, the elephant and Makara the crocodile here (as found in the episode 'Gajendra Moksham' in *Srimad Bhagavatham*).

The Kanchi Garuda Seva, Kanuma Utsavam, Ratha Sapthami and Vaikunta Ekadasi are celebrated here.

Ardhagiri Veeranjaneya Temple

At Aragonda, nearly 82 km from Tirupathi, this temple on the hill is believed to be the half of the Sanjeevini mountain that fell down (hence the name Ardhagiri) when Lord Hanuman was transporting it. On it grew the life-giving herbs that revived Lakshmana during the Lanka war.

Sri Rama Temple, Vayalpadu (Valmikipuram)

It is located 100 km from Tirupathi. The shrine of Pattabhi Rama has the idols of Sri Rama, Sita, Lakshmana, Bharatha, Shatrughna and Anjaneya. There is also a hill here called 'Veeranna Konda' with the shrine of Veerabhadra. It is said that the sage Valmiki sat on this hill while writing the *Ramayana*. Here the main idol faces north.

Sri Vinayakaswami Temple, Kanippakkam

This temple to Lord Vinayaka, also known as Varasiddhi Vinayaka, is supposed to have been constructed by Kulothunga, a Chola king, in the 11th century CE. It is 70 km from Tirupathi and stands on the banks of the river Bahuda. It was renovated by the Vijayanagara emperors in the 14th century CE.

It is said that the idol of Lord Ganesha is slowly outgrowing its silver *kavacham* or armour!

Subramanyaswami Temple, Tiruttani

This shrine to Lord Subramanya, 70 km from Tirupathi, is on a rock that rises 210 m above sea level. It is one of the six *padai veedu* (battlegrounds) where Lord Muruga fought to destroy evil forces. It is considered to be the place where the Lord stayed after slaying the demon Sura Padman. It is also the spot where the Lord married Valli.

The hill is called 'Thanikai'. The temple has four *Prakarams* and a series of towers. The tank at the foot of the hill is known as Saravana Poigai, the sacred pond where Lord Karthikeya was born. Its water is said to have curative powers and is rich in minerals.

In the lush garden on the southern side, the *saptharishis* are believed to have worshipped Lord Subramanya. The *sapthakannika* or virgins are enshrined in a tiny temple.

There is a pathway as well as a motorable road to reach the summit. The pathway has 365 steps.

The monthly Krithika festival attracts a large number of devotees. Besides this, the two major festivals held here are the Adi Krithikai and the New Year Step Festival on December 31.

Shiva Temple, Sri Kalahasthi

Located on the banks of the Swarnamukhi, a tributary of the Penna, Kalahasthi is 38 km from Tirupathi. According to legend, the river was originally called Uttaravahini. It changed its course and began to flow near the temple at Sage Agasthya's request.

Also known as Dakshina Kailasam, it has a famous ancient temple to Lord Shiva. It is one of the *panchabhootha linga* shrines where Lord Shiva is personified as the element of *vayu* or air. The flame of the oil lamp kept in the sanctum sanctorum flickers even in the total absence of a breeze inside.

There is a shrine to Kannappa, a great hunter and devotee of Lord Shiva who is believed to have attained liberation here, on a hillock that lies to the east of the main temple. The Durgamba Hill, that is mentioned as Kanakachala in legend, has a small shrine dedicated to Sri Durgamba. There is also the Kumaraswami Hill where there is a small shrine for Lord Subramanya.

Sukhabrahmasramam is located on the far bank of the river and Kailasramam, at a distance of 6 km from the temple. Battinayyakonda is in the midst of a forest that is 20 km from

Kalahasthi and it has a natural cave temple. The Malayalaswamiashramam is at Yerpedu. These are the important places of interest near Kalahasthi.

Pallikondeswaraswami Temple, Suruttupalli

About 70 km from Tirupathi, this temple is also dedicated to Lord Shiva and has an idol in a reclining posture. It is believed that Lord Shiva lay down here after consuming *halahala*, the poison that was meant to destroy the world.

There is a *sannidhi* for Parvathi Devi who is known here as Marakathambika and adjacent to it there is the *sannidhi* of Valmikeshwarar. The small Nandi in the outer *Prakaram* faces this sanctum. By its side is located the shrine of the main idol Pallikondeswaraswami.

There are three huge towers and beside the first entrance, there is a garden.

Shiva Temple, Yogimalleshwaram

It is a very ancient and famous Shiva temple said to have been built by a Chola king. It lies on the way to Tiruchanoor, 3 km from Tirupathi, and also has shrines dedicated to Ganapathi, Dakshinamurthy, Chandi, Kumaraswami and Brahma.

Places of Interest in and Around Tirupathi

SV Dairy Farm

The Sri Venkateswara Dairy Farm supplies milk and yoghurt to all the TTD temples for rituals, *prasadams*, abhishekams etc., and to all the institutions run by the TTD.

SV Museum

It has excellent exhibits depicting temple architecture, idols and ancient weapons. It is located near Sri Govindaraja temple. It contains many sculptures, idols of Sri Krishna and so on. Photographs of all the important 108 Vishnu temples are displayed here.

Grand World Amusement Park-cum-Resort

It is the only amusement park-cum-resort in the Rayalaseema region of Andhra Pradesh. It is a multi-dimensional theme park that is spread over 10 acres at the foot of the Tirumala Hills. It has 9 water rides. The water park has a ramp with simulated waves resembling a beach. There are also dodgem cars, boats and go-karts.

The 4,500-sq m air-cooled indoor amusement centre with food courts is an added attraction. There are also exciting video games like car racing, bike racing, shooting and skiing.

The laser show is only the second-such show in the country. Short films on spiritual themes are presented at the show.

There are 30 air-conditioned rooms, a multi-cuisine restaurant, a conference hall and huge party lawns.

Hasthakalamanram

Built by the Andhra Pradesh Tourism Development Corporation (APTDC) on the Tirupathi-Tiruchanoor Road, it is a showcase for Indian handicrafts and folk culture.

Chandragiri Fort

The fort is 14 km west of Tirupathi on a 56 m-high hill called Chandragiri or 'hill of the moon'. It is believed that Chandra, the Moon god, performed penance here to please Lord Shiva.

The fort is living testimony to the greatness of the Vijayanagara Empire. It contains the remains of palaces and temples constructed by the Vijayanagara kings. It was their second capital and also their last. It is said to have been built by Immadi Narasimha Yadavaraya in CE 1000. It was under the control of the Yadavarayas for about three centuries.

In 1646, the fort passed on to the Golconda rulers. Later, it came under the Mysore ruler who had it till 1792. It is now under the care of the Archaeological Survey of India.

The Shiva and Vishnu temples, the Rani Mahal and other structures are in a state of dilapidation.

The Raja Mahal, a brick-and-stone structure inside the fort, has now been converted into an archaeological museum.

The APTDC presents a daily *son-et-lumière* show based on the history of the fort.

S V Zoological Park

It is the second of its kind in Andhra Pradesh. Spread over an area of 506 sq.km, the wildlife sanctuary is dedicated to environmental studies. A unique feature here is the vast natural enclosure for animals to move around in freely.

Regional Science Centre

Established in 1993, the Regional Science Centre is affiliated to SV University and the National Council Of Science Museums. It is located at Alipiri, at the foot of the Tirumala Hills. It houses many attractive scientific and educational models and a planetarium. The centre conducts quarterly science exhibitions showcasing recent innovations in science and technology.

Kalyani Dam

The dam is 20 km from Tirupathi. It is constructed across the foot of the Seshachalam Hills.

Kailasanatha Kona

A natural waterfall that is 43 km from Tirupathi, Kailasanatha Kona is in Nagari valley near Tirupathi. The water here is considered sacred and is believed to contain minerals that have curative powers. An ancient but tiny shrine to Lord Shiva is found in a cave here.

Talakona

A 60 m-high perennial waterfall called the Talakona is located 40 km from Tirupathi in scenic surroundings. The place is also famous for the temple of Sri Siddheshwara Swami sited in the midst of a thick forest. Childless couples pray for progeny and name their children Siddiah or Siddhamma if their wish is fulfilled.

Horsley Hills

A hill resort located at an altitude of 1,265 m, Horsley Hills is about 150 km from Tirupathi. Originally known as Enugu Mallama Konda, it was later named after the-then collector of Cudappah, WD Horsley.

Mahathi Auditorium, Tirupathi

The enormous and beautiful TTD Mahathi Auditorium is located in the town and all cultural, religious and spiritual programmes organised by the TTD are held here.

Srinivasa Stadium, Tirupathi

This magnificent stadium is built in the shape of a giant hyperbola and is located in the centre of the sprawling campus of the SV University. It has a seating capacity of 2,500.

Municipal Park, Tirupathi

This sprawling park is located on the bypass road leading to Tirumala Hills. The dancing musical fountains are a special attraction here.

Mamandur Forest

It is a popular eco-tourism centre located 20 km from Tirupathi.

TIRUMALA

The Tirumala Hills (hereafter referred to as the 'Hills'), located between 13°N and 17°E, lie in the Eastern Ghats. They are believed to be a part of the mythical Meru mountain. This section of the Eastern Ghats starts from the Anamalai hills in the extreme south of India. It travels in a northeasterly direction up to the Talakona waterfalls, from where it deflects till it reaches Tirumala. To the east of Tirumala it ends in a gap. From Talakona to Tirumala, it is about 19 km as the crow flies.

Right from ancient times, this stretch of the ghat has been considered holy. The Kona or water course starting from Talakona Falls, which is the initial part of the waterfall, hence 'talakona', ends in Papavinasam. Rare herbs of medicinal value are found in plenty all over the Hills and particularly in the ravines. The Papavinasam Vanka is fed by many rivulets.

The height of the Hills at their northern face is about 1,074 m, at their eastern face about 825 m, at their southern side about 876 m, at their southwest about 1,086 m and to the west about 540 m to 600 m above sea level. The Hills slope sharply downwards to the plains. The tallest peak on the Talakona side is 1,074 m high while the Narayanagiri peak that is southwest of Tirumala temple, is 1,086 m high.

The Hills are made of rock that is the second-oldest in the world. According to scientists, the type of rock is granite and quartzite. The granite and gneiss that form the lower parts of these hills are more than 2,500 million years old.

The Venkatachalam range is also known as the Srisailam range or Seshachalam Hills, because it resembles Adisesha, the king of serpents. The *Puranas* compare this range to the celestial snake, Adisesha. Its hoods are at Tirumala, the abode of Lord Srinivasa, its middle is the abode of Ahobila Ugra Narasimha, its tail lies at the Srisailam temple and its mouth at Kalahasthi.

The temple of Lord Venkateswara stands in a shallow circular valley on top of the Venkatadri Hills or Vengadam Hills. This was once the northern border of the Tamil country and modern Karnataka and Andhra Pradesh that lay to its north, were then known as Vadugu.

The Tirumala Hills are around 26.8 sq km in area. They consist of seven peaks that represent the seven hoods of Adi Sesha. The first four peaks are almost flat and run in a continuous line, but the fifth, sixth and seventh peaks are separated by a deep gorge called Avasari Kona. The peaks are known as Seshadri, Neeladri, Garudari, Anjanadri, Vrishabhadri, Narayanadri and Venkatadri. The sacred shrine of Lord Venkateswara is located on the seventh peak, the Venkatadri. It is also known as Tirumala and the temple on it is one of the 108 sacred shrines in the Vaishnava tradition.

Adri in Sanskrit means 'hill'. It is referred to as 'Edu Kondalu' in Telugu. Seshadri means the Hill of Sesha on which Lord Vishnu reclines, Neeladri the Hill of Neela Devi and Garudari the Hill of Garuda, the *vahana* or vehicle of the Lord. Anjanadri means the Hill of Anjaneya or that of His mother Anjana Devi; Vrishabhadri refers to the Hill of Nandi, the *vahana* of Lord Shiva; Narayanadri means the Hill of Narayana; and Venkatadri means the Hill of Lord Venkateswara. The seven Hills are also supposed to represent the *saptharishi* or the seven sages.

Tirumala is 27 km from Tirupathi East railway station. The temple of Lord Venkateswara on the Tirumala Hills draws millions of devotees and is one of the biggest pilgrimage centres in the world. Till recently, it was the richest temple in the world (now the Padmanabhaswami temple in Kerala has been given that honour after a treasure trove was found locked in its vaults.)

In addition to the footway from Tirupathi town, there are two motorable roads to Tirumala. The starting point to go up the Hills is known as Alipiri and it is overlooked by an immense statue of Garuda in an *anjali* pose. There are two double-lane ghat roads, one to go up the Hills and the other, with 36 hairpin bends, to descend. Both the roads follow different paths along the Hills. The road coming down was laid in 1944. The other, ascending road, was laid in 1973. The distance from Alipiri is 22 km and it takes 40 minutes to reach the top.

The APSRTC buses ply daily between Tirupathi and Tirumala with a frequency of two minutes. During the Brahmotsavam, they run almost throughout the day and night. The APSRTC also has bus services (deluxe and ordinary) from nearly all the cities in Andhra Pradesh to Tirumala and from a few cities in the other southern states.

The APTDC also operates buses to Tirumala. Additionally, there is private transport available in the form of jeeps, vans and tourist taxis.

There are four footways to the Tirumala temple. One route starts from Tirupathi. The second is from Chandragiri, the third from Balupalli near the Mamandur railway station and the fourth footway is via Nagapatla.

The ascent was once made using a pathway paved with rough sandstone. In later years, a stone stairway was cut into the hill. This pathway is known as Sopana Marga. It covers a total of 11 km from Alipiri. This is the most important and the most popular pathway used by the pilgrims to climb up the Hill. The climb takes not less than 4 hours for an average person. After the steep and arduous ascent of the first Hill, the pilgrim approaches the big tower known as the Gali Gopuram that was built in the year 1628 by Matla Anantaraya. From here, there is a beautiful view of the landscape and the town below, the railway line, the river Swarna Mukhi, and the temples, towers and tanks dotting Tirupathi and Tiruchanoor. To the left rises a high, almost vertical, rock cliff.

At the Avachari Kona or Ammayar Koneru, there is a sharp descent and then a difficult ascent up the so-called 'knee-breaker' Hill that is known as 'Muzhangaal Mudichchu' in Tamil and 'Mokala Parvatham' in Telugu. Towards the top of this steep ascent there is a small mandapam and a shrine to Sri Ramanuja called Bhashyakar Sannidhi, which serves as a rest-stop. It is said that every day Sri Ramanuja studied the various inner meanings of the *Ramayana* under the guidance of Tirumalai Nambi here and this is where he was honoured after being bestowed the title of 'Emperumanar'.

All along the pathway, there are many mandapams. There is also a deep stepwell known as Muggu Bavi. At a short distance from the footway, is a structure called the Ghanta Mandapam where a bell was once kept. It was struck as soon as *naivedyam* was offered to the Lord at the temple. It is also said that Sri Ranganada Yadavaraya (1336-1356), a local chieftain who ruled this region, ate his noon meal only after hearing this bell at Chandragiri Mahal.

All along the footway from Alipiri, the TTD has provided rest-stops, security guards, canteens, drinking water, medical centres with ambulances at some points and toilet facilities. The luggage of the devotees who wish to walk up can be deposited with the TTD which transports it to Tirumala free of charge.

The ascent from Chandragiri is steep and the road is mainly used by traders and locals. It is only 6 km long but is very difficult to climb. There were also other paths once upon a time, like the one from Karakambadi and the forest path connecting Talakona in the west to the Hill.

The Glory and Sanctity of the Temple

Lord Venkateswara is also known as Venkanna, Venkatachalapathy, Balaji, Lord of the Seven Hills ('Edu Kondala Vadu' in Telugu and 'Ezhu Malaian' in Tamil), Srinivasa, Tirumal, Sripathi, Venkatapathi, Venkatanatha, Srivaru, Thiruvengadamudian, Maal, Manivannan, Thiruvengadanathan, Tirupathi Thinnappa, Venkataramana, Govinda and so on. He is called Kaliyuga Varada, that is, the wish-fulfilling Lord of Kaliyuga. Venkateswara means the supreme Lord who burns or destroys all past sins. 'Ven' means 'to burn', 'Kata' means 'past sins' and 'Ishwara' means 'the supreme Lord'. Venkatachalapathy means the one who resides in Venkadam. 'Ven' may also mean 'eternal', 'kata' may also stand for 'bliss' and therefore Venkateswara can mean the supreme God who grants eternal bliss to His devotees. Srinivasa refers to the Lord in whom Sri or the Goddess of Wealth Lakshmi resides, or the abode of Mahalakshmi. The Lord is usually referred as Balaji by the people hailing from northern India. Tirumal is another name for Lord Vishnu.

The idol's eyes are covered as it is said that His gaze is so powerful that it would scorch the universe. The holy *mantra* chanted here is *Om Namo Venkateshaya*.

The *prasadams* of this temple include the much-coveted *laddu*, *vada* and *dosa*. The *anna prasadams* or rice preparations offered to the Lord include curd rice, *puliyohara* and sweet *pongal*.

No one knows the exact sdate on which the idol was consecrated, so it is regarded as self-manifested or *swayambhu*. The sanctity and the antiquity of the temple that is constructed in the Dravidian style and the numerous *teerthas* found near it are described in several *Puranas* including the *Varaha Purana*, Padma Purana, Garuda Purana, Markandeya Purana, Hari Vamsa, Vamana Purana, Brahma Purana, Brahmottara Purana, Aditya Purana, Skanda Purana and Bhavishyottara Purana.

The ancient Vishnu Kautuvam describes the Lord as *soryarayan*, that is, 'the one who destroys evil and who protects'. The manifestation of Lord Srinivasa is described in *Venkatachala Mahatmyam* and *Varaha Purana*. The benefits acquired by a pilgrimage to Venkatachala are described in the Rig Veda and in the *Puranas*. The Sastras, *Puranas*, the Sthala Mahatmyams and Alwar hymns declare that one can attain *mukthi* in Kali Yuga by worshipping Lord Venkateswara (Balaji).

The Brahmanda Purana says:

Venkatadri samam sthaanam brahmaande naasthi kinchana
Venkatesha samo devo na bhuto na bhavishyathi.

It means that 'there is no parallel to Venkatachalam and there is no God equal to Venkateswara either in the past or in the future'.

It is also said that among all sacred places, Venkatadri is supreme and of all the *teerthas*, Swami Pushkarini is the holiest.

By singing the glory of Venkatachala, all sins are eradicated; so believe his ardent devotees. By saluting Sri Venkatachala all prosperity is attained. After a pilgrimage to Venkatachala, even the gods become worthy of adoration. Such is stated to be the glory of Venkatachala.

This temple was maintained and developed in the past by various dynasties like the Pallavas around the 4th century CE, the Cholas from the 2nd to the 10th century CE and finally by the emperors of Vijayanagara. Later the Mahants and the TTD took over the administration, maintenance and development.

From early times, many great saints have visited the temple and worshipped the Lord here. All three proponents of the Vedantha doctrine namely, Advaitha, Dvaitha and Visishtadvaitha, are believed to have come and sung the glory of the Lord. It is said that Adi Shankara, the proponent of Kevala Advaitha, worshipped the deity and placed the Sri Chakra at the feet of the Lord. The great Vaishnava *acharyas*, Sri Ramanujacharya and Madhavacharya paid obeisance and it was Sri Ramanuja who began the Vaishnava tradition here. The *Sri Venkatesa Ithihasamala*, a work belonging to the 13th century CE, mentions the association of Ramanuja with this temple and it relates how Ramanuja directed his disciple Anantaraya to supervise the rituals, worship and festivals, including Brahmotsavam. Sri Varadaradiraja Teertha, a Madhava saint, is believed to have climbed the sacred Hill on his knees and offered a garland of *saligrama* that represented Lord Vishnu.

Poets past and present have sung the glory of the Lord of the Seven Hills. Ilango's *Silappadikaram* and Saathanar's *Manimekhalai* that belong to Sangam-era literature dating to 500 BCE, mention Tiruvengadam. The Sangam literature describes the Lord and offerings to the Lord or *kainkaryam* in detail.

Nammalwar, the Tamil Vaishnava saint-poet, praised Lord Venkateswara as the medicine that cures all the ills of *samsara* or worldly life and that helps one escape the repeated cycle of births and deaths.

Kulasekhara Alwar prays to Lord Srinivasa to bless him with even the lowest of births such as a fish in the Swami Pushkarini or as a tree on the sacred Tirumala Hill, so that he can always be near the Lord. Poigai Alwar, Bhuthatha Alwar, Pei Alwar and the later Alwars have also sung the glory of the Lord. Till today, portions of the Tamil scripture *Nalayira Divya Prabandam* that consists of the songs of the Alwars, are sung everyday before the deity. Tirupathi, referring to Tirumala, is 'Kaliyuga Vaikuntam' according to the Alwars.

Talapakka Annamacharya, the great devotee of the Lord (1414-1503 CE) composed more than 32,000 hymns both in Sanskrit and Telugu in praise of Lord Venkateswara. Musicians like Purandaradasa, Thyagaraja, Muthuswami Dikshithar, Syama Sastri and several other well-known and lesser-known poets have also composed glowing paens of praise to the Lord of the Seven Hills.

The Temple has long been the beneficiary of the munificence

shown by devotees, both royal and common, from olden times. Contributions towards its upkeep and the daily performance of rituals were and are still made by private devotees and officials.

A number of centuries-old inscriptions on the stone walls of the temple record the names of the donors.

The Deity Represented by the Idol

It is said that till the time of Sri Ramanuja, the identity of the deity here was a matter of great dispute. The idol had no distinguishing marks or vehicles like most of the gods and goddesses in the Hindu pantheon. The conch and the disc that are usually associated with Lord Vishnu, were said to have been artificially fixed upon the shoulders of the idol at the time of Sri Ramanuja. The original image was not believed to have had them.

The original stone image is said to sport a crescent mark on the forehead and holds no divine weapons. It is also said that one can see matted locks, snake-shaped ornaments and a carving of a snake on the right arm of the idol. The Saivites also believe that originally the hands held the *trishula*, or trident and the *damaruka*, or the small drum, which are symbolic of Lord Shiva. Although the term Ishwara generally refers to God, it is usually meant to indicate Lord Shiva and the worship of the idol with *bilwa* leaves confirms this.

It is mentioned in the *Varaha Purana* that King Thondaiman was led by a parrot to a huntsman who took the king to Lord Venkateswara, who was seated under a Bilwa tree and this denoted His connection to Shiva.

The deity also has some associations with Sakthi, the female half of Shiva. The drapery resembles a saree. The deity is given a ceremonial bath on Fridays with sandalwood and turmeric paste and with turmeric water as in the case of goddesses. The ceremonial bath is accompanied by the chanting of *Sri Lakshmi*

Suktham. The Devi Bhagavatham is said to describe the Lord as 'Sri Venkateshwari'. The Tomala Seva to the Lord is also called 'Bhagavathi Aradhana' and Sri Suktha mantras are chanted during the abhishekam. Further Navaratri (Dasara) Brahmotsavams are also celebrated here. Usually Navaratri is especially dedicated to the worship of Goddess Sakthi. Further, Thiruppavada, a large quantity of rice symbolically coloured red and placed on a heap of margosa leaves, are offered to the deity as sacrifice. This appears to be a substitute for an animal sacrifice. It is also pointed out by some that the idol resembles the Durga idol at Thiruvanjikulam in Kerala. North Indians call Him Balaji, probably a name denoting Bala Tripura Sundari. So according to some, the idol represents Sakthi or Kali or Durga. The temple chariot and the temple walls also bear the 'Saktheya' symbol, depicting a lion.

The temple is located on top of a hill and a hunting festival is celebrated as is the case with Lord Subramanya. Further the holy tank is known as Swami Pushkarini. The term 'Swami' usually stands for Lord Subramanya. The *Vamana Purana* also states that Skanda performed penance here on instructions from His father Lord Shiva. So a few believe that the deity is a representation of Skanda.

It is also seen that the idol has a Srivatsam on the right side of the chest that is the emblem of Jains. Jainism thrived in southern India for a short period after the decline of Saivism and before the rise of Vaishnavism. Archaeological reports mention that ruins of Jain temples were found in the fort of Chandragiri and Narayanavanam which were the bastions of chieftains who ruled this region during that time.

The *Ithihasa Mala*, a Sanskrit work of the 12th century CE, states that during the controversy about the form that the idol represented, Sri Ramanuja is said to have requested the-then king to leave the weapons of Lord Vishnu and Lord Shiva in the temple and said that the matter would be resolved by the Lord

Himself. The king did as instructed and the doors of the sanctum were closed for the night. It is said that during the night, Sri Ramanuja approached the Lord as Adisesha and prayed that He assume the form of Lord Vishnu. When the Temple doors were opened the next morning, the Lord was found holding the conch and disc.

It is believed by Vaishnavaites that Kumaradhara, one of the holy *teerthas* located on the Hill, is the one associated with Lord Subramanya and that Swami Pushkarini has nothing to do with that god. It is also said that Bilwa leaves are acceptable to Goddess Lakshmi, the Lord's consort, therefore, to the Lord as well. Further it is said that Vishnu images are also permitted to have matted locks or *jata*. Lord Vishnu is also said to sport Naga figures in His ornaments as per *Padma Purana*. According to the *Bhavishya Purana*, the Naga jewels were presented by Akasha Raju to Lord Venkateswara, his son-in-law. The idol bears the Vakshasthala Lakshmi and the Srivatsa marks. It is believed that Lord Brahma and Lord Shiva visited this place to worship Lord Srinivasa.

Poigai Alwar, one of the early Alwars, saw both Hari (Lord Vishnu) and Hara (Lord Shiva) in this idol. Harihara is one whose vehicles are Nandi and the bird Garuda, whose residence is in the Kailasa Mountains as well as in the waters of the ocean, whose nature is both annihilation as well as protection of the Universe, in whose hands are the trident as well as disc and whose form is one of fire and clouds.

Bhuthatha Alwar and Pei Alwar saw the deity as one with *jata* or matted hair, the high crown, the shining dagger, the disc, the snake coiling His hand, and the golden *sutra* around His waist. He is the Lord of Tirumala in whom both the forms have merged into one. Another account, the authenticity of which is questionable, relates that once there was a dispute between Adi Shankara and Sri Ramanuja over the identity of the idol. Adi Shankara who was a devotee of both Lord Shankara as well as

Lord Vishnu, opined that the idol here represented Lord Shiva and not Lord Vishnu.

To prove his point that the idol represented Lord Vishnu, Sri Ramanuja placed the conch and disc in either hand of the idol and also drew a vertical *namam*, the marks of Lord Vishnu, on the forehead. It was a very dark night, so Sri Ramanuja could not see too well. He could not pinpoint the exact spot on the forehead, and this is said to be one of the reasons why the eyes of the idol are covered with the *namam*!

Sri Sitapathi, the former Commissioner of Archaeology and Chief Secretary to the Governor of Andhra Pradesh, in his book on the temple, says that the idol of Sri Venkateswara is not as per the Vaishnava *agamas*. Hence, it might not have been the image of Lord Vishnu originally but was later worshipped as Lord Vishnu.

He also says that the original idol must have been sculpted from the reddish igneous rock available in large quantities in the Tirumala area. Further, he mentions the records kept by a few British officers, like *Indian and Eastern Architecture – Volume 1*, that is based on JB Gibble's *The Temple of Vishnu on the Hill of Tirupathi*, published in 1875, and the district manual of North Arcot compiled by AF Fox in 1880 and revised by HH Stuart in 1895, which state that the idol was originally one of Lord Shiva.

Thus we find that the idol of the Tirumala temple exhibits features that support the differing claims made by different devotees.

However from the time of Sri Ramanuja, this idol has been worshipped as Lord Vishnu. Ramanuja, with the support of the local ruler Yadavaraya, gave the idol the form of Lord Vishnu by fixing the *shankha* and *chakra*, inaugurated the *vaikhanasa* form of worship, installed the other idols of Sri Rama, Sita and Lakshmana and introduced the recital of the Tamil *prabandams* composed by the Alwars.

These differing views about which deity the idol represents, only confirm the greatness of Hinduism. Hinduism is the only religion that gives complete freedom to the worshipper to view the deity in the form of his or her liking. The devotee can also see himself or herself in any relationship with the Divine that he or she chooses. After all, the different images are only the varied representations of the same supreme power or cosmic energy. It is like a ray of light passing through a prism and emerging in rainbow colours. So a dispute over which deity the image represents, is a sign of ignorance. The Rig Veda affirms that the Supreme is only one; the sages call it by many names.

As the great poet-devotee Annamayya has said, 'Brahmam Okade Para Brahmam Okade' and that it resides as the 'Antaratma' or the inner core in each and every being.

A legend goes that there was a contest between Vayu, the Lord of Wind and the great Adisesha on which Lord Vishnu reclines, to find out who was superior. During the fight, Sesha twisted his body around a portion of the Meru mountain and asked Vayu to lift it up. Vayu in turn filled the entire world with wind. When Sesha's hood was battered by the wind, he lifted it. Vayu entered the space and raised Meru. Sesha was also lifted along with the mountain.

After narrating this legend, Sri Jagannatha Rao in his book *Symposium on Tirupathi Venkateswara* states that in yoga, Meru is symbolic of *meru danda* or the vertebral column through which the physiological spinal cord and the psychological subtle *naadis* pass. While the spinal cord is visible to the naked eye, the *naadis* are so subtle, that they are visible only through yogic practices. *Merumukha* is the downward-turned or the *adhomukha swayambhu linga* located in the *mooladhara chakra*. Sesha represents the *kundalini shakthi*. The *kundalini shakthi* coils around the *linga* three-and-a-half times and its face or *brahma naadi mukham* is enclosed by its hood. This *linga* is of the colour of molten gold. When the yogi takes a deep breath (*vayu*), he fills the whole body with it and the anus is pulled up. The *apaana vayu* that unfurls the coils loosens the face of the *kundalini shakthi* that covers the *brahma naadi vivaram*. The *swayambhu linga* is raised upwards and forces the *kundalini shakthi* to pass through the *brahma naadi* to the *sahasrara chakra*—resulting in the realisation of Parabrahman.

According to the *Brahma Purana*, Meru is the Venkatachala Hills. Because of its molten red colour it was also called Kanakachala. So Venkatachala is the downward-facing *swayambhu linga* with the *kundalini shakthi*. Sri Rao feels that the seven hills represent the seven *kundalini chakras* that denote the different stages of ascent, beginning at the *mooladhara chakra* and reaching perfection at the seventh *chakra* namely the *sahasrara*.

Originally, the abode of the Lord was called 'Varaha Kshetra'. The first chakra is the *mooladhara chakra* that represents the Earth or Dharani or Bhoomi. According to mythology, Varaha is supposed to have rescued the Earth or Dharani. Sri *Varaha Purana* deals with *Dharani Varaha Samvada*. Dharani, that is the *kundalini shakthi* located in the *mooladhara*, is attended by two of her maids, that is the two *naadis* namely, Ida and Pingala. They prayed to Varaha and thanked Him for lifting Dharani up.

Rao points out that according to legend, Padmavathi Devi, the consort of the Lord is said to be the daughter of Akasha Raju and Dharani Devi. These parents represent the five *chakras*—from *mooladhara* that represents Dharani or Earth to *visudha* that represents *akasa* or space. The mind is related to these five elemental *chakras*. When the mind ascends to the sixth or *agnachakra*, it is lifted out of the five elements or *panchabhoothas*. It attains individuality or its own consciousness symbolised by the daughter Padmavathi Devi. Rising above the *agna chakra*, the mind enters the state of *unmani* or no-consciousness. This is the state when the yogi becomes Parabrahman.

The reason why the Lord has no consorts with Him inside the sanctum of the temple is that He represents the Parabrahman, the single Absolute without duality, who can only be experienced in the inner core of all beings, not explained in words.

The Temple Administration

Since 1933, the Tirumala-Tirupathi Devasthanams (TTD) has been looking after the administration of the Sri Venkateswara Temple on Tirumala and the other temples and their subsidiary shrines that are under its control. The TTD has undertaken several projects and schemes for the welfare of the pilgrims and for protecting and preserving the Hindu ethos and religion. It also provides several free facilities to pilgrims that include food, accommodation and amenities like a dormitory system with lockers, toilets and bathrooms, and free medical aid to the pilgrims who cannot afford to pay. These facilities can also be availed of on payment.

Besides these activities, the TTD has also taken up several projects in the fields of education, social service and all-round development of Tirumala and Tirupathi. The TTD receives donations from the devotees. The donations are deposited in a nationalised bank and only the interest is utilised for the schemes, along with a matching grant equal to the amount of the donation deposited by the TTD. Depending on the value of their donations, the donors are extended certain privileges by the TTD such as special *darshan* of the idol and *prasadam*.

There are many tanks and ponds in Tirumala including the Alwar tank, Mangalabavi and Ananthapalligunta, which provide the necessary water for the pilgrims and the gardens.

The TTD has 12 shrines and subsidiary shrines under its control. There are several temples dedicated to Balaji outside Andhra Pradesh. The temples outside Andhra Pradesh managed by the TTD are:

In Rishikesh:

Sri Venkateswaraswami Temple

Constructed in 1972, the temple is located on the left side of the

Andhrashram that is managed by the TTD. The Andhrashram was constructed by Sri Satchidananda Saraswathi Maharaj in 1942 and handed over to the TTD in the year 1969. The important festival held here is the annual Brahmotsavam in the months of May and June.

Chandramouleeswara Swami Temple

This temple was also constructed in the year 1972. It is located on the right side of Andhrashram. Besides the main deity of Chandramouleeswara, this temple has the idols of Goddess Parvathi, Vigneshwara and Subramanya.

Abroad

Lord Venkateswara temples abroad are located in Kenya (Nairobi), Botswana and Tanzania in Africa; Sydney, New South Wales (Helensburg), Victoria (Carrum Downs) and Melbourne in Australia; Singapore; Pittsburg, Pennsylvania, Penn Hills, Memphis, Malibu, California, Atlanta, Chicago, New Jersey, Livermore and North Carolina in the USA; Birmingham in the UK and in Mauritius.

Other Temples at Tirumala:

Sri Varahaswami Temple

Tirumala is also called Varaha Kshetram. This temple is located on the northern side of the main temple of Lord Venkateswara and is on the western banks of Swami Pushkarini.

In the small mandapam that is enclosed with iron grills one can see the idol of Gajalakshmi made of white cement in a sitting posture facing north. The idol is about 1.2 m high and has four arms. The uplifted hands hold two red lotuses in the *katakahastha* pose. The lower right hand is in *abhayahastha* pose and the lower left hand is in the *varadahastha* pose. There are two standing elephants on either side with their trunks lifted up in reverence.

There is another small stone mandapam here that has 18 pillars, out of which six form part of the inner temple on the western side. The mandapam is constructed in the Vijayanagara style of architecture and has many bas-reliefs on its pillars.

On the extreme right of this mandapam that faces the Swami Pushkarini is the Homa Vedika. The inner temple leads to another rectangular mandapam where the six pillars are seen clearly. Towards the right of this mandapam, the small shrine-like structure of Vishvakasena is located. The idol here is only 30 cm high. At its base there is a 30 cm-high stone statue of Sri Ramanuja. The covered Prakaram is about 1.8 m wide. There are *panchaloha panchamurthy* or five idols made of the five metals, in this shrine.

The inner temple has two small shrines. An Antarala Gruha measuring about 1.8 m x 2.1 m leads to a Garbha Gruha of the same size. The connecting chamber is about 3 m high. The two Dwarapalas of copper alloy are about 1.5 m tall and hold the conch and disc and display the *suchihastas* with the index finger pointing upwards.

Sri Varahaswami is seated in this Garbha Gruha under a small Simha Thorana. The stone idol of Bhu Devi, His consort, is about 90 cm high and is seen seated on His lap. Below the Moola Vigraha one can see the copper alloy icon of a standing Sri Varahaswami with Sri Venkateswara to His right and the Sudarshana and Saligrama stone between them.

The offering to Sri Varahaswami here is sugar candy. He is first worshipped by the pilgrims before they go into the main temple of Lord Srinivasa and He is also served first with the *naivedyam*. The worship in this temple is strictly as per Vaikhanasa Agama. A quantity of the food offerings prepared is sent to Varahaswami Temple and only when the bell there sounds to signify that the food has reached and is ready for offering, do the bells of Sri Venkateswara temple begin to ring. The *naivedyam* is offered simultaneously in both the temples.

The inscriptions reveal that the deity here was called Varaha Nayinar in 1380 CE and in 1476 CE, he came to be known as Gnanapiran. The temple itself is supposed to have been discovered in 1380 CE. According to legend, Tirumala was originally the abode of Lord Adi Varahaswami and it is believed that Lord Venkateswara took His permission to reside here. According to the *Brahma Purana*, devotees visiting this temple are to place their offerings here before they visit the shrine of Lord Venkateswara.

According to *Atri Samhitha,* that is also known as *Samurtar Chanadhikarana*, the Varaha Avatar of Lord Vishnu is revered in three forms namely, Adi Varaha, Pralaya Varaha and Yajna Varaha. The Adi Varaha form is worshipped here. The earliest mention of this temple is from an inscription. It records an agreement made in 1301 CE for offering of food to Varahaswami on the 2nd day of each of the Brahmotsavams held in Tirumala. In 1403 CE, Saluva Thimmaraja provided daily offerings to the deity. As per an inscription dated 1441 CE, the processional image of Malaiappa proceeded to Sri Varahaswami Temple on five days during each of the eight Brahmotsavams in the year, accompanied by the singing of *Thiruvaimozhi*, the devotional songs with 1084 stanzas composed by Thirumangai Alwar.

Sri Bedi Anjaneyaswami Temple

This temple is located in Sannidhi Street opposite the main temple and believed to have been built in the time of the Mahants. Anjana Devi, Lord Anjaneya's mother, is said to have performed penance here. Every Sunday, an abhishekam is performed and on Hanuman Jayanthi, special offerings are made.

Sri Anjaneyaswami Temple

Located opposite the Sri Varahaswami Temple on the northeastern bank of Swami Pushkarini, the temple was constructed when the administration of the main temple was in the hands of the Mahants. Here abhishekam is performed on Sundays.

Sri Venugopalaswami Temple

It is located on the way to Papavinasam.

Important Waterfalls (*Teerthas*) at Tirumala

Many sacred *teerthas* or waterfalls are found in the region of Papavinasam on the eastern side and Avachari Kona. The *teerthas* that flow from the northwest are Pasupu (885 m), Kumaradhara (810 m), Ramakrishna (675 m) and Thumburukona (675 m). The *teerthas* that flow from the southwest are Jablai (900 m), Akasha Sanga (810 m), Papavinasam (600 m) and Sanaka Sanadana (600 m). The other *teerthas* are Gogarbham (750 m), Vaikunta (660 m), Sesha (585 m), Sitamma (750 m), Bhima (630 m) and Alwar (210 m) on the Tirupathi side of the Hill. In addition to these, there are several other *teerthas* on the Tirumala Hils. These are Swami Pushkarini, Chakra, Vajra, Vishvaksena Sarovar, Jaraharadi, Markandeya, Vayu, Pandava, Varaha, Kayarasayana, Phalguna, Kataha, Galava, Yama, Agneya, Panchayuda, Agni Kunda, Brahma and Saptharishi *teerthas,* many of which are inaccessible.

Other Places of Tourist Interest at Tirumala

Deer Park

This is located at a point halfway to Tirumala.

Shila Thoranam

This arch-like structure is a rare and very ancient geological formation that is located 1 km north of the temple near Chakra Teertha. It is nearly 7.5 m long and 3 m high. It is believed to be 2500 million years old. This natural rock formation appears like an arch with a conch and a discus and the hood of a serpent. Geologists have classified this rock formation as Pre-Cambrian and to be older than the Jurassic Age. It is one of the three natural rock arches in the world.

Narayanagiri Padalu

After a 10-minute walk from Shila Thoranam one comes to a crossroads, one road leading to Dharmagiri and the other to the highest peak on the Tirumala Hills, the Narayanagiri. It is believed that this is the place on Earth where Lord Vishnu first set foot. The footprints are seen on top of this hill. One can also have a view of the Tirumala Temple from here. Nearby, there is a Shiva temple in a garden.

Musical Fountain

This is located exactly behind the Ananda Nilayam. The water springs from the fountain in time to the tunes of songs that praise the glory of Lord Srinivasa.

Vedagiri Vedapathshala (Veda Vignana Parishad)

It is 2 km from Shila Thoranam and is located on the Dharmagiri Hill. At the entrance, one can see an impressive idol of Lord Brahma displaying the four *Vedas*.

TTD Gardens

This garden in Tirumala maintained by the TTD has 200 varieties of plants and trees including some rare ones. It covers an area of roughly 460 acres. It is believed that the garden was planted by Sri Ramanujacharya, the great Vaishnava saint and his follower Sri Anandalwar during the 14th century CE. It supplies the 500 kilos of flowers required daily for worship to all TTD Temples in Tirumala and Tirupathi. Besides, flowers are donated by devotees under the scheme known as 'Srivari Pushpa Kainkaryam' that is transported free of cost by the APSRTC. During the annual Brahmotsavam, the Garden Department organizes Pushpa-yagnam and horticultural shows.

Asthana Mandapam (Sadas Hall)

The Dharma Prachar Parishad of the TTD conducts various cultural and devotional programmes that include discourses, music concerts, *harikatha* and *bhajan* in this auditorium near the temple complex.

Sri Venkateswara Museum and Photo Gallery

The SV Museum is located between Narayanagiri and the Sri Venkateswara temple. It was established in 1980 in the historical thousand-pillared mandapam. In 1983, it was shifted to the Nammalwar compound located near the Govindaraja Temple in Tirupathi. In 1997, the museum was again shifted to the present spacious building that is about 37,500 sq m in area. It has three floors and there are different galleries that exhibit photographs, historical personalities, copper statues, wooden statues, weapons and musical instruments. Traditional art and architecture, stone and wooden carvings and articles used for worship are also displayed here. There is no entrance fee.

Sri Venkateswara Dhyana Vignana Mandiram

This meditation hall was set up in 1980. It is kept open from 9 am till 6 pm on all days.

Lepakshi Emporium

There is an AP government-owned Lepakshi emporium selling attractive handicrafts in Tirumala.

Sri Hathiramji Mutt

The mutt is located on the South Mada Street near the temple. Hathiramji was a great devotee of the Lord. The mutt has a temple dedicated to Lord Krishna and also has Dasavatara idols. The mutt handled the administration of the Balaji temple from 1843 to 1933 when the Tirumala Tirupathi Devasthanams (TTD) took over.

2
Sanctity, Glory and Antiquity of the Deity and Tirumala

The origin of the temple of Lord Srinivasa on the Tirumala Hills is shrouded in mystery. It is believed to be extremely ancient, as even the Rig Veda (*Verse X.155.1*) makes an indirect reference to the temple and its deity We find references to the sanctity of the sacred Hill in the Epics. In *Kamba Ramayana* (Tamil), in the *Kishkinda Kanda*, it is said that the Hill reveals the Eternal Truth as contained in the four *Vedas* and all the Sastras.

In the *Puranas*, one can find many legends associated with the Temple. The book *Sri Venkatachala Mahatmyam* narrates the stories of the Lord's manifestation on Tirumala from the 12 *Mahapuranas*. The greatness of the Temple and the sanctity of the *teerthas* found on Tirumala are mentioned in the *Varahapurana, Padma Purana, Garuda Purana, Brahmanda Purana, Markandeya Purana, Skanda Purana, Brahmottara Purana, Harivamsa, Brahma Purana, Vamana Purana, Adithya Purana, and Bhavishyottara Purana*. The *Varaha, Vamana, Bhavishyottara, Brahma, Brahmanda and Padma Puranas* relate that Sri Venkateswara made the Hill His abode 28 Mahayugas or 7,77,60,000 years ago. (One Mahayuga is said to be equivalent to 43,20,000 human years).

The Seven Hills represent the seven hoods of Adi Sesha the cosmic serpent. By merely looking at its peak, it is said that Balarama attained the fruit of all pilgrimages. The sage Agasthya, after performing great penance here, had a vision of the Lord. King Dasaratha was supposed to have visited this sacred Hill and had a holy dip in the Swami Pushkarini. He meditated here and had a vision of Lord Narayana. Then he was blessed with four children, the eldest one being Sri Ramachandra who is considered an incarnation of Lord Vishnu. Sri Rama is also believed to have visited this Hill during His search for Sita. All the Devas, Gods and Rishis are believed to have come down to Earth and performed penance on this Hill to have a vision of the Lord.

The *Sri Venkatachala Mahatmyam* or *Thiruvenkata Mahatmyam Teertha* is a Sthala Puranam that was compiled by Pasindi Venkatatthuraivar alias Jiyar Ramanujayyan. It was first read out in the temple in 1491. This book contains the summary of tales from about 12 different *Puranas* along with the additions made by the author. It was translated into Telugu in 1884 when Sri Mahant Bhagavandasji was the administrator. It was later re-published by his grand disciple Sri Mahant Ramakishoradasji and reprinted in 1928 by his disciple Mahant Prayagadasji, the last Vicharakarta of the temple at Tirumala. Later Sri G V Chalapathi Rao translated this work into English and published the book in 1983.

Tales from the *Puranas*

The *Bhavishyottara Purana* contains a chapter on the greatness and glory of Venkatachala and Lord Venkateswara narrated by the sage Sutha to the sage Sounaka and others. In the entire Universe, the holiest and the most sacred Kshetra is Ananda Nilaya on Venkatachala. It is a cure-all for every disease and sin. It is the ultimate goal and sacred refuge for all. There is no Sastra that excels Vedantha and there is no God higher than Sri Venkateswara. There is none more blissful than Sri Venkateswara. His form is Sat-Chit-Ananda. Salvation is assured to one who visits Him. Even Lord Shiva enlightened Parvathi about the efficacy and glory of this holy Kshetra and the merit achieved by bathing in the sacred Teerthas particularly in Swami Pushkarini. Sage Sutha told the rishis who were listening to his narration, that it was impossible for a thousand Seshas to describe for a thousand years the glory of Sri Venkatachala. Even a minor part of it, if narrated, would bestow merit and longevity. If one reads or writes about or listens to the glory of Sri Venkatachala, one would attain prosperity and achieve one's desires.

So-called modern rationalists may belittle these tales as mere mythical claptrap. They may argue that the stories have no logic or reasoning behind them. They may say that these tales have been spun since time immemorial to fool the ordinary man and to condition the minds of children in a set pattern of behaviour and thinking. But one must understand that these Puranic tales were told, not by ordinary humans, but by ancient sages of advanced intellect. If the sages have passed them down to mankind, they must have had some deeper purpose. These incidents might have actually happened during ancient times, as people of those days were nearer to God the Almighty or the creator, or the divine energy, whatever one may call it. In olden times, spiritual well-being and material comforts and pleasures were given equal importance.

It is also possible that these tales were a combination of real incidents embellished by the creative imagination of the seers, who wanted to make the lofty truths of the *Vedas* and the spiritual quest palatable to the masses. Whatever their origin, one should not see only the outward meaning of the stories. Instead one should dive deep and gather the pearls of wisdom that lie within them. Merely listening to the stories is like eating the rind of a fruit and discarding the sweet flesh. The rind only protects the nutritious edible part of the fruit. The ancient rishis were magnanimous enough to come down to the level of ordinary humans to help them understand the one and the only truth through simple tales.

It is told that after compiling the *Vedas* and composing the Brahma Sutras, the great sage Vyasa was still discontented. It was Narada who made him realise the reason for his discontent. Vyasa was successful in explaining and demystifying the ultimate Truth through the *Vedas* and its gist, the Brahma Sutras, but he failed to reveal the path of Bhakthi or devotion that was suitable for the majority. So he asked Vyasa to compose the *Puranas*. The intention of the seers was to lift the minds of ordinary men to the higher level of spiritual knowledge or Jnana. They began with stories, for which of us doesn't like listening to stories?

From the lower level of Bhakthi that relates to the worship of the external forms of the divine, where the devotee prays for material comforts and well-being and in which he considers himself as different from that Supreme power, the sages tried to lift the devotee's mind to the higher level of Bhakthi where the Bhaktha seeks nothing from his deity but becomes one with Him; where emotion becomes devotion. To such a person everything that he sees and hears is the Paramatman. Somewhere along the way, the duality disappears and he becomes one with his chosen deity.

Just as the man who tries to rescue another person who has fallen into a pit, bends down a little to catch hold of the other person's hands to pull him upwards, similarly the sages of yore were generous enough to come down from the high perch of their intellect, to the level of the ordinary seeker.

The knowledge or Jnana that the Bhaktha gains in the initial stages through constant and continuous devotion to the Supreme power through idol worship, develops and culminates in Vijnana or wisdom, where he actually experiences the One without name and form. Thus Bhakthi that was at first emotional, then intellectual in content, transforms to Supreme knowledge or Vijnana, enabling the Bhaktha to become that which he worships.

As the great sage Ramakrishna Paramahamsa said, Jnana or knowledge means knowing all about a fruit and its taste, but Vijnana or wisdom is actually enjoying and experiencing the taste of the fruit. So to condemn and ridicule mythological tales and the beliefs of the people, only reveals an attempt to view the ancient wisdom through the lens of modernity. If the people who have no belief in scriptures want to really understand their inner meaning and purpose, then they need to conduct a thorough study.

The worship in the temple of Lord Venkateswara is conducted as per the Vaikhanasa Agama. According to the Bhavishyottara Purana, Sage Vaikhanasa after long *tapas* or penance, had a vision of Lord Krishna who told the sage that he should worship Him as Lord Srinivasa in Seshachala and that he would find the deity in an anthill with the help of His devotee Rangadasa. The sage then proceeded to Tirumala and with the help of Rangadasa, located the deity and started worshipping Him. Since he was the first to worship the Lord at Tirumala, his mode of worship is the one adhered to today.

According to the *Varaha Purana*, Adi Varaha manifested Himself on the western bank of Swami Pushkarini. When Lord Vishnu came down to Tirumala Hills, he met Lord Varaha and informed him about His desire to stay there till the end of Kaliyuga. Lord Varaha agreed and Lord Narayana took the form of Lord Venkateswara and remained on the southern bank of Swami Pushkarini.

According to a story in the *Brahma Purana*, Lord Vishnu asked Narada to suggest a place on Earth for him to visit and Narada indicated a place near Seshachala. In the meantime, Vayu, the Lord of Wind came to Vaikunta to pay his respects to Lord Vishnu. Adisesha, who was guarding the doorway to Vaikunta, prevented Vayu from entering. This led to an argument, with each boasting of his superiority over the other. Adisesha encircled the Ananda Hill that was an offshoot of the Meru

Mountain. Vayu tried to blow away the hill with all his might. The fight took a serious turn and the entire world trembled. All the devas led by Indra requested them to stop the contest. They consented, but Vayu had already blown away Adisesha and the hill to the bank of Swami Pushkarini. Adisesha was merged by the gods with the hill which became Venkatadri. Adisesha turned into Seshadri with his hood as Venkatadri, holding Lord Venkateswara. As suggested by Narada, Vishnu decided to stay there. It is said that Adisesha's middle became Ahobila supporting Lord Narasimha and his tail became Sri Sailam that became Lord Shiva's abode. His mouth became Sri Kalahasthi where Lord Shiva is represented as the element of Vayu or air.

The *Brahmanda Purana* narrates that the Lord ordered the Kreeda Parvatha from Vaikunta to be placed in Tirumala. In the last Kritha Yuga, a demon called Vrishabhasura lived on Kreeda and he was doing great penance near the Thumburu Kona Teertha. When Lord Vishnu appeared before him, the demon pleaded that the Lord fight with him so that he could know who was more powerful. In the end, the Asura was killed by the Lord using His Sudarsana Chakra. The hill came to be known as Vrishabhachalam.

During Tretha Yuga, a woman named Anjana Devi lived near Pampa Saras (Hampi). As she was childless, she did great penance here to beget a child and the god of wind Vayu appeared before her. He blessed her with a child who was Anjaneya. So the hill got the name Anjanadri.

Another tale, similar to the one about Venkatadri, says that in the Dwapara Yuga, when Lord Vishnu was with Sri Lakshmi, Vayu the wind God tried to enter His chamber. Adisesha forbade Vayu from disturbing the Lord and his consort. During the quarrel, Adisesha wound himself around Mount Meru and covered it with his thousand-headed hood. Vayu began to blow fiercely, throwing the three worlds into a panic. The inhabitants approached Adisesha and requested him to relent by lifting at least one hood for a split second. When he conceded to their request, one bit of Mount Meru whirled away and fell on the bank of River Swarnamukhi. It became the Tirumala Hills and came to be known as Seshachala.

According to one legend, Lord Vishnu bade Sesha to go to Earth and establish himself there as a mountain for the Lord to stay. Sesha accordingly became a mountain with his hood and tail at Kalahasthi, and Sri Sailam respectively and his body forming the sacred mountain of Tirumala, Lord Vishnu's abode.

Another tale relates, that after the great deluge, when the demon king Hiranyaksha hid the Earth under water, Lord Vishnu assumed the form of a boar or Varaha and lifted and brought back the Earth after a fierce battle, at the end of which the Lord killed the demon. It is said that after the battle, the Lord bade His vehicle Garuda to fetch Kridachala that was 30 yojanas long and 3 yojanas wide (1 yojana is equal to approximately 14 km) from Vaikunta. Kridachala was a huge hill with lofty peaks where gold and precious stones were found. It resembled the shape of Adisesha, the king of serpents on which the Lord reclined. It is believed that Garuda brought Kridachala on his powerful shoulders and placed it in a sacred spot to the east of Swami Pushkarini where the Lord was waiting for him. The Lord sat there as Adi Varaha. Since Garuda, the vehicle of Lord Narayana brought Kridachala or Kreedadri to Earth at the Lord's command, the Hill came to be known as Garudadri.

At the request of Lord Brahma and other devas, Lord Vishnu who had adopted a ferocious mien while destroying Hiranyaksha, assumed a gentle form and remained in that place permanently to protect His devotees. In course of time an anthill came up on this spot. Later, the king of the land consecrated Lord Varaha along with His consort Bhudevi in a shrine here. It is also said that all the devas headed by Lord Brahma went to Vaikunta to see Lord Narayana. There they were told that Lord Vishnu had gone to stay in a place called Narayanagiri on Earth. Lord

Brahma and the other devas proceeded to Narayanagiri. There, the Lord revealed Himself for the first time.

A legend goes that when the Lord was hit on His head by a shepherd, a small portion of His scalp became bald and this was noticed by a Gandharva princess Neeladevi. She felt that such an attractive face should not have a flaw. So she cut a portion of her hair and implanted it on the scalp of the Lord. Pleased with her act, the Lord promised that the hair offered by His devotees at the shrine would go only to her. It is believed that all the hair offered by devotees is accepted by Neeladevi.

Once, a Brahmin named Narayana meditated upon Lord Srinivasa near Swami Pushkarini. After a long *tapas*, Lord Narayana appeared before him. The Brahmin requested the Lord to name the Hill Narayanachala. The Lord agreed and said that the Hill would henceforth be known as Narayanachala.

A narrative about Rangadasa, a staunch devotee of Lord Vishnu, relates that during his pilgrimage to Tirumala, he had a *darshan* of Lord Vishnu's idol under a tamarind tree fully exposed to sun and rain. So the devotee erected a rough stone wall around the idol and started worshipping it. After some time, the frolicking of a Gandharva king and his wives distracted him. It was actually a *leela* of Lord Vishnu to test Rangadasa's devotion. After some time, it is said that Lord Vishnu revealed Himself to Rangadasa and told him that he would be reborn as a ruler of a province to enjoy all the material and worldly pleasures of life. At the same time he would continue to be a staunch devotee of Lord Vishnu and would construct a beautiful temple there.

Rangadasa was then reborn as Thondaiman, the son of King Suvera and queen Nandini and when he grew up, he inherited the kingdom of Thondaimandalam from his father. He then built a Prakaram and *dwara* gopuram for the temple and arranged for regular worship.

Later on in Kaliyuga, Akasha Raju who was a great devotee of the Lord, became the ruler of Thondaimandalam.

A second version of the story above goes like this. Rangadasa was a pious Brahmin ascetic. Lord Vishnu was at that time staying nearby in the guise of a shepherd and he was pleased with the penance of a devotee named Dhritavarma or Gopinath. As Gopinath had the extreme desire to have a vision of Lord Srinivasa, the Lord directed him to go to Venkatadri where Srinivasa resided near Swami Pushkarini. He said that he would find the idol of the Lord in an anthill there. He also told him that when he reached Venkatachala, he would meet Rangadasa, a devotee from the Pandya kingdom. The Lord further advised Gopinath to pray to the idol along with Rangadasa and promised that his desire to have a vision of the Lord would be fulfilled.

Gopinath then set out for Venkatachala. On the way he met Rangadasa and they together went up the sacred Hill and located the idol of Lord Varaha. Rangadasa got busy in planting a flower garden so that he would have enough flowers to prepare garlands for the Lord. Gopinath engaged himself in worshipping the idol under the tamarind tree. Together they erected a small hut for the idol. Then they constructed a wall around it and a hall in front of it. They covered the roof of the hut and began to worship the Lord.

A few months later, Kundala, a Gandharva and his wife came down to worship Lord Varaha near Swami Pushkarini. Rangadasa happened to see the couple's dalliance. He forgot himself for a moment but regained his poise immediately. He repented his impure thoughts. On his way to the shrine, he took a holy dip in Swami Pushkarini and collected fresh flowers.

Gopinath was angry with Rangadasa as he had failed to bring the flowers for the worship of the Lord on time. Unable to explain the reason for the delay, Rangadasa was silent. Meanwhile heavenly voices told Rangadasa that soon he would be born as a good king and enjoy all pleasures of life like the Gandharva and later he would renovate the temple, raise towers, construct walls and would continue to be a devotee of the Lord. The voices also said that the Conch and the Disc of the Lord would protect him from enemies and that finally, he and his family would be liberated.

Rangadasa commenced a fast-unto-death. It is said that he was reborn as Thondaiman, the son of King Suvera of the Lunar Dynasty. Thondaiman's brother was Akasharaju who in his previous birth was cursed by Lord Srinivasa for ordering a shepherd to strike the anthill. The blow had wounded the Lord's forehead.

The *Vamana Purana* legend goes like this. Once in Kaliyuga, a very pious and learned Brahmin by name Purandara Somayaji of Kalahasthi was blessed with a son after a prolonged penance. He named his son Madhava. Although he was learned like his father, he grew to be lustful. He took a fancy for a low-class woman who had a bad character. They lived together on the banks of the Krishna River for nearly 12 years. One day the woman passed away and unable to withstand her separation, Madhava lost his mind. He roamed around like a madman and one day, quite unaware, he followed the retinue of a king who was on a pilgrimage to Tirumala. He went up the Hill and stood along with the others in front of the Deity. A horrible smell emanated from his body which was soon engulfed in flames and burnt to ashes, washing away all his sins. Thereafter, the Hill came to be known as Venkatachala or the Hill that burns away all sins. It was also prophesied that Madhava would be reborn as the son of a Chola king and would rule over Thondaimandalam.

In the Tretha Yuga, an Asura called Kesari did penance to obtain the blessings of Lord Shiva for a son. However, Lord Shiva blessed him with a lovely daughter who, in course of time, would beget a charming son with all the qualities that the Asura wished for. Kesari named her Anjana. When she grew up, she was given in marriage to Kapi Kesari. She was childless for a long time. On the advice of a soothsayer, Anjana performed *tapas* for 7,000 years in Venkatadri. Sage Matanga also advised Anjana to perform penance. She lived on air and meditated on Vayu. After some time, Anjana gave birth to a boy. Years passed. Brahma visited her and told her that the child had been born for a purpose and that he would be invincible. He named the hill Anjanachala or Anjanadri in her honour.

Then there is the story of Lord Skanda. He asked Lord Shiva, his father, to point out the abode of Vishnu that would be the best for performing penance to wash away his sin of killing Tarakasura. Lord Shiva replied that the holy Hill Vrishachala was the best and asked His son to go and meditate there. He said the very sight of the Hill would liquidate one's sins and that anyone who recited the *Varaha mantra* for a month observing the austerities as ordained in the Sastras, would have all his desires fulfilled. Lord Shiva taught Skanda the *Varaha Mantra* and narrated the story behind the importance of the Hill. He told Skanda about the fight between Sesha and Vayu and asked him to choose a spot on the southern side of the Hill that was very beautiful and lush green. Rishis like Sukha and devotees like Prahalada and Ambareesha had performed *tapas* there. Lord Varaha had revealed Himself along with His consort Bhudevi to Dharma after his penance. In fact, the Hill was named Vrishachala because of Vrisha (Dharma). Skanda then proceeded to the Hill. There He spotted a lake and after taking a holy dip, he began to meditate on Lord Narayana. Soon His body acquired a scintillating golden hue.

There is one more explanation given for the name. There was a demon Vrishabhasura, (a great devotee of Narasimha) who offered his head to the Lord. But every time the head was cut, a new head sprang up in its place. After 5,000 years, Lord Narasimha appeared before the demon. The demon wished to do battle with the Lord but the wish was not fulfilled. Time passed and Lord Narayana came down to Earth and resided in Venkatachala. Once, when He was in the forest, Vrishabhasura challenged the Lord to a fight. A fierce battle took place between the two. Finally Lord Narayana cut the demon's head with His Sudarsana Chakra. At once, the demon realised who He was. He prostrated before the Lord and started worshipping Him. He finally requested the Lord to name the Hill Vrishabhachala after him. The Lord consented.

According to Bhavishyottara Purana, in the first three Yugas, namely Kritha Yuga, Tretha Yuga and Dwapara Yuga, Lord Vishnu as Sri Venkateswara remained in Venkatachala. When Kaliyuga began, He left for Vaikunta with His consorts Sri Devi and Bhu Devi by handing over charge of Venkatachala to Sri Varahaswami. When Sage Narada heard this, he went to Satyaloka and informed Brahma. He remarked that as long as Lord Venkateswara was in Venkatachala, people were pious and good. Lord Varahaswami would also find it difficult to manage the Brahmotsavam that Brahma had started for Lord Venkateswara, single-handedly. Brahma asked Narada to devise a plan to persuade Lord Narayana to return to Venkatachala.

Narada went to the bank of the river Ganges at Naimisharanya, where a number of sages had assembled to perform a *yagna* or sacrifice for the welfare of mankind. Narada wanted to know the name of the deity to whom they wished to offer the fruit of the *yagna*. The sages assembled there did not know know the answer. So they went to the wise sage Bhrigu. The sage through his intense *tapas*, had obtained a third eye (perhaps the eye of wisdom) in his foot. But he was highly conscious of his wisdom and therefore very proud of himself. Narada asked sage Bhrigu to answer his question.

So Bhrigu first went to Brahma Loka, the abode of the first of the Trimoorthis. But Lord Brahma did not notice the arrival of the sage as he was absorbed in chanting the *Vedas* with Goddess Saraswathi, his consort, sitting by his side. This irritated the sage and he cursed Lord Brahma saying that there would never be a shrine built for Him on Earth.

Then he hurried to Kailash, the abode of Lord Shiva, where

Lord Shiva was engaged in the performance of the cosmic dance along with his consort Goddess Parvathi and did not notice Bhrigu. This act enraged the sage. He cursed Lord Shiva saying that Lord Shiva would be worshipped mostly in the form of Linga on Earth.

Sage Bhrigu proceeded to Vaikunta, the abode of Lord Narayana. There also, the Lord who was with his consort at that time, did not notice the sage. The sage was humiliated by Lord Vishnu's behaviour. He thought the Lord had ignored him deliberately. He kicked Vishnu's chest in anger. Lakshmi, who resided in Vishnu's chest, was furious with Bhrigu's arrogant, insulting act. Vishnu's silence made it worse. Lord Vishnu tried to pacify his consort but the Goddess stalked out of Vaikunta in a huff.

Lord Vishnu caught hold of Bhrigu's leg, and while pretending to apologise, massaged the sage's foot and enquired whether his leg was hurt. He pressed the foot so hard that he crushed Bhrigu's extra eye! The Sage at once realised his mistake and he apologised to Lord Vishnu for committing such a great sin.

Goddess Lakshmi who was angry with Lord Vishnu, went to Karavirapura (Kolhapur). Unable to bear her separation, Lord Vishnu left Vaikunta and came down to Earth in search of his consort. He finally reached Seshachala and there he visited Varahamoorthy. With his permission, Lord Vishnu stayed at Varaha Mountain and he immersed himself in Dhyana inside an anthill.

In the meantime, Lord Brahma and Lord Shiva had transformed themselves into a cow and its calf. Goddess Parvathi disguised herself as a cowherd and she followed the cow and calf and sold them to the Chola king.

The king's cowherd usually took all the cows to the forest for grazing. However the new cow was not giving any milk after returning from the forest. The matter was reported to the king who ordered the cowherd to find out the reason behind this. So the cowherd began to follow the cow and to his surprise he saw the cow giving her milk to an anthill. The king was informed of the strange behaviour and went along with the cowherd to the forest. To his amazement, he saw the cow ooze milk on top of the anthill.

The cowherd immediately began to punish the cow by hitting it. At once Lord Narayana appeared with a bleeding head. The cowherd was aghast and he fell down unconscious. The king fell at Vishnu's feet and began to plead for mercy. Lord Vishnu at first cursed the king to become a devil, but as he showed great remorse and begged the Lord for forgiveness, Lord Vishnu relented. He then told the king that he would be reborn as Akasha Raju and that the Lord Himself would marry his daughter. At that time the king would be absolved of the sin committed by him. Since the cowherd noticed Lord Vishnu first, his race would be privileged to have the Lord's *darshan* first in the temple that would be constructed at the appropriate time.

Lord Vishnu set out on his wanderings once more. He reached the abode of Vakulamalika who was a great devotee of Lord Krishna and believed to be Devaki in her previous birth. When Vakulamalika saw the wound on the the forehead of Lord Srinivasa, she at once applied medicines. It is said that Lord Vishnu in his incarnation as Sri Krishna, had promised his foster-mother Devaki who could not witness His celestial wedding with Rukmini, that he would make amends. He told her that she would be blessed not only to witness but conduct his marriage when he incarnated as Lord Venkateswara.

Akasha Raju was the son of Chola king Sudarma. His younger brother was Thondaiman. His wife was Dharanidevi. King Akasha Raju and his queen were not blessed with children for a long time. Sage Sukha, their royal guru, advised the king to perform a Puthrakameshtiyagna, so that the couple would be blessed with a child. At the completion of the yagna, when the king ploughed the land with a golden plough, he came across a box. When he opened the box he saw a just-born, beautiful girl lying in a lotus inside the box. With great joy, the king took the child from the box and named her Padmavathi because she had been lying in a lotus or *padma*. In course of time, Pamavathi grew up into a lovely young maiden.

Once when Sage Narada visited the palace of the king, he predicted that Padmavathi, the princess would marry none other than Lord Vishnu. It is believed that in the Tretha Yuga, Padmavathi was born as Vedavathi. She wanted to get Rama as her husband. So she performed penance with that aim. However, Ravana the demon king wished to marry Vedavathi. When Ravana behaved in an indecent manner towards her, she cursed him saying that his lust would be the cause of his end and then, after saying this, she jumped into the fire. But Agni or fire saved her and she became the Maya Sita who was abducted from Panchavati by Ravana. At the end of the Rama-Ravana war, she entered the fire to prove her chastity, and the real Sita emerged from it. Sri Rama then told her that he would fulfil her wish in Kaliyuga when He would be Lord Srinivasa and she would be born as Padmavathi. It was not possible for him to fulfil her wish as Ramachandra because he followed Ekapatnivrata, meaning a vow to have only one wife.

Once, Lord Srinivasa who was staying with Vakulamalika, went hunting. He saw an elephant chasing a girl. To save the girl, he shot at the elephant with arrows. The elephant changed its direction and ran away. Even without knowing who the girl was, the Lord fell in love with her. The girl, who was none other than Padmavathi, the daughter of the king, was also attracted towards him. She began to spend her days thinking about him by recollecting her experience. She was very sad as she did not know who he was and his whereabouts.

Lord Srinivasa, on His return, told Vakula Devi what had happened. For the first time, He revealed Himself to her and told her the story of Padmavathi's earlier birth. He knew that the girl whom He had saved from the elephant was the princess of the kingdom. He disguised himself as a gipsy woman and went to the palace. The princess extended her palm to the 'gipsy' for reading. Lord Srinivasa who pretended to read it, told the king that the reason for the princess's sorrow was the hunter who had saved her life and with whom she had fallen in love. He said that the hunter was none other than Lord Vishnu. The 'gipsy' then asked the king to conduct the marriage of his daughter with the Lord without any further delay. The King was very pleased to hear the words of the 'gipsy' and he readily agreed.

Accordingly, the wedding was fixed for the 10th day of Vaikasi, a Friday. Lord Srinivasa then bade sage Sukha to inform all the gods about his wedding with Padmavathi Devi. The Lord approached Kubera for a huge sum to meet the expenses of his marriage. He assured him that he would repay the loan at the end of Kaliyuga and till then he would pay him the interest. It is believed that the Lord sought a loan of one crore and 14 lakh gold coins from Kubera who immediately supplied the treasure.

The Lord asked Vishvakarma, the divine architect to create celestial surroundings on Tirumala for His wedding. Lord Brahma and Lord Shiva marked their presence as two peepal trees on the banks of Pushkarini. In the presence of all the gods and their consorts, the celestial wedding of Lord Venkateswara with Padmavathi took place.

After the demise of Akasha Raju, his brother Thondaiman and his son Vasudana fought for the throne. Lord Srinivasa who was the son-in-law of the late king, intervened and divided the kingdom between these two claimants. Thondaiman became the king of Thondairaj and Vasudana was crowned as king of Narayanapuram. Thondaiman was a great devotee of Lord Vishnu and in his last birth as Rangadasa, had built a small temple. It is thus believed that it was Thondaiman who constructed the original temple after he had a vision of Lord Vishnu in his dream. It is said that the Lord directed

Thondaiman in his dream to build a temple. He is said to have taken the deity from an anthill and installed the idol in a temple constructed by him. The Brahmanda Purana confirms this story.

As per the wishes of Lord Srinivasa, Thondaiman constructed the temple near Swami Pushkarini after obtaining permission from Lord Varahaswami. He constructed two gopurams or towers facing the east, three compound walls or *Prakarams*, seven gates with orchards and festoons, a *dwajasthamba* or flag post, a court hall or *asthana mandapam*, a mandapam for yoga, cowshed or *goshala*, granary, a storehouse for cloth, oil, ghee etc, dining hall, stables for horses and elephants, a flower room, a perfumery, kitchens for cooking food and the food offerings, a jewel house and so on.

He also completed the freshwater well which he had sunk in his previous birth as Rangadasa and inlaid it with copper plates. In addition, he constructed a *vimana* with *chathur murthis* and Garuda and crowned it with a golden *kalasa*. He laid the pathway over the Hill measuring one yojana or around 16 km, built mandapams en route for the pilgrims, dug wells and built tanks for supplying water. It is also said that the main temple constructed by Thondaiman was named 'Ananda Nilayam.'

Once when Thondaiman was attacked by enemies, the Lord gave him His Shankha and Chakra to eliminate them. After his victory, he requested the Lord not to hold the Shankha and Chakra that a mere king had used, in his divine hands. The Lord agreed to hold them invisibly and since then He has stood there without his weapons.

It is also said that Lord Brahma lighted the two lamps in the shrine of Venkateswara for universal prosperity and human welfare. He then prayed to Lord Venkateswara to grant him his wish that the two lamps would shine till the end of Kaliyuga. It is believed that the Lord assured Lord Brahma that His avatar as Lord Srinivasa would end when the *vimana* fell and the lamps were extinguished.

He then directed Lord Brahma to celebrate His wedding ceremony with Padmavathi every year, commencing with the flag-hoisting ceremony and ending with the car festival. Since then, on the second day of the month of Kanya, the Lord's flag is hoisted and there is a celebration with all pomp and pageantry. The deities are taken round in procession on a palanquin. On the second day, they are taken out in procession on the Sesha Vahana and swan vehicle. On the 3rd day, on the lion vehicle and pearl mandapam; on the 4th day in the Kalpavruksha and Sarvabhoopala Vahana; on the 5th day on Garuda Vahana with the Lord in the guise of Mohini, on the 6th day on Hanumantha Vahana and elephant vehicles, on the 7th day in the Surya Prabha Vahana and Chandra Vahana, on the 8th day in the Ratham or car and Aswa Vahana and on the 9th day in the Palanquin.

The deities are anointed with turmeric and vermillion before they are taken out in procession. Brahma and other gods are supposed to lead the procession through the temple streets. The festival concludes with *avabhrita*, the final bath and *pushpayagna* on the Sravana Nakshatra day.

It is believed that Lord Brahma had once observed the festival in the brighter half of the month of Bhadrapada on the day of the star Chitra. Those who offered even simple worship in the month of Bhadrapada (September-October) were well-rewarded.

Sage Sanaka is supposed to have said that whoever takes a holy dip in Swami Pushkarini on the concluding day of the annual Brahmotsavam ensures that all the sins of his previous births are destroyed instantaneously.

A pleased Sri Venkateswara asked Brahma what desire he had. Lord Brahma requested Lord Srinivasa to stay on at Venkatachala blessing and granting the wishes of His devotees. The Lord agreed to stay on at Tirumala for the welfare of mankind.

According to another legend, a boy called Bala was accused wrongly as a thief. He was chased by the people who wanted to punish him. When they caught him, they began to hit him on the head. The bleeding boy somehow escaped and took shelter in the temple. When the people reached the temple they searched for the boy, but could not find him anywhere. Instead they saw the deity bleeding from its head.

There is also a legend about Lord Varahaswami. Once there was a hunter by name Vasu who lived on Sri Venkatachala. He grew crops on the Hill. He took the grain from his field, mixed it with honey and offered it to Sri Varahaswami before he ate his food. His wife, Chitravathi was also a pious lady.

One day the couple went out to collect honey for the Lord. They left their son Veeraman at home and when it was time to offer food to the Lord, Veeraman boiled some rice and offered it to Varahaswami who was installed under a tree. Later Veeraman ate the *prasadam*.

When the couple reached home, they learnt from their son that *naivedyam* or the food offering to the Lord had already been made without mixing it with honey. At this, Vasu became so angry that he rushed to kill his son. But at that moment Lord Varaha revealed Himself, snatched the sword from the hunter and threw it away. The Lord then decided to remain on the banks of the lake.

According to another version, Lord Varaha was wandering in the fields, when Vasu the hunter saw him and beat his drum and sounded his bugles. Varaha vanished. In the night, Vasu saw Varaha entering an anthill. When he began to dig the anthill, Varaha appeared. On seeing Varaha in the anthill, Vasu fell unconscious.

Veeraman, his son, saluted Varaha the boar. Pleased with his act, Varaha told him that He was the Lord of Lords. He then asked Veeraman to inform the king that he should consecrate Varaha there and worship Him by purifying the anthill with a black cow's milk. He had to install Him there as per the procedure laid down in the scriptures.

Veeraman then went to the palace and narrated all he had seen and heard to Thondaiman the king. Thondaiman was very happy. That night in his dream, he saw an underground passage leading from his palace to the spot where the boar was seen entering the anthill. The next morning, he located the passage and identified the anthill. He planted a tamarind and *champaka* saplings there. The tamarind tree later became the abode of the Lord and the *champaka* tree that of Goddess Mahalakshmi.

Then he cleared the spot and erected a temple there as per the insructions already given by the Lord in his dream. In his dream the Lord also revealed to Thondaiman that a *vimana* would be constructed later on by Narayana, his descendant. Thondaiman arranged for the daily worship of the Lord in the temple. He visited the temple daily through the underground passage.

The Tamil Alwars

The Tamil Alwars (or Azhwars) have also sung about the antiquity, sanctity and glory of the Hill and the deity in many places in the *Nalayira Divya Prabandam*.

Poigai Alwar

Poigai Alwar (500-550 CE), one of the early Alwars, wrote the first 100 verses of the *Nalayira Divya Prabandam*. He refers to Venkatachala as Vengadam and the Lord as Venkatapathy or Venkadathumeyan. He describes the Vengadam Hill in his 'Mudal (First) Thiruvandhadi' as an unexplored wilderness of bamboo groves inhabited by the Kuravas or Kurbas, a hunting tribe. There were elephants and serpents. The Hill did not have a proper temple at that time.

Poigai Alwar's *Mudal Thiruvandhadi* mentions five temples in 11 verses and eight verses out of the 11 verses are in praise of Vengadam. He makes nearly 12 to 15 direct references to Tirumala. In his 5th and 74th hymn he refers to the place as a sacred one where the Lord has manifested as Harihara. About the image, he says that the Lord here is both Ara (Hara) and Narayana; His vehicle is the bull and the bird; His word, the book and the *Murai* or basis; His house of residence, the mountains (Kailasa) and the waters (ocean); His function, destruction and protection; the weapon in His hand, the trident and the disc. He has ashes all over His body. He is Jatadari (has long matted locks of hair); the one who has the sacred Ganga on His head and the one who has a tall crown; His form, though one, is both fire and dark cloud. He burnt the castle (Tripura) and broke open the heart (of Hiranyakasipu). His colour is sapphire blue. Part of His body is Parvathi and on one side is the woman born of the Lotus (Sri Lakshmi). It is Vengadam that enlightens the Gods, it is Vengadam that the Brahmajnanis worship and its Lord is the Lord of the four *Vedas*. The 26th stanza has a reference to the sacred Hill, His abode.

Bhuthatha Alwar

The description of the Hill, the wild animals and of the primitive inhabitants given by Bhuthatha Alwar (around 600-650 CE) is similar to that of Poigai Alwar. His 2nd *Thiruvandhadi* also consists of 100 verses wherein he refers to 12 temples in 17 verses. Seven out of the 17 verses are devoted to praising Vengadam. He says that Vengadam is the highest object to be desired and the Lord of Vengadam is the Lord of the *Vedas*, the God of all Gods. In stanzas 25, 28, 33, and 45, he describes the idol here as a form of Lord Vishnu. He, however, says that the form of the idol here has matted locks, the high peaked crown, the shining dagger and the *chakra*, the snake coiling around Him and the golden *sutra* around His waist.

He says, 'My father on Tirumala is two forms gracefully blended into one'. He found the deity on the Hill decorated with flower garlands and dressed up as Balakrishna with the tuft tied up into a knot over the forehead. In his *Prabandam,* he describes the deity as being smeared all over the body with the hill-grown sandalwood paste and divine ornaments, dressed in silk and profusely decorated with highly-fragrant white jasmine flowers. He says that His image itself is the manifestation of Brahman. He desired to stand on the Hill to allow His devotees to worship Him and that He has been there from time immemorial.

Pei Alwar

Pei Alwar describes the Hill and the deity in more or less the same way. He also says that the deity on this Hill is self-manifested. The term 'Tirumala' is used for the first time by this Alwar in stanzas 40, 63, 69, 70, 72, 73 and 93. In the 40th hymn, he also mentions the deity as the one who measured the Earth with His foot as Vamana (an Avatar of Lord Vishnu). In stanzas 62 and 63, he describes the Lord as Harihara, just like Poigai Alwar. He says, 'the two may pass as separate ones but the one is really the other' (maybe referring to both Lord Shiva and Lord Vishnu). He also identifies Him with Krishna and Vamana or Thrivikrama.

He says that the sanctity of Vengadam is equal to if not more than that of Vaikunta (the celestial abode of Lord Narayana) and Parkadal (the ocean of milk); He is the four *Vedas* and their essence and is the Being who is seated in the hearts of all. He refers to Vengadam and the idol here in stanzas 14, 26, 30, 32, 58, 59, 69, 70, 71, 72, 73 and 75. He describes Vengadam as being full of very tall bamboos growing up to the sky. Its summit is so high as to touch the sky; that elephants, monkeys, swine and the Yali or Sarabha, the imaginary wild animal that is supposed to be stronger than the lion, lives on it. The Hill contains numerous streams; its ridges are glazed and reflective. He further says that the original inhabitants of this Hill, the Kuravas, were cultivating a dry crop, Thinai or Korra, in addition to hunting.

In his 3rd *Thiruvandhadi* of 100 verses, he refers to 12 temples in 19 verses. Ten verses out of the 19 are devoted to praising Vengadam. In five more verses, it is sung about along with other places.

Thirumalisai Alwar

Thirumalisai Alwar (around 656 CE), who was also known as Bhakthisara, was the third Alwar. He has sung about the Lord in both his collection of hymns: 'Tiruchchanda Vruttham', a set of 120 verses and 'Nanmugan Thiruvandhadi', containing 96 stanzas. Both these are included in the *Prabandam*.

In hymn 42, he asks people to go and pray on the high Hill Vengadam, that by its very nature is capable of dispelling the sins of devotees and on which Brahma and Shiva are worshipping the deity's feet with lotuses.

He refers to Vengadam and the deity in stanzas 34, 40, 42, 43, 44, 45, 46, 47, 48, 60, 81 and 90. In stanza 47, he says that Vengadam consists of forests from where gold, gems, pearls and flowers from the trees are washed away by rapid torrents. It is also the place where the God of the blueberry complexion resides. In the 48th hymn, he states that Vengadam is the most valued resort of the celestials and it is the destroyer of all human sins and diseases. It is also the dwelling place of the Lord who raises the disc or *chakra* to slay the demons or the wicked ones and to protect the good ones. It is the mountain of that Lord who defeated the Danavas with His disc and saved the Devas.

He says that the deity was standing on a unforested plot of ground, had flowers placed on Him by worshippers and that the image was tall and clearly visible from all directions.

In the 60th hymn of the 'Thiruchchanda Vruttam', he says that towering bamboos grow on the Hill and that the frost and snow fall on it. He describes in his hymns, the rivulets and the wild animals and the tall bamboos that fall to the ground, dry up, decay and sprout again and grow to great heights. He asks every

Bhaktha to go to Vengadam Hill as it possesses the virtue of steadily rooting out all *karmas*.

He has sung about 13 temples in 26 verses; 17 in 'Thiruvandhadi' and nine in 'Thiruchchanda Viruttam'. Out of the 26 verses, 14 verses are in praise of Vengadam. The deity in all these is referred to as Vengadanathan or Vengadathumeyan.

Thiruppanalwar

To Thiruppanalwar, Vengadam is the place where 'Vanavar' or the celestials worship the Supreme Being at *sandhi*, that is at dawn and dusk. He contributed a hymn of 10 stanzas about this Lord. In his first hymn, he identifies Sri Venkateswara with Sri Ranganatha.

Thirumangai Alwar

Thirumangai Alwar who lived around the middle of the 8th century CE, was one of the most learned Alwars. He contributed the greatest number of stanzas to the *Prabandam*. He sang nearly 64 stanzas in praise of Vengadam. He mentions Sri Venkateswara and the sacred Hill in hymn 53. He identifies the Lord on the Thiruvengadam Hill with Lord Krishna, and the one who resides in Sri Rangam, as Thrivikrama, Rama, the dweller of Bhadarika Ashram in the Himalayas, Narasimha, the healer of the moon's diseases, the moulder of Pancha Bhuthas or the five elements, the thousand-named, the birthless, the Lord of the celestials and the spouse of Sri Lakshmi.

In the 9th hymn, he urges the mind to seek the Thiruvengadam Hill which shines as the *thilakam* among the Hills on Earth, that is surrounded by vast gardens filled with fragrant flowers and on which stands the Lord who affords easy *darshan* to his devotees, who by the chanting of His *Ashtakshara Mantra* – *Om Namo Venkatesha* would be liberated from the repeated cycle of birth and death.

In the 10th hymn, he says that those who recite these nine verses composed by him in chaste Tamil as garlands in adoration of the Lord of Thiruvengadam, would become his ardent devotees and saviours of their followers and also attain heaven.

Kulasekhara Alwar

Kulasekhara Alwar lived around the 9th century CE. He was a royal saint. He contributed 11 stanzas in praise of Thiruvengadam. Kulasekhara Alwar's hymns are known as 'Perumal Thirumozhi'. He mentions a *koil* or temple in Vengadam built with wood from *thumbaka* and *champaka* trees. He also mentions the sacred tank or Koneri. He further says that this is the place where Rudra, Brahma and Indra come daily to worship the Lord of Vengadam. It is also inferred that there was some kind of worship carried on by an *archaka* or priest while the devotees stood outside.

During the time of Kulasekhara Alwar, who was a prince, elephants seem to have become scarce on the Hill. In his evocative hymns, he says that he desires to render service to Lord Venkateswara. He wishes to be born in the Swami Pushkarini on the Vengadam, preferably as a fish or as a *champaka* tree, so as to have a glimpse of Lord Venkateswara's feet. He wishes he were lucky enough to have been born as a bush on the beautiful Hill.

He tells us about his dislike of all worldly pleasures and of the status of a king. He says that the only wish he has is to become the golden summit on Vengadam that is filled with the melodies of the singing beetles, but for which he would have to perform extraordinary penance. He sings about the forest stream on Vengadam that is more fortunate than he and of the gardens of flowers overflowing with honey. If only he were the pathway on the Vengadam Hill covered with cool and fragrant flowers, where the God praised in the *Vedas* resides! Or the steps at the entrance to the Lord's sanctum used by the devotees, gods and other celestials, so that he can have a continuous glimpse of the Lord! He expresses his reluctance to rule over the world and his longing to be any object on the illustrious Vengadam where his patron God resides. His heartfelt prayer is that he might be born again as bird, fish, or beast, or a stream, stone or tree, or a post, a statue or a doorstep in the temple of the Lord. He would vastly prefer to be an inanimate object on the golden hill of Vengadam to owning all the earthly riches and even a kingdom.

Nammalwar

It is said that after listening to the ten verses of the 'Tiruvaimozhi' by Nammalwar (early 10th century CE), his young disciple Sri Tirumalai Nambi went to Tirumala with his guru's blessings. Tirumalai Nambi is believed to be a descendant of the sage Narada. He dedicated his whole life to the daily service of Sri Venkateswara as instructed by Nammalwar in his songs.

The first 100 verses of Nammalwar's *'Thiruvaimozhi'* a work that is regarded as highly as the *Vedas* by Tamilians, are devoted to the precise exposition of the philosophy of the *Upanishads* and *Puranas*; of the celestial and cosmic creations; of how the formless supreme being assumes innumerable forms with special attributes and powers, so that it is comprehensible to the individual Jivas. His work consists of four different 'Pasurams'—stanzas, hymns or songs in praise of the Lord. The 'Thiruviruttam' consisting of 100 'Pasurams' expounds the Rigveda, the 'Thiruvasiriyam' of seven 'Pasurams' expounds the Yajurveda, the 'Periya Thiruvandhadi' containing 87 hymns expounds the Atharva Veda and the 'Thiruvaimozhi' of 1,102 hymns expounds the Sama Veda.

Out of these 1,102 hymns, he sang 35 in praise of Sri Venkateswara. He identifies the Lord here with 'Thiruvikrama' in the 8th hymn. In the 'Thiruvaimozhi', he mentions the Hill and the Deity in hymns 5,6,7,8,9,10 and 13. He identifies the Lord with Lord Vishnu, Sri Rama and Vamana. He says that for both the people who live on Earth and for those who abide in Heaven, the Lord abiding in Thiruvengadam is the protector, like the eyelids protects the eyes. He also says that the deity of the Vengadam Hill alone destroys all *karma*, good as well as bad and puts an end to this body with its cycle of birth and death. He gives salvation even to the Devas, who for that purpose, worship this deity daily.

He further says that the Lord of Vengadam is the truth of the *Vedas* and He has freed him (Nammalwar) of all sins and helped him attain the supreme bliss. He describes the Lord of Vengadam as the 'Adi Murthy' or the earliest Lord and the Hill as one that gives *moksha* or salvation.

He devoted 10 hymns of his 'Thiruvaimozhi' to Tirumala itself and makes a detailed reference to the temple here. In another one or two groups of 10 verses he makes an indirect reference, which in all likelihood, indicates the Tirumala temple. He also believed that the Lord of Tirumala is a combination of Rudra, Brahma and so on. He says that the Lord merged in Himself Rudra, Brahma and Lakshmi after destroying their separate identities.

It is said that Sri Anantalwar, a disciple of Sri Ramanuja, was working in the Lord's garden and his pregnant wife was assisting him. When she became very tired, the compassionate Lord assumed the form of a lad and began helping her. Anantalwar did not like this. Furious, he hit the chin of the lad with a spade. At once the lad disappeared. Anantalwar was perplexed. However, when he visited the temple, he found that the Lord's chin was bleeding. With great remorse, he apologised to the Lord and applied *pachcha karpooram* (camphor) on the wound. The Lord not only pardoned Anantalwar but he also smilingly told him that He would display the camphor forever on His chin to honour his devotion.

In Sanskrit Literary Works

The Hill is also mentioned in Sanskrit literary works. For example, in the *Vishvagunadarsa Champu* composed during the 17th century by Venkatadhvari, the glory of Venkateswara is described. It says that Lord Vishnu found the temple a better place than Vaikunta and therefore made it his permanent abode. The author says that the Lord here is the essence of all *Vedas*. He is nearest to the hearts of all His devotees and an incarnation of Lord Krishna.

Nattipalli Narakanthiraya Sastri of the 20th century composed two sets of Sanskrit stanzas in praise of the Lord; one set of five stanzas and a second set of nine verses called the *Sri Venkatesha Satakam*.

In Telugu Literature

In Telugu literature too, one can find many references to the temple and the Lord.

Sri Krishnadevaraya talks about Lord Venkateswara in his work *Amukthamalyada* in 1516 CE. It dealt with the life of Andal or Goda Devi and her foster-father Vishnuchittha, along with stories and episodes of saints from the *Puranas* and other sources.

Chayapathi of the 18th century dedicated his Telugu work *Raghavabhyudayam* to Lord Venkateswara.

There are several Telugu songs in praise of Lord Venkateswara.

The *Venkatachala Vihara Sathakam* describes the hardship faced by the Hindu pilgrims who climbed the Hills of Tirumala at the hands of the Muslim armies.

In the *Venkatachala Dhama Taravali*, the poet expresses his deep devotion to the Lord.

The *Venkateswara Panchaka* makes a reference to the upright *namam* and black hair of the Lord.

In the *Venkatachalapathi Sathakam* the poet surrenders totally to the grace of the Lord.

The *Venkata Nagadhyaksha Sathakam* says that the spot on which the temple stands is Vaikunta. It also describes the *shankha* and *chakra* of the Lord and His holy feet saying that they radiated all the eight *siddhis* or paranormal powers.

The *Sri Venkateswara Kalyana* makes a reference to the story of Bhrigu Maharshi that culminated in the celestial wedding of Lord Venkateswara with Goddess Padmavathi.

Tarigonda Vengamamba praises the Lord in many of her works. She also describes the celestial wedding of the Lord and her intense devotion to Lord Krishna is evident in her poems.

Yerra Pragada Kavi in one of his verses, completely surrenders his soul to the Lord.

Chadalavada Mallayya Kavi refers to Lord Venkateswara in his poem.

Talapakka Annamacharya, the great devotee of Lord Venkateswara, who was born in the year 1408 and who lived for 96 years, composed *sankeerthanas* both in Sanskrit and in Telugu in praise of Lord Venkateswara. He was known as 'Sankeerthanacharya'. His grandson Chinna Tirumalacharya in his poetical work *Annamacharya Charithamu,* mentions that his grandfather composed 32,000 *sankeerthanas*. Annamayya also wrote a book called *Venkateswaraaka*, pertaining to Goddess Alamelu Manga, the consort of Lord Venkateswara.

Pedda Tirumalacharya, Annamacharya's son, translated the *Suprabhatham* as *Sri Venkateswara Prabhatastava.*

Revanuri Venkataraya, Annamayya's son-in-law, who lived in the 16th century, wrote *Sri Padarenu Mahatmya* describing the divine qualities of Sri Padarenu and he requests the Lord to bless him always with 'renu' or the divine inspiration to compose poems. He says that the *Sri Padarenu* has the power to cure the deaf-mute, the ignorant and those who stammer. The power comes from the Lord in the form of Dhanvantari.

In the 1920s, from a small cell sealed with loose stones in the

Vimana Pradakshinam inside the Temple, about 3,000 copper plates were recovered by the TTD, each with three *sankeerthanas* of Annamayya engraved on both sides. Some of the plates also have the compositions of his son Pedda Tirumalacharya and his grandson Chinna Tirumalacharya. Out of the total of 18,000, about 10,000 *sankeerthanas* were authored by Annamacharya, 5,000 by his son Tirumala and around 3,000 by his grandson. The rest of the songs are believed lost.

It is said that when Annamacharya was on his deathbed, he told his son Tirumala to compose at least one song each day and sing it in front of the Lord. Pedda Tirumalacharya and his son, Tirumala, who was proficient in 8 languages and therefore given the title of 'Charutara Ashta Bhasha Chakravarthi', composed several *sringara keerthanas* as well as *adhyatma keerthanas* on Lord Venkateswara. A few *sankeerthanas* that were found in Ahobilam were acquired by the TTD and it is said that some were in Srirangam Temple.

Purandaradasa was a Kannada musician known as 'Dasaru'—one among those who are highly devoted to Lord Vitthala or Panduranga of Pandharpur. He lived in the latter part of the 15th century and early part of the 16th century. Purandaradasa heard about the fame of Annamacharya and came all the way to Tirumala to meet him. Each had great respect for the other. They jointly composed one song. Although the song is one, each addressed his favourite deity in that song.

Vyasaraya who was also known as Vyasa Teertha and who was the teacher of Purandaradasa, composed a song on Lord Venkateswara in Kannada.

The triumvirate of Carnatic music, Thyagaraja, Muthuswami Dikshithar and Syama Sastrigal, belonged to the 18th and 19th centuries CE. Thyagaraja was born in 1759. He visited the temple once and sang two *keerthanas* dedicated to the Lord.

Muthuswami Dikshithar was born in 1775. He composed five songs in praise of Lord Venkateswara.

Syama Sastrigal, whose original name was Venkata Subramanya, was born in 1763. Out of his 300 *keerthanas*, one was on Lord Venkateswara. His second son Subbiah Sastri, also composed a song in praise of Lord Venkateswara.

Vina Kuppier was a direct disciple of Sri Thyagaraja. He composed *pancharatna keerthanas* on the Lord.

Patnam Subramanya Iyyar (1845-1902), Ramanathapuram Srinivasa Iyyangar and so on have also composed songs in praise of the Lord.

Kakamani Murthi Kavi who lived in the 16th century, dedicated his work *Raja Vahana Vijaya* to Sri Venkateswara. In it, he praises the Lord as Thimmappa, a shortened form of 'Tirumala Appa'. He concludes by saying that there is no other god as benevolent and magnanimous as Sri Venkateswara, the Lord of Seshachala, in bestowing gifts on all His devotees.

Siddhi Raju Thimmaraju who was the governor of Kondavidu and nephew of Aliya Ramaraya of the Aravidu dynasty, in his poem, refers to Lord Venkateswara's divine pose, His left hand resting on His lap, His gold ornaments, His right *varadahastha* posture pointing to His feet, His merciful looks, His strings of pearls and His sacred Skanda and Chakra Teerthas.

Tari Goppula Mallan, a native of Chandragiri, in his poem, *Chandrabhanu Charitham* describes the journey of innumerable pilgrims who come to worship Sri Venkateswara undergoing all kinds of physical inconveniences and pains.

Pingali Suranaraya, in his work *Manikhandara* narrates the story of a disciple of Narada who made a pilgrimage to Tirumala and to the temple of Sri Venkateswara. He gives a graphic description of the Temple as it looked around the 16th century when he composed this poem.

Sreshtaluri Venkataraya in his *Srinivasa Vilasa Sevadhi* lists the nine *teerthas* found in the Swami Pushkarini namely, the Varaha Teertha at the northwest corner; Kubera (Dhanada) Teertha on the north; Galva (Arishi) Teertha on the northeast; Markandeya Teertha on the east; Agni Teertha on the southeast; Yama Teertha on the south; Vasishta Teertha on the southwest; Vayu Teertha on the west in the shade of the Asvatha tree and Saraswathi Teertha in the centre of Swami Pushkarini.

His work, besides containing legends, also describes the work of King Thondaiman who built this temple and the various *vahanas* and festivals of the temple. These are the Sesha Vahana marking devotion, Hamsa Vahana which symbolises the instruction given to Brahma as a swan, Simha Vahana indicating the slaying of Hiranyaksha, Pushpaka Vahana indicating that the Lord and Goddess Padmavathi travelled in it, Garuda Vahana as a mark of Gajendra Moksha, Hanumantha Vahana to denote the Bhakthi or devotion of Lord Anjaneya who carried Lord Vishnu as Rama on His shoulders, Gajavahana denoting royalty when Sri Rama rode an elephant called Satrunjaya, Surya Vahana denoting Surya or sun, Ratha Vahana to denote Lord's *hitha* as a *sarathy* or charioteer, Thuranga Vahana to indicate the Lord's victory over demons and Sibhika Vahana or palanquin indicating the Lord's desire to protect His devotees.

There are numerous other authors, including Ganapavarapu Venkata Kavi who composed a work called *Venkata Vilasa* and dedicated it to the Lord; Challapalli Narasa Kavi who lived in the early part of the 18th century, who in his work, *Venkateswara Vilasa*, describes the Lord's wedding with a Chenchu woman; Krishna Kavi, a poet of the 20th century, who dedicated his translation of Kalidasa's *Shakunthala* to Lord Srinivasa; Veturi Prabhakara Sastri who compiled 19 *sathakams* in praise of Lord Venkateswara (he designated this volume as 'Sri Venkateswara Laghu-Kruthulu') and other poems and prose from several manuscripts. All of them address Lord Srinivasa as 'Sathru Samhara Venkatachala Vihara', 'Venkata Satha Nayaka', 'Venkataramana', 'Venkateswara', 'Venkatachalapathy' and so on.

A few of the works are complete, others are incomplete and the authors of numerous other works are unknown. Another work *Venkatachala Vilasini* composed by an unknown poet, describes the pilgrimage of certain rishis to the Hills of Venkatachala. Divakara Tirupata Sastry and Charlapalle Venkata Sastri, of the late 19th century and early 20th centuries, wrote more than 100 works dedicated to Lord Venkateswara.

Many other modern poets, who are less well-known, have also composed songs on Lord Srinivasa. It is said, that when the famous Saivite saint Appayya Dikshitar visited the holy Hill, he was refused *darshan* because he was a staunch devotee of Lord Shiva. When the doors of the temple were opened the next morning, the priests saw the Lord in the form of Lord Shiva. They realised their mistake, welcomed the saint and begged for forgiveness.

Another story is that Lord Venkateswara played dice with a great *bhaktha* Hathiram Bhavaji who is supposed to have come to Tirumala around 1500 CE. When the Lord lost the game he became a servant of this devotee and this is said to be the reason why the management of the Temple went into the hands of Mahants in 1843. This tale is found in the *Venkatachala Mahatmyam*.

3
Sanctity of the Teerthas of Tirumala

The sacred Hill of Tirumala was also known as 'Teerthadri' once upon a time because of the presence of many sacred springs on the Hill, a number of which are inaccessible. It is said that there are 1,008 Teerthas on the Hill of Venkatachala. It is also said that once, the thousand sons of Daksha did severe penance at each of the Teerthas on Venkatachala. Narada advised them to excavate 108 more Teerthas. It is believed that Swami Pushkarini, Akasha Ganga, Papavinasam or Papanasam, Pandu, Kumaradhara, Thumburu and Krishna are the most sacred among them. Again, it is said that those who take a dip in these Teerthas attain the supreme state. Further, bathing in any one of these Teerthas when the Sun is in Capricorn on a full moon day, is considered most auspicious.

It is said that 68 Teerthas in Venkatachala and its surroundings are important. The very recital of their names liquidates all the sins of a person. Some of these are: Chakra, Vajra, Vishvaksena, Panchayuda, Halayantha, Narasimha, Kasyapa, Manmada, Brahma, Agni, Gowthama, Dyva, Vishvamitra, Bhargava, Astavakra, Durarohana, Bhyrava, Maha, Pandava, Vayu, Asthi, Markandeya, Jablai, Valakhilya, Jwarahara, Vishahara, Lakshmi, Rishi, Sathananda, Vybhandhika, Bilwa, Vishnu, Sarabha, Brahma, Indra, Bharadwaja, Ambara Ganga, Prachetasa, Papavinasa, Saraswathi, Kumara Dharika, Gaja, Rishya Sringa, Thumburu, Asthadeva, Dasavatara, Helayuva, Saptarshi, Gaja

Karna and Gajakara. It is also said that Lord Shiva advised Lord Subramanya to go to Venkatachala where there are several Teerthas. Of these, He said the Chakra, Swami, Matsya, Pandava, Naga, Bilwa, Jabali, Akashaganga, Papavinasa, Thumburu, Vamana and Kumaradhara are the most important and one who sings the glory of these Teerthas would be relieved from all his past sins. It is believed that Markandeya bathed in several of these Teerthas.

Swami Pushkarini and other Teerthas

Swami Pushkarini is the holy tank near the main temple. The Varahaswami temple is located on its southern bank. The float festival of the Lord is held here during February-March and the Avabhredha Snanam, also known as Chakrasnanam, is held on the last day of the annual Brahmotsavam. Pilgrims take a holy dip in the Pushkarini before entering the main temple.

The *Varaha Purana* describes the greatness and sanctity of this sacred tank. It is believed that of all the Teerthas, the Swami Pushkarini is the holiest. Sri Varaha recounted the greatness of Swami Pushkarini and other Teerthas to His beloved consort Dharani Devi. He said that Swami Pushkarini equalled in merit all the Teerthas in the three worlds combined. It is only to serve the Pushkarini that all the other Teerthas abide on the sacred Hill of Tirumala.

It is supposed to have been brought down to Earth by Garuda, the vehicle of Lord Vishnu, for the Lord's sport. It is believed that it contains all the sacred Teerthas. A holy dip in it would bring about material prosperity and spiritual fulfilment. By merely seeing, touching or even remembering Swami Pushkarini, one will be able to fulfil all one's desires. Even physical deformities are said to be cured by observing religious rites near Swami Pushkarini.

It is said that Lord Subramanya expiated His sin of killing

Tarakasura after taking a bath here. King Dasaratha did penance near this holy tank and obtained a boon by which Lord Narayana Himself was born to him as Rama his son. Janaka also is believed to have bathed in the tank. Sri Rama is supposed to have vanquished Ravana after the sacred bath in Swami Pushkarini. Markandeya took a bath in Swami Pushkarini in order to gain the merit of taking a holy dip in all the sacred Teerthas. Even Goddess Saraswathi is believed to have come down to have a holy dip here.

Brahma was once performing austerities near Swami Pushkarini. Pleased with His penance, Lord Vishnu appeared before Him and agreed to stay there until the end of the Kalpa along with His consort Sri Devi, Bhu Devi, Neela and all His attendants, Sesha, Garuda and Vishvaksena, for blessing the humans and saving them from their sins. Brahma also obtained the Lord's approval for conducting Brahmotsavam.

The glory of Swami Pushkarini is sung by all the sages like Atri, Vyasa and Vasishta. They have repeatedly emphasised the sanctity of the tank. Its sanctity and glory were also lauded by Brahma to Vamadeva.

It is said that King Dharmagupta who was the son of King Nanda, a descendant of the Soma Dynasty was cursed by a bear to become a lunatic. King Nanda took his son to the hermitage of sage Jaimini and requested him to cure his son's insanity. Jaimini advised the king to take his son to Swami Pushkarini for a holy dip. Dharmagupta was cured completely and was absolved of his sin.

Sumathi was the son of a pious Brahmin Yagnadeva who was an expert in the *Vedas*. Due to bad company, Sumathi was led astray and he left his parents and wife and ran away to Utkal. There he met Yuvamohini, an immoral woman and in course of time became a pauper because of his friendship with her. Sumathi began to steal to maintain himself and the woman he loved. Once while stealing in the house of a Brahmin, he killed the Brahmin. The sin committed by him followed him wherever he went. He at last returned to his parents. But even his father could not save him from the sin of killing a Brahmin. At that moment, sage Durvasa came there. He advised Sumathi to take a holy dip in Swami Pushkarini to get rid of the sin. As soon as Sumathi did so, all his sins were washed away.

Sankhana was a bad king, so he was driven away from his kingdom by the feudatory chiefs. Sankhana reached Rameshwaram and from there he came to the northern bank of Swarnamukhi River. He took a dip, proceeded to Padmasarovar and stayed there. In his sleep, he heard a heavenly voice asking him to travel further northwards to Sri Venkatachala and bathe in Swami Pushkarini. Then he was to go towards the west where there was an anthill and construct a small hut there. He was to reside in it, bathe in Swami Pushkarini thrice a day and meditate on Lord Venkateswara for six months continuously with unflinching devotion. Then he would regain his kingdom. Sankhana obeyed the heavenly voice. As prophesied by the voice, he had a vision of Lord Vishnu who said that he was about to regain his kingdom. When the king returned to his capital, circumstances had changed in such a manner that there was no ruler. Sankhana, who had turned over a new leaf, now ruled the kingdom well.

Sankha, who was the son of King Srutha of Hyhaya dynasty, was a great devotee of Lord Narayana and he yearned for a vision of Sri Hari. Once the Lord appeared in his dream and asked Sankha to go to Narayanachala (Narayanadri), take a dip in Swami Pushkarini and perform *tapas*. He said that after 1,000 years, when the sage Agasthya came there accompanied by his disciples, he would have the vision of the Lord. Sankha did as the Lord commanded and 1,000 years passed. When sage Agasthya came there, both he and Sankha had a vision of the Lord.

It is said that sage Sukha visited Venkatachala and did *tapas* near Padma Sarovar. Due to his *tapas* everything came to a standstill. Indra sent an *apsara* in order to disturb him. But Sukha could not be disturbed. He did not waste the powers of his *tapas* by cursing the *apsara*. Instead he began to meditate on the Lord with more intensity than before. A pleased Lord appeared before him. The Lord then blessed sage Sukha and said that the sage would go to heaven in the flesh and at the end of the *Kalpa* or aeon, he would merge with the Lord's divine body. Saying this, the Lord disappeared.

Sage Kasyapa had the power to save anyone from any poison, whatever its potency. However, he did not save King Parikshit from the bite of Thakshaka, the king of serpents. Instead, he took the precious gems and other gifts given to him by Thakshaka and returned to his ashram. He knew that Parikshit was destined to face death from the poison of Thakshaka. Later Kashyapa approached Sage Sakalya for relief from the sin that he committed in not saving the king, although he was capable of it. Sage Sakalya asked Kashyapa to go to Venkatachala and take a bath in Swami Pushkarini and worship Sri Varahaswami and then worship Lord Srinivasa, so that his sin would be washed away.

Atmarama was a pious Brahmin. When he lost all his property after the death of his father, he proceeded to Venkatadri. He took a holy dip in all the Teerthas. There he found Sanatkumara who was engaged in deep meditation. Atmarama saluted the great sage and sought his blessings. He told Atmarama that his misery was due to his evil deeds in the past. Sanatkumara asked the Brahmin to go to Venkatachala and chant the *mantra* of *Vyuhalakshmi*, that is, mother of the *Vedas*, with a clean body and pure mind after bathing in Swami Pushkarini. Atmarama followed the advice of the sage. He had a vision of Lord Venkateswara with His consorts and he was freed from all his miseries.

Sarvabaddha was an atheist and evil, but he was unusually devoted to sage Vasishta. So Vasishta asked Brahma to tell him a way in which he could rid himself of his sins because of his association with Sarvabaddha. Lord Brahma asked him to go to Venkatadri and have a dip in Swami Pushkarini. He also mentioned Ghona Teertha that had the power to wash away sins if one took a bath in it when the Sun entered Pisces, on a full moon day.

Vasishta accompanied by his disciples and Sarvabaddha, went to Swarnamukhi River and later to Kapila Teertha and thence to Swami Pushkarini. He bathed in all the three Teerthas and offered prayers to the Lord. He proceeded to Papavinasa Teertha on an Ekadasi Day and fasted for five nights. Sage Vasishta went into deep meditation and entered a state of *samadhi*. Lord Venkateswara appeared and comforted Vasishta and told him that He would make Sarvabaddha a virtuous person. Not only that, he would remove all the sins that had befallen Vasishta on account of Sarvabaddha.

It is believed that a dip in Swami Pushkarini on Mukkoti Dwadasi day, that usually falls on the 12th day of the fortnight of Dhanurmasa (December-January), is equivalent to taking a bath in the holy Ganges and would destroy all sins. All one's desires would be fulfilled and one would attain liberation, as on this day, more than three crore Teerthas merge in the tank.

There are nine other holy Teerthas near Swami Pushkarini like Dhanada and Galava.

Papavinasam

It is located 5 km north of the temple. It is believed that the water that one uses for the sacred bath becomes discoloured in proportion to the number of sins that one has committed. The *Varaha Purana* says that a sacred bath in this Teertha on the seventh day of the bright fortnight combined with the star Uttarasadha; Sunday on the 12th day of the bright fortnight combined with Uttarabhadra star; Sunday in the month of Aswayuja; and the 7th day of the bright or the dark fortnight in the month of Vaishakha combined either with the star Pushya or Hastha on a Sunday, is considered to be extremely sacred.

Nowadays, the supply of water here is maintained with water from the dam. The dam was constructed for meeting the increased demand for water in Tirumala. The temple and Tirumala town get water supply through a reservoir. The Gogarbham Dam is on the way to Papavinasam. A bypass enables the devotees to take the sacred bath.

Kumaradhara

This Teertha is about 10 km to the northwest of the temple. A festival is held here on Magha Poornima. It is said that on the full moon day in the month of Kumbha, all the Teerthas congregate at Kumaradhara and a dip is considered highly auspicious. It confers all the goodness of bathing in the Ganga and other sacred rivers. It is said that Lord Shiva asked His son Lord Skanda to go to Kumara Teertha, salute it and recite the mantra *'Om Sri Venkateshaya Namaha'* and perform *tapas*. Skanda bathed in the Swami Pushkarini and Chakra Teertha and sang the praise of Lord Venkateswara in the shrine. He proceeded to Papavinasa Teertha and after a dip there, continued to the sacred waterfalls that lay in the southwest. He bathed again and began to meditate.

At midday of a full moon day in the month of Kumbha, God revealed himself to Skanda. He directed Skanda to perform *tapas* for 12 years to attain peace and happiness. The Lord then told Skanda about the sanctity of Kumaradhara. He said that a dip in the Kumaradhara on the day Lord Hari manifested before Skanda would elevate all those who bathed there. Every year all the gods and men would congregate for a holy dip. He instructed Skanda to stay on there till the end of the Kalpa. After 12 years of penance, Skanda was relieved of the sin of killing Tarakasura.

In *Varaha Purana*, it is said that once Lord Venkateswara in the guise of a charming youth, was roaming about on Venkatachala. He saw an old man with poor eyesight wandering around weeping of great hunger and thirst, calling out to his son Koundinya. Lord Venkateswara told him that there was no one there. He wanted to know why he wished to keep on living at such an old age and in an impoverished condition. The old man replied saying that he wished to live only to fulfil his desire to perform rituals and religious offerings to the gods and his ancestors.

Lord Venkateswara took the old man near the water source and asked him to have a dip there. As soon as the old man bathed in the sacred waters, he emerged as a sixteen year-old boy. The youth was really none other than the Lord with 1000 hands and heads. Since then, this spot with the sacred waters came to be known as Kumaradhara. It is believed that whoever bathes in this Teertha thrice a day for three months while leading a life of restraint is freed from all illnesses. His body would become strong like a diamond and he would get rid of all his sins and reach the highest region, the realm of Lord Vishnu, in the end.

In the Markandeya Purana, the same story is told in a different way. Once there was an old man, who was disgusted with life. He left his family and reached River Swarnamukhi wanting to end his life. He climbed Venkatachala and was about to throw himself down. Lord Venkateswara who was hunting at that time in the guise of a prince, saw the old man and told him that the Sastras prohibit suicide. Then he took the old man with Him to the north of Papavinasa Teertha and asked him to take a dip there. As soon as the old man had a dip, he became a charming youth. Meanwhile the Lord disappeared. But the old man heard a heavenly voice that told him that the prince was none other than Lord Venkateswara. All his wishes were granted and the voice said that he should go back home and perform all the Dharmas as prescribed in the Sastras.

Seeing this, all the gods said, "Let this Teertha be known as

Kumaradhara. Anyone who bathes here will live happily and will be free from all sins."

The man then returned to his village and lived a pious and virtuous life and finally reached Vaikunta, the abode of the Lord.

Thumburu Teertha (Also known as Ghona Teertha or Phalguna Teertha)

This Teertha is about 16 km north of the temple in the midst of thick forest. A festival is held here on Phalguna Poornima day. According to tradition, many sages lived here once. It is a favourite place for wild animals like tigers. It is said that at one spot there is a cave that has a secret passage leading to the Sri Venkateswara Temple. It is also said that during the Muslim invasion in the 14th century, the idol of Sri Ranganatha in the Srirangam Temple was brought to Tirumala for safe-keeping. The idol is said to have been dropped into a deep ravine and was worshipped there for some time. It is assumed that the small mandapam that is seen in the middle of the Teertha might have been that spot. According to the *Varaha Purana*, in the month of Meena, on the full moon day when the star Uttara Phalguna is ascendant, three crore Devas bathe in it and a dip in this Teertha at that time would release one from the cycle of birth and death. It would confer great merit not only on the person but also on his ancestors. It would confer the same merit as that of a holy dip in the Ganges, Narmada, Chandrabhaga or Sarayu Rivers. It is said that Arundhathi, wife of Sage Vasishta, visited several Teerthas on the sacred hill, including Swami Pushkarini, worshipped the Lord here and spent 12 years in penance without food at Thumburu Teertha. Pleased with her *tapas*, the Lord appeared before her on the full moon day in the Phalguna month. She requested the Lord to tell her about the sanctity of the Teertha.

The Lord told her that those of His devotees who bathed in

the waters of Swami Pushkarini would be blessed with longevity and prosperity. Those who bathed in Thumburu Teertha would earn the grace of the Lord and that of His consort Goddess Lakshmi. Those who bathed in the waters of Thumburu Teertha on the full moon day of Phalguna, the day he appeared before Arundhathi, would gain the merit of bathing in all the Teerthas. The Teertha would also thus be known as Phalguna Teertha. Those who bathed here would get rid of all sins of mind and body and all their desires would be fulfilled.

Another legend relates that once Narada and his friend Thumburu were floating in the sky with veenas in their hands. Narada wanted to know why Thumburu's veena was not as resplendent as his. Thumburu replied that this was because the veena had been presented to him by King Pracheenabarhis for singing his praises. Narada was furious and yelled that Thumburu was not worthy of his (Narada's) friendship. Thumburu's veena should sing the glories of Lord Vishnu alone and not of a mortal king. He cursed him to lose the power of flying. At once, Thumburu fell down in the midst of a wild forest near Ghona Teertha on Venkatachala. He took a bath in the Teertha and meditated and prayed to Lord Narayana for a year. On the full moon day of Phalguna (March), the Lord appeared before him and asked him to have a holy dip in the Teertha to get rid of all sins. Thumburu then requested the Lord to name the Teertha after him and the Lord agreed.

There is also a story that on a winter's day, a Gandharva called Thumburu asked his wife to follow him to River Malapaha for a sacred bath. The water in the river had the capacity to save sinners. But Thumburu's wife was reluctant to accompany her husband. Thumburu cursed his wife in anger, saying that she would be born as a frog under a peepul tree with no water near Ghona Teertha on Venkatachala. When his wife repented, he took pity on her. He said that the curse would be lifted when she listened to sage Agasthya who would visit the Teertha with his disciples and expound its glory. This came true. Agasthya stated that Venkatachala is the most sacred place on Earth and that the Lord here pardons even the worst sins of His devotees who worship Him. When the frog listened to Agastya, it regained its original form and prostrated before the sage. Then the sage told her that since she had listened to the glory of Ghona Teertha, she would be rid of her sins.

Akasha Ganga

It is a waterfall that is about 2 km to the north of the temple. The origin of this Teertha is believed to be from the holy feet of Lord Narayana. Anjana Devi performed severe penance here for 12 years in Tretha Yuga and begot Anjaneya.

It is said that Tirumalai Nambi used to fetch water from a far-off waterfall in Papavinasam for the daily abhishekam and worship of the Lord in the temple. One day the Lord, in order to test the depth of Nambi's devotion, appeared as a hunter and asked for some water to quench His thirst. When Tirumala Nambi refused to give him water, the hunter struck the pot with an arrow and drank it without Nambi's knowledge. Nambi reached the temple with an empty pot, but he found that the Lord had had His abhishekam already. Tirumalai Nambi was about to set out again for water, when the hunter told Nambi that there was an equally pure water source much nearer to the temple. He shot an arrow into the ground and water began spouting from that spot. It came to be known as Akasha Ganga. From that day onwards, Tirumalai Nambi fetched the water from there.

Even today, three silver pots of this Teertha are brought each morning for the abhishekam by one of the seven families of Acharya Purushas who recite the *Mantra Pushpam* before the Deity. They belong to the family of Tirumalai Nambi. It is said that a dip in the Akasha Ganga in the early morning on the full moon day when the Sun is in Aries and the star Chitra is ascendant with the moon, is highly beneficial and ensures salvation.

Chakra Teertha

It is located 3 km to the northwest of the temple. At this Teertha, there are the images of Sri Lakshmi Narasimha and Sudarshana Chakra. On the 12th day of the dark fortnight in the month of Karthika, *payasam* (sweet pudding) from the Temple is offered to the images here. According to Skanda Purana, Lord Vishnu sent His Sudarsana Chakra here to destroy the demons. The Utsavamurthy is brought here during Brahmotsavam..

Sundara, a Gandharva who had become an evil demon due to the curse of sage Vasishta, regained his previous form when the Chakra of Lord Vishnu cut his head off in order to save Sage Padmanabha who was about to be eaten by him. Sage Padmanabha requested the Chakra or Disc to stay there so that the water source might be named after Him and the sages could live there fearlessly. The water source came to be known as Chakra Teertha. The Sudarsana Chakra also assured the sage that those who bathed in the Teertha would prosper in every way.

During the month of Karthika, the Kheerabdi Dwadasi festival is held here.

Vajra Teertha

It is located above Kapila Teertha. It is said that a dip ensures a place in the realm of Indra. A legend about Devendra or Indra is connected to the Teertha. Devendra fell in love with the sage Gouthama's wife. The sage cast a curse on him that his body would grow 1,000 female organs. Devendra prayed to Vishnu at the Teertha and saw a vision of him as Varaha who granted him a boon. The 1,000 female organs dropped off and the scars left behind were converted to 1,000 eyes. The Teertha at Vrishabhadri was named Vajra Teertha after Indra's weapon, the lightning bolt.

Vishvaksena Sarovar

It is located above Vajra Teertha. It is said that Varuna's son did severe penance at Vishvaksena Teertha and was blessed with a form identical to that of Sri Hari. The Lord then appointed him as the commander-in-chief of His army and he became Vishvaksena.

Jabali Teertha

This Teertha is located at a distance of 5 km from the main temple. It is believed that Jabali Rishi lived here for some time along with his disciples.

According to one story, Durachara was a Brahmin living on the banks of River Kaveri. He was a bad person and therefore he was possessed by a goblin or Bhetala. He ran from place to place and finally reached Venkatachala and fell into the Jabali Teertha. Immediately he regained his previous form of a Brahmin. On the way back to his home, he met sage Jabali who gave him an insight into his earlier life.

Then the sage stated that a dip in the Jabali Teertha would redeem anyone from the gravest sins. Even those who were wandering the Earth as ghosts would be relieved of their sins and attain salvation. According to the *Varaha Purana*, Agasthya also stayed here for a long time along with his disciples.

Hanuman Jayanthi is celebrated every year as Sri Rama is believed to have stopped here.

Jaraharadi Teertha

In a cave east of Swami Pushkarini there is a sacred Teertha called Jaraharadi Teertha. It is said that there are precious stones and costly metals buried in its banks. It is also said that there are two other Teerthas in its vicinity. A true devotee who climbs the Hill after bathing in this Teertha it is believed, can notice its miraculous effects.

Pandava Teertha (Also known as Gogarbha Teertha)

It is located on Narayanagiri, about a km to the northeast of the temple. It is said that Lord Krishna advised the Pandavas to visit this Teertha, hence the name. They followed His advice and after the sacred bath, the Pandava brothers worshipped the Lord here for a year. Yudhishtira had a dream in which the Lord announced that anyone who stayed on the Hill for a year would be rid of all sins and would recover his lost property and kingdom.

Beside it, there is a small cave with carvings of the Pandava princes. It is also called Gogarbha Teertha on account of a depression in the western side of the channel that resembles a cow's stomach.

It is said that one who bathes in this holy Teertha on the 12th day of the bright fortnight in Vaishakha when the Sun is in Taurus and in conjunction with Mars, would be freed of all kinds of difficulties in life.

On a Sunday of the bright fortnight or on Tuesday in the same month during the dark fortnight, all the sacred rivers including Ganga congregate in this Teertha and a dip on that day confers great merit.

Ramakrishna Teertha

It is about 10 km to the north of the Temple. According to Skanda Purana, sage Ramakrishna who performed penance on Venkatachala, dug a tank for taking his daily bath. In course of time, an anthill grew over the body of the sage. The sage was unaware of this as he was in deep meditation. The heat given off by his body due to the penance was such that Indra had to send incessant rain for seven days. Consequently, the anthill broke down. From it sprang Lord Narayana with conch and disc in His hands.

He was pleased with the sage and said that anyone who bathed in the Teertha on the full moon day when the Sun was in Capricorn and the Moon was aligned with the star Pushyami, would be rid of all sins. All the gods and men would be purified by taking a dip in the sacred waters of this Teertha on the day when Lord Narayana revealed Himself to the sage. Having said this, the Lord disappeared. Since then, this Teertha has been known as Ramakrishna Teertha.

A festival is held here on Pushya Poornima day in the month of Magha.

Varaha Teertha

Varaha Teertha is located to the northwest of Swami Pushkarini. When Lord Vishnu in the incarnation of a boar, lifted the Earth from underwater and killed Hiranyaksha the demon, the sages consecrated Lord Narayana in the form of Varaha there. They gave the idol a sacred bath in a Teertha that later came to be known as Varaha Teertha.

Sanaka Sanadana Teertha

This Teertha is located about 6 km north of Papavinasa Teertha. It is said that this Teertha is worshipped by Siddhas. Those who encounter obstacles in yoga are advised to bathe here to attain success. They should first bathe in Swami Pushkarini at sunrise on the 12th day of the bright fortnight in the month of Margasira, that is December, with a pure mind. From the next morning onwards, they should bathe in the Sanaka Sanadana

Teertha and should invoke Lord Narayana 1000 times a day. This Teertha is not visible to the common man. The *Varaha Purana* explains the procedure to be followed by those who practise yoga for bathing in this Teertha.

Kayarasayana Teertha (Also known as Asthi Saras)

It is located near the Sanaka Sanadana Teertha. It is said that the body of one who drinks the waters of this Teertha would be instantaneously purified. It is said that even a rotting yellow-coloured leaf thrown into its waters would at once turn green. This Teertha is hidden from view for the common man and is visible only to the Mahatmas. It is believed that the source of this Teertha was blocked with stones by Sanaka and other rishis.

Kataha Teertha (Also known as Thotti Teertha or Tub of Holy Water)

It is located on the northern side of the Vimana Pradakshinam in the temple. Here the Abhishekam Teertha of the Lord is collected after His holy bath.

Padmanabha, a pandit, once lived on the banks of river Tungabhadra where Brahmins well-versed in the *Vedas* resided. Kesava, his son, fell into evil ways and was excommunicated by the other Brahmins of the village. The rest of the story is similar to the one about Sumathi narrated earlier, except that it was the sage Bharadwaja not Durvasa who told father and son to drink the water of the Kataha Teertha to the north of the Venkatachala shrine. The waters of this Teertha had originated from the feet of the Lord. Afterwards they worshipped both Varaha and Venkateswara. They were at once redeemed of their sins.

Viraja Teertha

It is a small Teertha the water of which is collected in a stone tub in the Sampangi Pradakshinam of the Temple. The heavenly river Viraja was believed to flow below the sacred feet of Lord Venkateswara. The feet of the idol were always wet. Attempts were made to arrest the seepage but it was effective only temporarily. So a borewell was sunk in the street behind the Temple and the oozing of water in the sanctum was reduced to a great extent.

According to *Varaha Purana* and *Skanda Purana*, Lord Vishnu who appeared before His devotee who was doing penance, said that those who bathed in this Teertha in the month of Chaitra on the full Moon day when the star Chitra was ascendant, would live happily and would avoid rebirth.

Galava, Markandeya, Yama and Vayu Teerthas

The Galava, Markandeya, Yama and Vayu Teerthas associated with the eponymous sages and gods, are all believed to confer longevity, happiness and salvation on those who drink their waters or bathe in them.

Deva Teertha

It is a tank located in the thick forest to the northwest of the Temple. A bath in this Teertha on Thursday when the star Pushya is on the rise, or on a Monday when the star Sravana is ascendant, destroys all sins and bestows merit, longevity, progeny and happiness in this world and beyond.

Vaikunta Teertha

It is located 3 km to the northeast of the Temple. Its water comes out of a cave called Vaikunta Guha. In *Varaha Purana* it is said that Lord Vishnu who gave His vision and that of Vaikunta to some of the vanaras who accompanied Sri Rama and Lakshmana on their way to Lanka to vanquish the demon king Ravana, resided in this cave in order to give *darshan* to His devotees.

Kapila Teertha

This Teertha flows down the hill where the shrine of Lord Kapileshwara is located. As sage Kapila worshipped the *linga* it is known as 'Kapileshwara Linga'. It was called 'Agneya Linga' in Tretha Yuga, as Agni worshipped it. In the Dwapara Yuga, Chakra worshipped it. In the Kaliyuga, it is called 'Kapila.'

It is said that those who bathe in this Teertha or drink its waters would overcome old age and death. It is also believed that sage Kapila worshipped the sacred Kapila Linga in *patala* or the underworld with the celestial cow's milk. The Teertha here is supposed to be in the cavity which was formed when the *linga* sank down into the Earth along with Kapila Muni. The huge *linga* is multi-coloured. It is silver coloured at the base, golden at the centre and red at the top. It is five-faced and three-eyed. It is said that all the Teerthas of the three worlds congregate in Kapila Teertha on the noon of the full moon day in the month of Karthika, that is, November, and stay there for about four hours. A dip in these sacred waters at that time will wash off all sins and finally one will reach the realm of Brahma.

In addition to the above-mentioned Teerthas, there are also several other sacred Teerthas on the Tirumala Hills, like the Sesha Teertha, Sitharama Teertha and Pasupu Teertha. It is also said that above the hermitage of Vishvaksena, there are five other holy Teerthas called Panchayuda after the five weapons of Lord Vishnu namely Shankha (conch), Chakra (disc), Gada (club), Saranga (bow) and Nandaka or Khadga (sword). In one of these, Agni is said to have performed *tapas*, so it is known as Agneya Teertha.

Above the Agneya Teertha, is said to be the Brahma Teertha near which are located the Teerthas of the seven sages or Saptarishi who had their hermitages here. The Saptarishi Teerthas are named after Kasyapa, Atri, Bharadwaja, Vishwamitra, Gauthama, Vasishtha and Jamadagni.

4

History of Tirupathi, Tirumala and the Temple

The history of the temple of Lord Venkateswara is shrouded in mystery. The temple is believed to be extremely ancient. It is referred to in the old scriptures and Tamil literature. It is said that Lord Venkateswara is mentioned in the *Rigveda* and Tirupathi and Tirumala together are considered as 'Kaliyuga Vaikunta'. However, the exact period during which the temple was constructed is not known. According to tradition, the idol here is *Swayambhu* or self-created (not installed).

History of Tirupathi and Tirumala region

The region in which Tirupathi and Tirumala are located, was once considered the border area between the Tamil country and the country of the Vadugars, or Vaduga Nadu, inhabited by the Kannada- and Telugu-speaking people. The area was a part of Thondaimandalam. The villages around Tirupathi were known as Thirukkodayur Nadu.

In Tamil literature, the region is also referred as 'Aruva Nadu', that is the country of Aruvalars or Kaduvars, a tribe of hunters who had first inhabited Vengadam. Their chieftain was Puli, who was a powerful ruler.

The region was also home to the Tiraiyar who had migrated from lower Burma a very long time ago and mingled with the Aruvalars. One of their chieftains, Thiraiyam, ruled over a wide territory.

The region's political history starts with the Mauryas who overthrew the Nandas. After the Mauryas, it came under the control of the Satavahanas who ruled for more than four centuries. Then it passed into the hands of the Pallavas. The inscriptions on the walls of the temple reveal the history beginning from the Pallava regime.

During the Pallava era, Vengadam was located in Thiruvengada Kottam (*kottam* means *place* in Tamil) within Thondaimandalam and this region was further divided into 24 Kottams and 75 Nadus. Of these, the border area was Thiruvengada Kottam that included Kadukurai Nadu, Pottapi Nadu and Thondamanadu and was considered a place of strategic importance. It comprised of roughly the present Chittor, Chandragiri, Thiruchokkanur, or the modern Tiruchanoor and Kalahasthi.

In the middle of the 4th century, the region passed out of the hands of the early Pallavas when Samudra Gupta of the Gupta dynasty invaded Kanchi and defeated the Pallava ruler Vishnugopa. However, the Pallavas re-established their rule after some time, only to relinquish hold to the Cholas. The Cholas changed the name Thondaimandalam to Jayankonda Cholamandalam. Karikala Chola was the first Chola king and he subjugated the Aruvalar and expanded his kingdom. Ilam Thiraiyan was his contemporary and ruled over Thondaimandalam from Kanchi.

Towards the end of the 1st century CE, Thondaimandalam became a part of the Sathavahana Empire as a result of the death of the Chola king Karikala and the resultant chaos in the south. During this period, Thondaimandalam was ruled by the Aruvalar and Nagas.

During the last days of the Sathavahanas, around the second decade of the 3rd century CE, particularly during the time of the last Sathavahana king Pulumavai III, Mahasenapathi Skandanaga became the governor of a vast region in the south that included Thondaimandalam. The Pallavas were originally the inhabitants of the southeastern part of the Sathavahana Empire bordering Thondaimandalam. The founder and the first ruler of the Pallava dynasty Simhavarman alias Virakurcha, married a Naga princess and inherited her kingdom. He was a powerful ruler. The Pallava realm that was established during the period of Simha Vishnu (560 CE–580 CE) shrank during the period of Mahendra Varman 1 (580 CE–630 CE) as much of the northern territory was captured by Pulakesi II. But later Narasimha Varman 1 (630 CE–668 CE) established the Pallava rule in this region once again.

Pallavas

The reign of the Pallavas is the first major landmark in the history of Thondaimandalam, Tirumala, Tirupathi and the temple on the Tirumala Hills. The founder and the first ruler of the dynasty, Simhavarman alias Virakurcha, invaded the coastal region and ended the Ikshavaku rule and annexed some of the regions of present Andhra Pradesh that included the district of Rayalaseema where Tirupathi is located. Till the end of the 9th century, the Pallavas ruled this land and later it was conquered by the Cholas. The Banas, a family of Pallava feudatories ruled the region around Tirupathi and Tirumala. The early inscriptions on the temple walls mention the name of one Bana Vijayaditya who flourished during the early half of the 9th century CE.

The first of the last three rulers of the Pallava dynasty was Danti Varman (775 CE–826 CE). After two more generations of Pallava kings, the Chola king Aditya I (871 CE–907 CE) invaded Thondaimandalam and defeated the Pallava king Aparajitha and this region came under the control of the Cholas. Thondaimandalam remained in their hands till around the middle of the 13th century (900 CE–1250 CE).

Cholas

During the time of Paranthaka I (907 CE–955 CE), who was the son of Aditya I, the Chola kingdom expanded further. The Rashtrakuta ruler Krishna III, along with several others, fought with Paranthaka I and defeated him. Later Arinjaya and his son Paranthaka II (957 CE–973 CE) regained several regions of their lost kingdom. Parthivendra Varman alias Aditya II who was the son of Paranthaka I, was the viceroy of Thondaimandalam for nearly 15 years from 956 CE. Kulothunga III was the last great Chola emperor. During the reign of the last Chola ruler, Rajendra III (1246 CE–1279 CE) the Chola power weakened. After the fall of the Cholas, their empire disintegrated and there was no central power ruling the land for a number of centuries.

Telugu Pallava Chiefs

A number of Telugu Pallava chiefs like Vijayagandagopala, Rajagandagopala and Thripuranthaka governed parts of Thondaimandalam as subordinates of the Chola kings.

With the Chola power declining, they began to rebel. When the Pandyas, in the form of Sundara Pandya, entered the field, the Pallava chiefs temporarily acknowledged his sovereignty.

The Telugu Pallava chief Vijayagandagopala emerged as an important figure in the history of this region. He along with Kopperunjinga, another Pallava chieftain who was also an ally of the Pandyas, shared Thondaimandalam with the Pandya king. Kopperunjinga or Kadavaraya raided Thondaimandalam in 1220 CE and occupied a part of it. His son Khadgamalla crowned himself as king in 1243 CE and invaded Thondaimandalam and fought with Narasinga Yadavaraya, a local chieftain.

Pandyas

Jatavarman Sundara Pandya I became the Pandya King in 1251 CE. He extended his empire extensively. By the middle of the 13th century, the Pandyas under Mahavarman Sundara Pandya I became very powerful. This king invaded Thondaimandalam, reached up to Nellore and established his rule.

Yadavarayas

The Yadavarayas were the local dynasty and the most important chieftains in the Tirumala-Tirupathi region. They governed part of Thondaimandalam, first as Chola subordinates and then as Pandya feudatories. They had limited authority in a portion of Thondaimandalam under the last Hoysala ruler, Vira Vallaja III and the kings of the Vijayanagara empire in the 14th century. Later they became independent rulers. They exercised authority over the northern and eastern portions of Thondaimandalam.

The greatest chieftain among them was Veera Narasinga Deva. He reigned between 1209 CE and 1262 CE. Veera Narasinga Deva was originally a subordinate of Veera Gandagopala, the Telugu Pallava chief whom Jatavarman Sundara Pandya I defeated. Later he became a powerful feudatory of Rajaraja Chola III. When the Pandyas came to power he became a feudatory chief of the Pandya Kings. He was in charge of a portion of Thondaimandalam that included the modern Kalahasthi, Karveti Nagaram, portions of Chingelpet in the present Tamil Nadu and Chittoor district including Tirupathi.

His son was Thiruvenkatanatha who ruled over the land between 1310 CE and 1336 CE.

Then Sri Ranganatha Yadavaraya became the ruler in 1337 CE and ruled for nearly 20 years. When the Vijayanagara empire was established he ruled as a subordinate to Harihara I. Even at the inception of the Vijayanagara empire in 1336 CE, Thondaimandalam was a part of it.

The Muslim Rule in the north and the Hindu Kingdoms in the South

During this period, Muslim rule was established in northern India. The Khilji dynasty came to power in Delhi towards the end of the 13th century. At this time, there were two great Hindu Kingdoms in the Deccan, the Yadava kingdom with its capital at Devagiri or the modern Daulatabad and the Kakatiya Empire that covered the Telugu-speaking region. To the southwest there was the kingdom of Hoysalas in Mysore state. In the Tamil country, the Pandyas were powerful at that time.

The Khilji general Malik Khafur led an expedition to the South and plundered huge wealth from all the southern kingdoms. Later the Khiljis were succeeded by the Tughlaks who became the rulers of the Sultanate of Delhi. The crown prince Ulugh Khan, son of the ruler Ghiasuddin, led a strong army to the south and captured many places. It was during this time that the processional deity of Sri Ranganatha was smuggled out of Srirangam by Pillai Lokacharya and other devotees. After wandering from place to place, they finally reached the Tirumala Hills. There the idol was suspended in a ravine and later kept in the Tirumala temple for a long time. But during both these invasions, Tirumala and Tirupathi area escaped attention, as the route the armies took did not pass through this region. Ulugh Khan then killed his father, assumed the title of Mohammad bin Tughlak and ascended the throne.

After a few years, the feudatories and generals under the Kakatiya Prataparudra, liberated large areas by driving away the Muslim governors who were appointed by Ulugh Khan. Harihara and Bukka, the two brothers who were the sons of Sangama, the guard of the Kakatiya treasury, fled when the Tughlak army attacked Prataparudra. Guided by the saint Vidyaranya, they returned and founded a new kingdom called Vijayanagara for protecting Hindu religion and culture. They settled on the southern bank of the Tungabhadra in 1336 CE. Thondaimandalam came under the rule of the Vijayanagara emperors from 1336 CE till 1680 CE.

Vijayanagara Empire

Sangama Dynasty

Chittor district then came under the Rayas of the Vijayanagara Empire. Four dynasties namely, the Sangama, the Saluva, the Thuluva and Aravidu dynasties ruled over this kingdom from 1336 CE to the last quarter of the 17th century. Harihara founded the Sangama dynasty in 1336. He was succeeded by his brother Bukka I whose son was Kumara Kampana. During this period, Saluva Mangideva, one of his subordinates, ruled the Chittoor region that became the capital of the later Saluva chiefs.

Harihara II succeeded the throne of Vijayanagara Empire in 1377 CE and ruled till 1404 CE. Devaraya II (1406 CE–1447 CE) was the greatest ruler of the Sangama dynasty and an ardent devotee of Sri Venkateswara. He restored the Veda *parayanam* in the Tirumala temple. Mallikarjuna was the last king of the Sangama family.

Saluva Narasimha who was a general and the de facto ruler during the last days of the Sangama dynasty, was a great patron of the Tirumala and Tirupathi temples.

Saluva Dynasty

With the coronation of Saluva Narasimha, who was the son of Saluva Gunda, the chief of Chandragiri in the Tirupathi region, the Saluva dynasty came to power in the Vijayanagara empire. Saluva Narasimha ruled the kingdom till 1490 CE. His reign opened a new chapter in the history of Tirupathi. He was the great-grandson of Mangideva Maharaja who had gilded the Vimana and Sikharam of the temple in 1359 CE. Saluva Narasimha installed the idol of Lakshmi Narasimha at the starting point of the pathway to Tirumala. After his death in 1482, his son Immadi Narasimha ruled till the middle of 1505 with Narasa Nayaka, the chief minister and commander-in-chief, as his regent.

Thuluva Dynasty

In 1505, when Narasa Nayaka died, Vira Narasimha, his eldest son, overthrew Immadi Narasimha and proclaimed himself king. He established the third and the final dynasty called Thuluva. He ruled the empire till his death in 1509 CE.

His half-brother Krishnadevaraya (1509 CE–1529 CE) ascended the throne. During his reign, the glory of the temple reached its pinnacle. Nearly 50 inscriptions belong to his reign. He was a great devotee of Lord Venkateswara. He visited the Tirumala temple seven times. Each time he gifted valuables, lands and villages to Lord Venkateswara.

In the last years of his rule, Krishnadevaraya set free his half-brother Achyutaraya from the prison at Chandragiri and nominated him his successor. But Aliya Ramaraya, the emperor's son-in-law, proclaimed an infant son of Krishnadevaraya as emperor and attempted to seize power.

However, Saluva Nayaka, the most powerful nobleman in the empire, seized the throne and held it until the arrival of Achyutaraya from Chandragiri. Achyutaraya celebrated his coronation in the Tirumala temple and then in Kalahasthi and finally the coronation was celebrated for the third time at Vijayanagara, the capital city. He ruled between 1529 CE and 1543 CE.

After his death, Sadasivaraya was crowned in 1543 CE. He was the son of Achyutharaya's younger brother. He was also a great devotee of Lord Venkateswara. Although Sadasivaraya was the king, Aliya Ramaraya was the power behind the throne. He conspired against the emperor, threw him into prison and usurped power. The kingdom had to face several internal troubles as well as external crises in the form of Muslim invasions.

Aravidu Family

The Sultans of Delhi combined their armies and attacked the Vijayanagara Empire. Aliya Ramaraya faced the attack with the help of his two younger brothers, Tirumalaraya and Venkatadriraya. In the battle at Tallikota in 1565 CE, Aliya Ramaraya was killed and the Vijayanagara army was routed. The capital city of Vijayanagara was reduced to ruins and all its wealth was plundered by the Sultan's army.

Tirumalaraya fled the capital. He gathered all the valuables he could, took his family and the imprisoned emperor Sadasivaraya with him and fled to Penukonda with gold, diamonds and precious stones laden on 550 elephants, the state insignia and the celebrated jewel throne of the king.

The Muslim army attacked Vijayanagara, stayed there for six months and destroyed the great capital city. Tirumalaraya of the Aravidu family, the younger brother of Aliya Ramaraya, who was the chief minister of Sadasivaraya in 1565 CE, administered the southern part of the empire in the name of Sadasivaraya till 1568 and later assumed power as Tirumalaraya in 1570 CE, after the death of Sadasivaraya. His name is associated with the Tirumalaraya Mandapam at Tirumala temple.

During this period Krishnappanayaka, commander of the forces of Ginjee and son of Vishvanatha Nayaka, the governor of Thiruvadi Rajya seized parts of Thondaimandalam. The confusion during this period was favourable to the Sultans of

Bijapur and Golconda and they led frequent attacks against the empire that came to be known as the Carnatic Empire at that point of time.

Tirumalaraya made his eldest son Sri Ranga the viceroy of the Telugu-speaking area of the empire. He appointed two of his other sons as viceroys of the Kannada- and Tamil-speaking regions and made Chandragiri his headquarters.

Soon the armies of Bijapur attacked this region but Tirumalaraya played a political game and averted the danger. His second son Sri Ranga II succeeded him and ruled between 1572 CE and 1585 CE. In 1578, the capital was shifted from Penukonda to Chandragiri. Sri Ranga II's younger brother Venkatapathi I succeeded him. He had been the governor of Chandragiri. He ruled between 1585 CE and 1614 CE. He died without an heir. A war broke out for the throne. After some unrest Sri Ranga III, the nephew and the nominee of Venkatapathi I, became the king but was deposed, confined in the palace and later murdered by his wife's brother Jaggaraya.

However, Ramadevaraya (1614 CE–1630 CE), the only surviving child of Sri Ranga, was rescued from the hands of Jaggaraya and crowned king. He ruled from 1616 to 1632. During his reign, the Bijapur armies attacked twice, in 1620 and 1624. The armies of Golconda also attacked in 1624 and the Vijayanagara armies were defeated.

Ramadevaraya died issueless. Venkata II (1630 CE–1642 CE) became the next ruler, but the war of succession continued. There was anarchy and confusion, compounded by the Bijapur sultan's repeated attacks. Finally, the emperor sought refuge in the hills of Chittoor district.

In 1642, Sri Ranga IV succeeded him and reigned till 1672. Sri Ranga IV made great efforts to retain possession of Tirupathi and Chandragiri and the adjoining areas. But the Bijapur and Golconda armies constantly attacked the empire. The people of this region had to face untold miseries at the hands of the Sultans.

The Sultans' armies plundered the temples, looting them, and disfiguring and breaking the idols in lower Tirupathi. Sri Ranga had to escape to Mysore.

With this, the Vijayanagara Empire collapsed completely. Although Sri Rangaraya made a last-ditch attempt in 1664 to regain lost glory, he failed and the end of the Vijayanagara Empire came in 1665.

The Fall of Vijayanagara Empire and the Mughal Rule

Thondaimandalam was part of the Vijayanagara Empire until its total collapse. By the middle of the 17th century, the Tirumala-Tirupathi region came under the rule of the Sultans of Bijapur and Golconda. The Muslim rule in this area lasted from 1650 CE to 1800 CE. It was a bad time as there was no proper government during that period. The Muslim armies of Sultan Abdulla Kutubshah of Golconda took possession of this region after 1656. Mir Jumla, his general, first conquered this region.

When Jumla tasted defeat at the hands of Aurangazeb, this region became part of the Mughal Empire. The Tirupathi region was administered by the Golconda viceroys with their headquarters at Tirupathi until the Golconda Sultanate was completely overthrown by Aurangazeb in 1668. With that, the Golconda region of the Carnatic passed into the possession of the Mughal Empire. Mir Jumla who had deserted the Golconda sultan at the first sign of trouble, received the region as jagir from Emperor Shahjahan. It was Tupaki Krishnappa Nayaka who managed the jagir for the General.

After Mir Jumla's death the jagir was given to Neknam Khan. He managed the jagir through Chintapalli Mirza, his representative. The Mughal Emperor turned the Carnatic into a separate Nawabi. Sadathulla Khan became the nawab in 1710. Todarmal was his advisor.

Then Asaf Jha Nizam, a Subedar of Deccan declared himself as an independent ruler and claimed authority over the Nawab of Carnatic. In 1733, Asaf Jha appointed Dosti Ali as the Nawab of Carnatic.

Seven years later in 1740, the Marathas invaded the region under Raghoji Bhonsle and killed Nawab Dosti Ali and his son in a battle at Damalacheruvu near Tirupathi. Raghoji then visited the Tirumala Temple to pay his respects to Sri Venkateswara. He also made several offerings, including jewels, to the Lord here. Saftar Ali, another son of Dosti Ali, sued for peace at Vellore. He paid Rs 50,000 from the treasury of the Tirumala temple as compensation to the Marathas who retreated. Anwaruddin became the Nawab of Carnatic in 1744.

Soon both the Nizam of Hyderabad and Anwaruddin died and a war of succession broke out. The time was opportune for the English and the French who were competing for dominance in India, to begin their machinations.

The English East India Company

Mohammad Ali, son of Anwaruddin, became the Nawab of the Carnatic with the help of the English East India Company (EEIC). Mohammad Ali reimbursed the Company's expenses of two lakh rupees from the treasury of the Tirumala temple.

In 1748, the EEIC acquired a portion of the Carnatic from Nawab Mohammad Ali. The Nawab of Arcot assigned the revenue of the temple on Tirumala to the EEIC so that he and his son Raja Saheb could retain control over this region.

In 1753, Mohammad Kamal, who served under the Nawab of Arcot, set out to raid Tirupathi, but the EEIC sent a small force and Kamal was captured and killed.

In 1756 Nazibulla, the brother of the Nawab of Arcot, rebelled and attempted to capture the temple, but he was defeated by the English army. He then waylaid many pilgrims and looted them.

In 1761, Hyder Ali became the king of Mysore. In 1782, he took possession of Chandragiri Fort along with Tirupathi. Hyder Ali did not interfere in the temple administration. However, the manager of the temple was his appointee and the annual revenue of about a lakh of pagodas was paid to Hyder Ali.

At the end of the Fourth Mysore War in 1799, and after the death of Mohammad Ali in 1795 and his son in 1801, the EEIC entered into an agreement with Azim-ul-umara, the second son of Mohammad Ali in 1801, by which he handed over the Carnatic to the EEIC in return for an allowance. From then onwards, the English had control over this region, the temple, its properties and its income.

Thus, the EEIC appropriated the income of the Sri Venkateswara Temple and at the beginning of the 19th century, it took over its direct management. All the property and the revenue of the Temple came into the possession of the East India Company. Without money, the rituals and festivals could not be conducted and they stopped. Later, the EEIC prepared a report on the Sri Venkateswara temple and all the other temples in Tirumala, Tirupathi and Tiruchanoor, a total of 19 temples. The report was published in 1818. Another one was prepared in 1819 with an account of the deities in the temples and their structural measurements.

The *Dittam Book* described the quantites of provisions used and their mode of distribution for the daily offerings to the deities at different times and on special occasions. This procedure became the standard and is in force even today.

A fourth record known as *Bruce's Code* provided details of the temple administration. Food offerings were provided to the deities six times daily. To pay for this, 432 villages near Tirupathi were donated by the kings and devotees in olden days. Besides, a large number of villages were also donated to the Temple up to the time of Talikota in 1565. When the possession of the temple and its income passed to the sultans, then the Nawab of Arcot and finally to the EEIC, the number of offerings and their quantities were reduced to three times (morning, noon and night) a day, as per the rations specified by the ruler. The Company enjoyed the revenue till 1843.

In 1842-43, during the reign of Queen Victoria, the English East India Company was stripped of the power to administer Hindu temples in India. Accordingly, the administration of the Sri Venkateswara temple at Tirumala and the other temples in Tirupathi was handed over in 1843 to the Mahants. As per the agreement, the administration was supposed to be carried on without any money set aside for the purpose. After strong protests, a sum of Rs 5000 was given. From 1843 till 1933, six generations of Mahants administered the temple and its properties. They exercised authority as Vicharanakarthas. Finally, the Temple administration was handed over to the TTD in 1933.

History of the Sacred Hill Tirumala, the Idol of Lord Venkateswara and the Temple

Early History of the Hill and the Idol

The earliest mention of the Hill is found in Sangam literature. At that time, northern Vengadam (Vada Vengadam) was the border between the Tamil areas and that of the Vadugar. It was the northernmost boundary of the Tamil kingdom. A verse from *Agananuru*, a Tamil work, speaks of the people who were in the land beyond Vengadam where the language changed from Tamil to Telugu. The people of the Tamil country called Telugu, Vadugu.

According to the work of Tamil grammar, the 2nd century BCE *Tholkappiam*, considered to be the oldest example of Tamil literature, Tamil was spoken in Vengadam. Vengadam or Thiruvengadam was the name of the sacred hill that was located at the border. The Sangam poet Mamulanar (2nd or 3rd century CE) also mentions the name of this Hill at least seven times in his work, both directly and indirectly. But both the *Tholkappiam* and Mamulanar do not mention any temple or deity here. He says that an important feature of Vengadam was its festivals and therefore it is possible that a temple that attracted people might have existed here. Vengadam is also mentioned as a prosperous place. Mamulanar in his 295th poem refers to Tirupathi as 'Pullikunram', the hill belonging to the chieftain Pulli, which was covered by a forest where elephants roamed.

Poets like Kanakkayyanar and Tasyam Kannana have also referred to the Hill. In Ilango's *Silappadikaram* and Saatanar's *Manimekhalai,* two of the greatest Tamil epics of the Sangam era, written around the 5th and 6th centuries CE, one can find many references to the deity.

Ilango calls the sacred Hill 'Nedion Kunram', that is, the Hill of the tall deity. He also describes the Vengadam Hill and the deity fully decorated with flowers and holding the Shankha, Chakra and bow. The epic describes how the Sun and Moon shone on the idol, which implies that the deity was in the open. The Kadankathai describes the standing posture of Lord Vishnu on top of the high hill called Vengadam. As mentioned in the *Silappadikaram,* till the middle of the 13th century, the Lord on Tirumala was mentioned as 'Uchchiyil Ninran', that is, the one who stands on the summit.

The Tamil Alwars (3rd to 8th century CE)

The Tamil Alwars have also sung about the Hill and the Lord in their hymns in the *Nalayira Divya Prabandam*. The *Prabandam* is a collection of 4,000 stanzas of Tamil poetry describing the 108 sacred Vaishnavite places of worship. This collection throws some light on the early history of Tirumala. It covers a period of

500 years from 300 to 800 CE. However, the hymns also do not mention any temple on the Hill although they praise the Hill, its sanctity and the Deity there. Of the 12 Alwars, Poigai Alwar, Bhuthatha Alwar and Pei Alwar are considered as contemporaries. They belonged to Thondai Nadu of which Tirupathi formed a part. They are also considered as the early Alwars.

Later History of the Temple

As far as recorded history goes, up to the 8th century CE, there is no evidence to suggest the existence of a proper temple with enclosures that housed an idol on the Tirumala Hill, although there seems to have been a deity that stood on a height, and which was visible to people from a distance. Around the 8th century there may have been a small temple for the deity inside an enclosure, during the time of Thirumalisai and Kulasekhara Alwars. So before then, there might have been a forest temple. As per the inscription dated 830 CE a proxy image of this deity then known as Thiruvilan Koil Peruman Adigal, a representative of the deity on the Tirumala Hills, was worshipped in Thiruchchokkanur now known as Tiruchanoor. A regular temple might have come up on the Hill only in the latter part of the 8th century CE.

The centuries-old inscriptions on the walls of the Tirumala temple and those on the walls of the temples at Tirupathi give us a detailed account of the temple, the daily routine of the Sevas and worship, the offerings, its festivals, the Vahanas, the flower gardens and its feeding houses and so on that were in existence even in the past. Further, these inscriptions also give us a historical account of the South Indian dynasties.

As per certain inscriptions, the second or inner enclosure wall or Prakaram was built by King Parikshit and the outer Prakaram by his son Janamejaya. Further it is seen that King Vikramaditya made several improvements to this temple six centuries later. Some historians point out that Thondaiman Chakravarthy, an ancient king, lived in the 1st century BCE. If that is so, then this Temple might have been built around that time. However the present structure was constructed with cut stones that have carvings in the Pallava style of architecture. Epigraphers point out that cut stone architecture developed only after the 6th century CE. So the previous temple constructed by Thondaiman might have been a rock-cut cave temple. The probable date of construction of the temple of cut stone is taken as 900 CE and as per an inscription, the ritualistic worship was started in 966 CE when the silver idol was installed and consecrated.

According to other evidence, the history of the temple dates back almost 2000 years. A temple with sanctum and Antarala and so on seems to have been built originally by the Pallavas. Then it was renovated by the Cholas from the 2nd century BCE to the 10th century CE and by the Pandya and Pallava kings around the 4th century CE. Later renovations were by the Yadavarayas, the emperors of the Vijayanagara Kingdom and by the Mahants in the 19th century. The literature of the Mauryan and Gupta periods is said to have mentioned the Hills here as Adi Varaha Kshetra. The temple as it is seen today was not constructed at any one time, as there were improvements and extensions carried out by several kings down the centuries. To start with there might have been only a small stone temple in the Pallava style of architecture with a 3.6 m sq. chamber as the sanctum and an ante-chamber or Sayana mandapam for the devotees to stand in. It was probably lit with one or two ghee lamps and the deity propitiated with some sort of food offering. There may have been an inner Pradakshinam path about 1.5 m wide on the south and west and about 5 m wide on the northern side including a deep receptacle to collect the Abhishekam water through a hole in the north wall of the sanctum.

The Pradakshinam path was closed when the original shrine

was extended with the construction of the Ramar Medai and Mukha Mandapam in front of it where ghee lamps were lit throughout the day and where the jewels of the Lord were preserved in huge wooden boxes and iron safes. This interior Pradakshinam pathway is now called Mukkoti Pradakshinam as it is opened for devotees only on Mukkoti Ekadasi day and closed again the following night. The Garbhagriham or the sanctum and the Mukha Mandapam or Sayana Mandapam seem to have been built as one block about the end of the 9th century or early 10th century CE. This was followed by the covered pathway for Pradakshinam or circumambulation and its enclosing walls or Prarthanavaranam or the Mukkoti Pradakshinam. The Tirumamani Mandapam was constructed in front of the Mukha Mandapam around 1417 CE. The establishment of the Tiruvilan Koil and the regular ritualistic form of worship might have been around 966 CE.

An inscription on the north wall of the first Prakaram walls of the Tirumala Temple tells about the gifts and arrangements made by Samavai for the offerings to the Lord and the festivals in Tiruvilan Koil. Whether this Tiruvilan Koil refers to the temple at Tirumala we do not know. An inscription of 826 CE found in Tiruchanoor temple mentions the existence of a sacred proxy or a second deity called Tiruvengadatthu Perumanadigal also known as Tiruvilankoil Peruman in Tiruvilan Koil in Tiruchanoor. Probably there was a proxy temple of Lord Venkateswara at Tiruchanoor around 826 CE, as the Hill was difficult to climb.

However, another inscription belonging to the period of a Chola king Paranthaka (945 CE) gives details about the burning of a perpetual lamp in front of Tiruvengadam temple. During this time, the *dwajasthambam* and the Balipitam might have existed in the inner Prakaram. Around 960 CE during the time of Alavandar and his grandson Tirumalai Nambi, it can be presumed that Sri Ramanuja might have planned to enlarge this temple. In the latter part of the 11th century, after the death of

Sri Ramanuja, that is around 1160 CE, the temple might have developed to its present structure.

The next stage in the development of the temple came after the end of Chola supremacy and the emergence of the Yadavarayas and other feudatories. The presence of the Utsava Murthy with His consorts is known during the period of Sri Ranganada Yadavaraya in 1339 CE.

The evolution of the temple structures continued into the 15th and 16th centuries. It is found that Saluva Narasimha endowed the village of Durgasamudram in 1482 CE for the construction of gopurams in Tirumala and Tirupathi and for constructing the Narasimharaya *Mandapam* in the temple at Tirumala. In the 16th century, Talapakka Tirumalayyangar constructed the Swami Pushkarini steps. In the latter part of that century, the Tirumalaraya Mandapam was constructed.

The Garbha Griham and Sayana Mandapam form a monolithic structure and are also presumed to have been constructed in the late 16th century. It is also possible that it was in this Tiruvilan Koil or Stapana Mandapam or the Snanapana Mandapam that the silver idol of Lord Srinivasa presented by Queen Samavai was consecrated. At that time, most probably the temple consisted of the Garbhagriham, the Sayana Mandapam together with the Antarala Mandalam or Pradakshinam corridor and Tiruvilankoil in front of the Pradakshinam.

It is found that there are two sets of walls in the Garbhagriham. The Vimana was constructed when the new wall was built between 1244 and 1250 CE. The old walls were demolished, so the inscriptions on them were lost. The stones that were salvaged from the old wall were used to line the inner face of the new walls. The outer side of the new wall has only the ancient inscriptions that were copied from the walls of the temple.

According to the inscriptions, Vira Narasingaraya Yadavaraya financed the reconstruction work. He was a feudatory chief under the Pandya king Sundara Pandya. During the renovation between the 12th and the 13th centuries, a second wall was built around the first, perhaps to take the weight of the Vimana which was constructed only then. After building the Vimana, he covered it with gilded copper plates. King Sundara Pandya gilded the Kalasam on top of the Vimana around 1262 CE. At this time the Mukkoti Pradakshinam was enclosed on all the four sides to make it the first Avarana.

Later, many kings and chieftains particularly those of the Vijayanagara Empire, developed and extended the temple. The first Pradakshinam path or Avaranam was closed. Inscriptions reveal that the closure might have taken place sometime after 1262 CE. Two inscriptions, one complete and the other fragmentary, on the south wall of Ramar Medai, show that it was formed by closing the first Prakaram some time between 1262-1285 CE, probably to increase safety. The covered corridor surrounding the old temple might have been demolished.

The 16-pillared Tirumamani Mandapam or the Mukha Mandapam as it is called now, in front of the Garbha Griha, was constructed in the early Vijayanagara style of architecture by Mallanna alias Madhavadasa of Chandragiri around 1417 CE. During this time, the *dwajasthambam* and the Balipitam might have been shifted to the present place. The Garuda temple facing the sanctum is supposed to have been a later addition.

The Tirumalaraya Mandapam was renovated by Saluva Narasimha in the middle of the 15th century for celebrating the Anna Unjal Thirunal instituted by him in 1473 CE. This structure was later extended in the 16th century by Rangaraja Tirumalaraya. Saluva Narasimha also constructed the four-pillared mandapam at the four corners of the Sampangi Pradakshinam in 1470 CE. He is also credited with the construction of Vasantha Mandapam in the Tiru Koneri for the Tiruppali Odai Tirunal during the last 10 days of the Kodai Tirunal. He also constructed four mandapams on the bank of the temple tank and purchased the Teerthavari Mandapam from the priests of the temple. He planted a flower garden on the banks of the temple tank and another on the banks of Narasingaraya Koneri. It is also probable that he excavated the Achyutaraya Koneri on the west bank of Swami Pushkarini that was filled up most probably in the 19th century. A coconut grove was raised over it along with a place where free meals were provided.

The 1,000-pillared mandapam was constructed by Saluva Mallayadeva Maharaja, cousin of Saluva Narasimharaya. The Prathima Mandapam is comparatively modern and might have come up after the 16th century when festivals became numerous and attracted large crowds of pilgrims. The earliest mandapam in the Sampangi Pradakshinam must have been the Ranga Mandapam with a small shrine at the back that housed the Utsavamurthy of Ranganatha of Srirangam during the time of Muslim invasion of the south during 1310–1360. Sri Ranganatha Yadavaraya, the local ruler, constructed this mandapam to accommodate the idol and the refugees who followed the deity.

From the inscriptions it can be concluded that the outer wall was renovated during the time of Sundara Pandya and the outer Gopuram as we see it today might have been constructed in the reign of Saluva Narasimha. There are no inscriptions indicating the period of construction or the name of the mandapam or the donor or purpose for which the Aina Mahal came up originally. This was in the form of a Yagnasala originally but later converted into the Unjal Mandapam.

Between the closing years of the Sangama dynasty of the Vijayanagara Empire around 1450 CE, to 1830, when the English East India Company relinquished the direct management of the Temple which they had assumed in 1801, inscriptions are available only for the years between 1450 and 1638 CE.

A glimpse of the history of the temple during Muslim rule can be obtained from the contemporary records of the English and the Dutch and the English East India Company. The last king of Vijayanagara retained the title till 1665 CE and then the temple passed into the hands of Mir Jumla, former commander of the Golconda forces in July 1656. The temple was under the control of the Nawab of Carnatic till 1801 CE except for a short period from 1758-59 when it was captured by the French. In the early 19th century, the EEIC took possession of the temple. It is understood that during the Muslim and EEIC rule, the temple and its properties were leased out annually by auction to a tenant, who paid the Nawab the bid amount. The tenant collected the bid amount through poll tax, the Kanukas, Arjithama Sevas and so on. These became the permanent sources of income for the bidder.

The EEIC relinquished their connections with the religious institutions and transferred the administration of the Sri Venkateswara temple and all other temples of Tirupathi and Tiruchanoor to the Mahants in 1843. From 1843 till 1933, six generations of Mahants exercised authority over the temple as the Vicharanakartas. Their administration of the Temples came to an end in 1933 when the Tirumala Tirupathi Devasthanams (TTD) was formed.

The Surroundings of the Temple

The Temple at present, is surrounded by the four Mada streets. The north and south Mada streets of the Maha Pradakshinam around the Temple each measure about 240 m long and the west Mada street is about 270 m long. The east Mada street, running in front of the main Temple and alongside the east bank of Pushkarini, is the shortest at 225 m. The ground slopes from west to east. The area where the Temple stands is at a much lower level. The Mada streets are about 4.5 m lower in level than the other areas, as the ground beyond them rises sharply on all sides. The entire area is spread over roughly 16 acres including the temple proper, the Swami Pushkarini, Varahaswami temple and the site of the Patha Pushkarini, where a tank was constructed by Achyutaraya Maharaja in the 16th century and subsequently filled up by the Mahants in the 19th century. The area behind the temple was once a garden that supplied the flowers needed for worship. Out of the total area, the temple covers 2.20 acres, the Swami Pushkarini 1.50 acres and Patha Pushkarini around 2.50 acres. The remaining 10 acres are occupied by Matams and lanes that once consisted of Nandana Vanams or flower gardens.

The old landmarks in this area include the Tirumalai Nambi Tirumaligai. Tirumalai Nambi lived in the last quarter of the 10th century CE. It was the first building in the south Mada street, a stone mandapam enclosed by mud walls. The Ahobila Matam or the Van Sathakopan Mandapam and some other mandapams are located in this street. At the end of the south Mada street where it joins the west Mada street, stood the garden 'Tirumalaikki' meaning 'for Tirumala' where Sri Anantalwar, the famous disciple of Sri Ramanuja lived in the last quarter of the 11th century. The garden and tank are outside the temple area. At the southwest corner, the pathway from Chandragiri joins the Mada street with a mandapam at the junction.

In the west Mada street, there are a number of choultries and matams facing the east.

The Patha Pushkarini and the Swami Pushkarini form a large part of the north Mada street.

The east Mada street has the Swami Pushkarini and the temple to its west and a few matams. The Ratham is kept there. The Vahana Mandapam that is located facing the temple is used for placing the processional deity on the particular Vahana that is earmarked for that day of the festival. The procession starts from here.

The Ghanta Mandapam is opposite the main entrance of the temple. It has a huge bell that is rung to announce the coming of the priest to the temple in the morning and evening. It indicates the opening of the temple doors for the devotees. Locally it is called the Golla Dani Mandapam.

Since the TTD took over the administration of the temple, several renovations have been undertaken. Certain old structures were demolised and new ones were built. To mention a few, the 1000-pillared mandapam was demolished and the Museum and the Asthana Mandapam were shifted to a new location. A new Kalyanakatta complex and a new Pottu for the preparation of the Laddu Prasadam are currently under construction. A musical fountain that attracts the visiting pilgrims was built behind the Ananda Nilayam outside the Temple. The Ananda Nilayam Vimana was gilded, the Vaikuntam queue complex was constructed and another road for vehicles going uphill was laid. A modern spacious toll gate has come up and the pathway used by pilgrims who climb up on foot has been provided with shade and several amenities.

5

Important Contributions of Kings, Mahants, TTD and other Devotees

The inscriptions found on the walls of the main temple at Tirumala and the other temples at Tirumala and Tirupathi cover the medieval period from the 9th to 17th centuries. They provide a lot of information about the association of different dynasties and kings with the temples. However, many of the inscriptions are beyond recovery and are damaged and some are fragmentary and incomplete. The complete inscriptions clearly indicate that the temple of Lord Venkateswara enjoyed the patronage of several kings and chieftains of different dynasties who ruled this region.

One of the earliest inscriptions mentions the Bana Prince named Vijayaditya who ruled in the early half of the 9th century and it is seen that he had made some gifts to the temple at Tiruchanoor.

Pallavas

Several kings donated lavishly to expand this temple, among them the Pallavas, who built the present temple. In the third century CE, the Pallavas became the rulers of southern India, from Amaravathi to Kanchi, a territory that was previously ruled by the Andhra Satavahanas from 274 BCE to 200 CE. The territory was called Thondaimandalam and its boundaries were

Important Contributions of Devotees

marked in the north and south by the Penna and Amaravathi rivers.

The Pallavas ruled till the end of the 9th century when the Cholas succeeded them. A large number of inscriptions on the north wall in the first Prakaram dating back to the 9th century, describe in detail the contributions made by the Pallava kings. One of the earliest inscriptions alludes to Samavai, daughter of Pallava Pergadaiyar and queen of a Kadava subordinate Sakthi Vitankan. She presented a Kiritam or crown, a necklace of four strings and other ornaments for the hands, waist and feet of Lord Venkateswara. She consecrated a silver image of the deity, provided for processions and endowed the temple with lands in Tiruchchokkanur, the present Tiruchanoor, some time in the third quarter of the 10th century CE. The jewels she presented included Thirumudi, Malas, Udarabandams, Thirumarai-Patthikai, Bahuvalayam, Thiruchchandan, Vadiyal, Korai, Padachayalam, Prabha etc. She arranged for the daily offering of a plate of cooked rice and performance of the holy Abhishekam of the silver idol on the occasions of Ayana Sankranthi and the two Vishu Sankranthis. She instituted the celebration of the Purattasi festival for nine days, beginning with the Ankurarpanam on the day of the Chitra star and another festival of two days' duration before it. She also gifted land comprising several villages towards the expenses of a festival twice a day for seven days prior to Margazhi-Thiru Dwadasi, that is, Mukkoti Dwadasi for Manavala Perumal.

Volume 1 of the early inscriptions reveals that the Pallava kings, particularly during the period of Koppatra Mahendra Varman and Sarvagra Khadgamalla and so on, contributed to the temple. Inscriptions also reveal the contributions made by Dantivikrama Varma of the Pallava lineage in 839 CE. Ulagapperumanar of Chola Nadu, a subordinate officer of the Pallava king Vijayadanti Vikrama Varma, gifted a lamp to the Tiruvilankoil Perumanadigal.

The Cholas

One of the earliest Chola inscriptions of the Temple belongs to the period of Maduraikonda Ko-Parakesari Varman alias Paranthaka I, who ruled between 905-953 CE. He gifted a lamp to the temple.

A gold Pattam set with precious stones weighing 52 *kalanju* and set with six rubies, four diamonds and 28 pearls was gifted around 1001 CE, by Paranthaka Devi Amman, most probably the queen of Paranthaka II, or Sundara Chola and the daughter of Cheraman who ruled the Chera kingdom.

Kodungalluran of Malai Nadu, during the reign of Paranthaka I (936 CE), deposited 40 *kalanju* of gold for maintaining a lamp in the shrine. Ulagamadevi the queen consort of Rajaraja Chola I, probably gifted 29 cows to the temple for ghee used in lighting the permanent lamp in front of Thiruvenkatamudian. Arulakki, alias Rajaraja Moovendavelan of Sonadu on the south bank of Kaveri, an officer of Rajaraja I (985-1016 CE), deposited 40 *kalanju* of gold for a lamp. The inscriptions on the temple walls point out that during the reign of Rajendra I, Rajendra Chola II, Kulothunga Chola II, and Rajaraja Chola, gifts were made to the temple of Lord Venkateswara. The queen of Kulothunga I made arrangements for offering of milk and curds to the temple.

Telugu Pallavas

During the reign of Telugu Pallava king Vijaya Ganda Gopala Deva (1250-1285 CE), his queen presented cows for supplying ghee to light three lamps in the temple.

Pandyas

The Pandya kings also made contributions to the temple. Jatavarma Sundara Pandya I (1250-1275) placed a gilded *kalasam* over the Ananda Vimana of the temple.

Yadavarayas

Vira Narasinga Deva, one of the earliest Yadavarayas, gifted a village to the temple for supplying rice, vegetables and ghee everyday. He and his queen also presented cows, bulls and jewels. The inscriptions mention the contributions made by Thirukkalathi Deva, Vira Rakshsa, Vira Narasinga Deva, Thiruvenkatanatha, Ranganatha and so on. Thirukkalathi Deva gifted some land in the village of Avilala to the temple. Vira Rakshasa Yadavaraya, son of Thirukkalathi Deva granted some land. Yadavaraya Nachiyar, the queen of Vira Narasinga Yadavaraya, presented 64 cows for ghee and two bulls for lighting two perpetual lamps, around 1217 CE. Vira Narasingaraya gifted 32 cows for lighting one ghee lamp. He issued orders to Sthanathars to permit Thiruppullanidasar to undertake the renovation of the central shrine and to re-engrave the old inscriptions found on the earlier walls before any reconstruction. He also weighed himself in gold and presented it to the temple. Thiruvenkatanatha gifted a village for conducting Adi Thirunal. He granted two villages to the temple as Sarvamanya or tax-free income for the daily food offerings to the Lord. Mahapradani Singaya-Dannayaka instituted an offering called Sitakara Sandhi. During the reign of Ranganatha, flower gardens and *matams* were set up and he also arranged for the hunting festival or Padiyavettai. Vasanthotsavam is also mentioned during this period. Hobala Yadavaraya presented an ornament for the hand of the deity.

Vijayanagara Kings

The first dynasty of the Vijayanagara empire also made lavish gifts to the temple in the form of villages, ornaments, costly gems and so on. During their time, the fame and popularity of the temple increased remarkably. A large number of services and charities were also instituted during the Vijayanagara period in the form of Nitya Naivedyam, Tirunals with processions and offerings, Nandanavanams, flower gardens, mandapams, gopurams, Ramanuja Kutams (poor feeding houses) and lands that yielded permanent income to meet the expenses of daily and festival day offerings to the deities.

The kind of endowments made during the rule of Saluva and Vijayanagara kings were different in three ways from the endowments made during the Pallava, Chola and Pandya regimes. The latter devoted more attention to the burning of perpetual lamps or Nanda Vilakku/Nithya Deepam. The food offerings or Nithya Naivedyam during their time were also just enough to meet the requirements of the temple during ordinary days and festivals. The private feeding houses catered to the visiting pilgrims.

We find a departure from these practices starting from the rule of Saluva Narasimha. The food offerings and the feeding of pilgrims were given more importance by the later kings. Lands, jewels, villages, income from irrigation channels, money, Nitya Naivedyam, flowers from flower gardens and so on also became important gifts to the temple. The offering of Teertha and Prasadam to the worshippers in the temple during festivals and important days, the recitation of *Vedas* by Brahmins and Prabandams by Brahmins and non-Brahmin Vaishnavas, were initiatives supported generously by the Vijayanagara kings.

Sangama Dynasty

The early inscriptions on the temple walls mention the names of the Vijayanagara kings like Bukkaraya I, Harihararaya II, Devaraya II and Mallikarjuna who made significant contributions.

During the reign of Bukkaraya I, a village was gifted for Sandhi or offering twice a day for the Lord that was known as Bukkarayan Sandhi, meaning 'in the name of Bukkaraya.'

Mahamandaleshwara Misaraganda Mangi Deva, who was a

prominent feudatory, fixed a golden Kalasa on the Shikhara of the temple Vimana in 1369 CE. He gilded the sanctum as well.

A minister of Kumara Kampa gifted 28 cows and a bull in 1388.

Mullai Thiruvenkata Jiyar instituted the Masi Thirunal in the name of Harihararaya the-then king. Kodai Thirunal and Vidyadari day of each of the festivals is mentioned during this period.

Harihara II also instituted a festival in the month of Masi and made arrangements for its conduct through the payment of 100 *panam* each year, that being the income from Pengodu village.

Devaraya II revived the Veda parayanam on the basis of a representation made by one of the Sthanathars, Mudaliyar Thirukkalikanri Dasar Alagappanar. He granted three villages and paid 2,200 gold Varahas or coins to be used for the daily offerings of 30 plates of cooked rice, one of sweet pudding or Payasam and one plate of Appam and presented two big cups for holding spiced water and Punugu for smearing the deity. He also arranged for the celebration of a festival in the Asvayuja month (September–October) for nine days starting from the day of Punarvasu star. It ended on the day of Svathi star with Teerthavari or the sacred bath.

Vira Pratapa Devaraya, the chief minister or Amatya, granted three villages.

Sekhara Mallanna, who was given the governorship of Chandragiri and later became the ruler, made arrangements for a Naivedyam and Nitya Deepam to Lord Venkateswara. He offered one Thirupponakam and gifted 82 heads of cattle for ghee for food offerings and for lighting two ghee lamps in the sanctum. He made arrangements for two Sandhi offerings. He also constructed the Tirumamani Mandapam in front of the sanctum and renovated the Ananda Nilayam. During Sangama rule, the festivals with the flag hoisting ceremony increased to seven spread over 10 days each. Besides these, other festivals such as Kodai Thirunal in summer, Adyayanotsavam in the month of Margazhi with the chanting of Prabandam, were celebrated. Vedaparayanam was revived and permanently established.

The Bhakthas or ordinary devotees also gifted cows, jewels and lands and dug irrigation channels.

The income of the Temple grew significantly.

Saluva Dynasty

In 1446 CE, Peri Mallayyadeva Maharaja and Kathari Saluva of the Saluva family paid 1,000 *panam* for one Thirupponakam to be offered daily to Thiruvengadamudian. Another Saluva chieftain Siru Mallayyadeva Maharaja paid 1,200 *narpanam* for the daily offering of one Thirupponakam to the Lord from the interest on the capital.

Saluva Narasimha (1454-1500) who was the most influential general, was the viceroy of Chandragiri from 1450 till 1485, when he became the Emperor. It is seen from the inscriptions on the Tirumala-Tirupathi temple walls (Volume 2) that Saluva Narasingadeva Maharaja or Saluva Narasimha was the great-grandson of Mangideva Maharaja who was given the governorship of the erstwhile Yadavaraya country by the Vijayanagara king Bukkaraya I. He shifted the capital to Chandragiri. He gilded the Vimana and Sikharam in the year 1359 and offered gifts to the temple in various years. His queen, the crown prince, his other sons, their grandmother, his eldest brother, secretary, general, the palace dance master, the feudatory chiefs and his subordinates also made generous offerings to the temple. Saluva Narasimha gifted 18 villages located in several parts of his kingdom. A Sandhi was instituted by him. He also constructed a gopuram and arranged for feeding the pilgrims. It was he who instituted the Dola Mahotsavam or Anna Unjal Thirunal, a festival in which the idol was placed on a swan-shaped swing twice. The swing was installed in the Tirumalaraya Mandapam constructed by Saluva.

Thimmanna Dandanayaka, the military commander of Chandragiri, provided for an offering to the deities on the first day of the five-day swing festival as he did for Pavitrotsavam. He also made an offering during Thoppu Thirunal, a festival conducted in the garden or grove for 20 days.

For Margazhi Thiru Dwadasi, Saluva Narasimha provided huge offerings to Sri Venkateswara and to Malai Kuniya Ninra Perumal in the Tirumamani Mandapam. He gifted a village for the construction of Gopurams at Tirumala and Tirupathi and Narasimharaya Mandapam at Tirumala. He also provided for the offerings during the different festivals including the seven Brahmotsavams. It was he who constructed the Vasantha Mandapam in the midst of Swami Pushkarini. He instituted the Thiruppali Odai Thirunal or floating festival. He purchased the Teerthavari Mandapam from the temple priests, constructed four mandapams on the bank of Swami Pushkarini and four mandapams inside the temple in the Sampangi Pradakshinam. He provided food offerings at these mandapams to the processional images in his name and in the name of his sons. He arranged for a large quantity of food offerings on the first night of the swing festival in the name of his mother.

He constructed the front Gopuram and other Gopurams in the temple and the unfinished Gopuram at the entrance of Tirumala village and the big Gopuram at the foot of the first Hill. During his reign several villages were gifted to the temple by those connected to the palace and by other devotees. Thus, by the end of the second half of the 15th century, the temple owned around 50 villages in and around Tirupathi. Some villages also maintained gardens for supplying flowers to the temple. A stone-stepped well was also constructed during his rule. More than a 100 offerings or Sandhis were provided by the innumerable devotees that included 57 Sandhis daily with 68 measures of rice, some sweets stipulated by Saluva Narasimha and one Appa Padi offering, one Thirukkannamadai and one Payasam. Several other devotees including his family members, made varied food offerings. So the offerings made during his reign increased significantly.

Saluva Narasimha's cousin Saluva Mallayyadeva Maharaja, instituted the Thirupavitra Tirunal or Pavitrotsavam, the purificatory ceremony for the Lord for five days in the month of Avani. Thimmanna Dandanayaka, a Brahmin military commander of Chandragiri, made an offering of one Appa Padi to the processional images on the first day of the Pavitra Thirunal and many other devotees also gave various food offerings to the deity during this festival. Thus the foundation for the fame and popularity of this temple was laid by Saluva Narasimha.

Saluva Parvatharaja, his son, constructed a mandapam at Muzhangal Mudichu or Mokala Parvatham along the pathway to Tirumala and erected the Gali Gopuram. He set up a water tank in it for the pilgrims.

Thuluva Dynasty

Krishnadevaraya (1500-1528)

Krishnadevaraya is considered the brightest star among the Vijayanagara kings. The emperor gifted ornaments set with precious stones and gold and silver vessels both for the main idol of Sri Venkateswara and the Utsavamurthis. He also gifted several villages to the temple which were located in the districts of Chandragiri, Udayagiri and Penukonda. His two queens accompanied him to Tirumala during his visits and they also made offerings to the Lord along with the Emperor. Amatya Sekhara Mallanna, the minister, completed the construction of Tirumala Mandapam and arranged for the Nitya Deepam and Naivedyam for the Lord. Krishnadevaraya adored the Lord as his patron God and dedicated his excellent work 'Amuktha Malyada' to Him. During his reign, he visited the temple seven times.

In the year 1513, the emperor visited Tirumala three times. After defeating Kapileshwara Gajapathi, the monarch of Orissa, he visited Tirumala along with his queens and gifted one Navaratna Kireetam, that is a crown, that weighed 3,308 carats, was set with 9 kinds of gems, one Trisaram, or three-stringed necklace, containing pearls, diamonds and sapphires and Addigas, or chokers, set with precious stones, a Pathakam or pendant embedded with five kinds of gems all weighing 225 carats and one pendant weighing 61 carats. He gifted 25 silver plates for offering camphor Harathi to the Lord, one Vududhara ornament weighing 66 units that included five diamonds, 17 Addigas set with emeralds, rubies, diamonds, gems and gold strings, and a Katari, or sword with a tasselled sheath, set with diamonds, rubies and saphires. The tassel was composed of small and big pearls and rubies with a total weight of 326 units in which the rubies, diamonds and emeralds alone weighed 165 units. There was also a Nischala sword with sheath weighing 132 units and set with rubies, a small sword with a tassel of pearls and a sheath containing rubies, pearls and diamonds, one Pathakam, weighing 87 carats, set with diamonds, rubies, emeralds etc. There were Bhuja Kiritis or Vankis gifted to the Lord, one pair weighing 573 units set with pearls, rubies, sapphires and diamonds, one Vanki for daily use weighing 198 units and two pairs of Bhuja Kirtis for daily use, one gold string with 17 Addigas, 30 more Addigas in the shape of peepul leaves, set with pearls, rubies, diamonds and emeralds weighing 205 units in all, another similar string weighing 276 units, three crowns weighing 380 units, studded with pearls, diamonds, rubies, cat's eyes and sapphires for the Utsava murthy and for His Nachimars.

His queens Chinnajidevi Amman and Tirumaladevi Amman gifted a gold cup each weighing 374 units for offering milk to the Lord.

The emperor also made certain endowments for the merit of his parents Narasa Nayaka Udaiyar and Nagalammangaru. The gifts consisted of a few ornaments set with 9 kinds of precious stones together with a saffron cup and 300 betel leaves, 600 betel nuts and an annual Brahmotsavam in the Tamil month of Tai for which he gifted the villages of Chatravadi, Thuluru and Karikambadu in Godagurnadu. The number of Brahmotsavams was increased to eight.

After capturing the Udayagiri Fort defeating Pratapa Rudra Gajapathy, the Emperor visited the temple for the fourth time in 1514. At that time he performed Kanakabhishekam with 30,000 Varahas apart from gifting Talippakkam village for the daily food offerings to the Lord, a three-stringed ornament weighing 250 units inclusive of gold wire, gold clips, rubies, pearls and sapphires and one pair of Kadiyam and Bahuvalayam or bracelet and armlet of gold set with diamonds and rubies.

His queen Chinnajidevi Amman gifted one Kantha mala with a Padakkam set with diamonds, rubies, emeralds and pearls and a central ruby with a pendant weighing 200 units and Mudiyur village for the daily offerings to Sri Venkateswara. The other queen Tirumaladevi gifted a gold pendant or Chakra Padakkam weighing 225¼ units that contained diamonds, rubies, emeralds and pearls and Piratti Kulathur village for the daily offerings to the Lord.

In the year 1515, returning from his victorious eastern expedition againt the Kalingas and capturing Katakapuri, the present Cuttack in Orissa, in October 1515, he issued an edict donating one Navaratna Prabhavali or Makara Thoranam (an arch carved with the head and face of a crocodile at the centre). The arch weighed 27,287 units and contained 25 Kiritimukha leaves, 13,835 Vommachchu beads, gold wire weighing 16 units and solid gold beads numbering 7,978; the silk and gold fringes weighed 5,474 units and contained 10,994 rubies, 754 emeralds, 530 sapphires, 40 cat's eyes, 45 agates, 74 topazes, 920 diamonds,

3,933 pearls, four large sapphires, six corals and 30 conch shells. The total weight was 14,711 units, with the cost of the Makara Thoranam or Prabhavali coming to 3,112 Varahas.

In the year 1517, returning from Simhadri Potnuru where he installed a triumphal pillar after capturing Kalinga Desa, Krishnadevaraya made his fifth visit to Tirumala. This time, he donated one Kantha Mala, one Padakkam and 30,000 Varahas or gold coins for gilding the Vimana over the sanctum. Another 1,000 Varahas from Godagurnadu went for the weekly Punugu Kappu expenses for the Lord. Certain taxes worth 1,500 varahas collected from Godagurnadu were given for conducting the daily morning offerings to the Lord.

In the year 1518, the gilding work taken up by the emperor was completed.

In the year 1518, he visited the temple along with Tirumaladevi Amman after the birth of his son, for the sixth time and presented a Pitambaram (yellow silk cloth) set with 9 kinds of precious stones, a Kullavu or head-dress set with pearls, rubies, emeralds and sapphires, two Chamarams set with 9 kinds of gems, 10,000 gold Varahas and a Padakkam. His queen Tirumaladevi presented a Navaratna Padakkam.

In 1521, the emperor made his seventh visit to the shrine along with his sole surviving queen Tirumaladevi and his son Tirumalaraya Maharaja who was only a few months old. At that time, he granted some lands to the Temple for the merit of the prince; unfortunately, the child died young.

During the reign of Krishnadevaraya, a number of his officers, temple employees, merchants, spiritual and religious leaders and Bhakthas also made large donations to the temple. All the 24 courtiers of the emperor and several other officers of the Empire also made huge contributions.

Appa Pillai who was a very successful General of the Empire made three endowments as a token of his gratitude to the Lord during the reign of Krishnadevaraya's elder brother Vira Narasimha.

The commander-in-chief of the empire, Periya Obala Nayakar Rama Nayakar made a grant of Kadalur village and 100 cows for the daily offerings and donated towards the Lord's Prasadams.

Timmarasa the chief minister, who was also a general and who was well-known for his intimacy with Krishnadevaraya, made an endowment of Parantalur village in 1512. He also presented one Pithambaram to the Lord.

Tirumala Nayakar excavated an irrigation channel in 1512 in Parittiputtur and from the extra income that accrued with this scheme, he made a variety of offerings to Sri Govindaraja (who is supposed to be the brother of Lord Srinivasa) at the flower garden in Tirupathi.

Pradhani Saluva Thimmarasayyangar, his wife Lakshmi Ammangar, his brother Saluva Govindaraja, Rayasam Kondamarasayyar who was a governor, Mannar Pillai, brother of Appa Pillai, Ellappa Nayakar and his son Tirumala Nayakar, Thimmu Nayakar a general, Thiruvenkatayyar, Vasalam Ellappa Nayakar, who was a member of the King's household, Karanikka Basavarasa, Udiyam Ellappa Nayakar, Ekkadi Thimmannan, Adaippam Bhaiyappa Nayakar, Tryambaka Devar, Bahur Mallarasar, Lakka Nayakar, Subhuddi Ramadasar and Ambika Mudusala also gave gifts to the Lord of Tirumala.

These people contributed towards the expenses of food offerings, gifted lands and villages, excavated irrigation channels, constructed mandapams, offered money towards development and extension works, Abhishekams, rituals and so on.

During Krishnadevaraya's rule, the daily offerings during the festivals and other auspicious days as well as the landed property and the jewels for the Lord increased significantly.

Achyutaraya (1528-1540)

In the year 1529, Achyutaraya who was a captive in the Chandragiri fort, was freed by his half-brother Krishnadevaraya and crowned his successor. He also made several endowments to this Temple. He was crowned thrice, first at Tirumala in the presence of Sri Venkateswara, for the second time at the Kalahasthiswara Temple and finally at the capital city of Vijayanagara.

His first act on becoming the king was the construction of pavements with granite stones together with two rows of mandapams at Kapila Teertha or Alwar Teertha. He renamed it Chakra Teertha. He visited the Tirumala temple thrice.

During his first visit in 1533, he performed the Kapila-Pasu (brown cows of gold) and Swarna Varsham (raining of gold coins) ceremonies, presented valuable jewels and ornaments to Sri Venkateswara, including a Kapha (gown) set with precious stones, a gem-set Kiritam (crown), four Bahuvalayam (circlets for shoulders) and necklaces and ornaments for the head, eyes, neck and chest. It is seen from the inscriptions that he performed Srinivasa Sahasranamarchana personally along with his queen Varadaji Amman and his son Kumara Venkatdri while the Archakas or the Nambimars were asked to recite the Sahasranama of the Lord.

He excavated the Achyuta Koneri between 1530 and 1533 at Tirumala.

In 1535, he introduced the Lakshmi Mahotsavam that was described as Thirunal or festival of Sri Venkateswara and Alarmelumanga and a festival for Sri Rama. For the expenses, he granted 300 *Rekhai pon*, or gold coins, from the income of the villages in Kondavidu Sinha. He also constructed seven mandapams where Malaiappa was given the offerings stipulated by him. On this occasion, he also arranged for a festival for Raghunatha, Sita Devi, and Lakshmana enshrined in the sanctum.

The officers who accompanied the king during his second visit also provided for the offerings. His queen Varadaji Amman granted six villages that yielded 920 *Rekhai pon* for the daily offerings, with 20 food offerings and five kinds of Paniyaram to be offered to the Lord in her name. Her previous offerings were termed as Krishnaiya's offerings and Achyutharaya's Avasaram or offerings.

Achyutharaya's third visit was in 1537. Six officers and his youngest brother-in-law who accompanied him, paid 15000 *narpanam* for providing 300 Appa Padi yearly to Malaiappaswamy. Saluva Thimmarasa at the suggestion of the king, granted the village of Mallapuram for offering one Appa Padi on the seventh day of each of the eight Brahmotsavams conducted during that period. He also granted money and gifted a village for the daily worship at the temple. His queen Varadaji Amman gifted six villages. The temple dancers sent by Achyutharaya also made their share of offerings.

His father-in-law Thimmaraja Salakaraja constructed a mandapam and paid 600 *narpanam* in 1533 CE for maintaining a water tank in it.

Periya Kommamman, the queen of Salakaraya Periya Tirumalayyadeva Maharaja paid 1300 *narpanam* in 1534 for offering 9 Athirasa Padi to Malaiappaswamy on the seventh day in each of the 9 Brahmotsavams at her mandapam and in other mandapams.

The youngest brother-in-law of Achyutharaya, Singraja, paid 15,000 *narpanam* in 1537, for offering 300 Appa Padi each year to the Lord during Brahmotsavam, Kodai Thirunal, float festival and on other festival and auspicious days. Again in 1542, he paid 15,000 *narpanam* for offering 300 more Appa Padi to Malaiappa.

During Achyutharaya's regime, around 35 villages and some lands were granted to the Temple. Thalappaka Pedda Tirumalayyangar, son of Annamayya, gifted a dozen villages for providing about 50 food offerings and certain sweet and savoury Padis to the Lord everyday. He also paid 2,000 Varahas for celebrating a new Brahmotsavam for the Lord in the Tamil month of Ani (June-July) for 13 days.

Several devotees also made different kinds of offerings to the Lord in the form of money, villages and food. At the commencement of Achyutharaya's reign, there were only nine Brahmotsavams. By the end of it, the number of Brahmotsavams had increased to 10.

Sadasivaraya (1540-1565)

Sadasivaraya was the co-regent of Achyutaraya in 1537. By 1541, he became the king and by 1543, he became the undisputed successor to the throne of Vijayanagara. During his reign, all the 10 Brahmotsavams were continued and a new Thirukkodi Thirunal or Brahmotsavam was started. A large number of festivals were also celebrated, although the emperor himself did not institute any of these in his name. He seems to have made two visits to the temple. During his reign, very many old festivals were made more elaborate by several devotees. A few of these festivals were: the Nityotsavam held for 30 days during Tai-Masi month every year, Mukkoti Dwadasi which was made a grand festival, Vanabhojanam and Kalyanotsavam instituted by Talapakka Tirumalaiyyangar, Pallavotsavam during the last five days in the month of Vaikasi, Phalotsavam in the month of Masi, Adyayanotsavam, Vasantotsavam for five days in the month of Masi, Sahasranamarchana for five days, civet oil Abhishekam on all the 53 days in Tirumala and Ratha Sapthami festival for five days.

During the era of Sadasivaraya, the members of the Aravidu family, the Matla family and the Manamapoli family seem to have donated to this Temple.

Matla Kumara Anantarajayya during his pilgrimage offered three golden asva or horse, gaja or elephant, Samarabhupala/Ratham or chariot, vahanas or vehicles, one Padma Peetam, the lotus-shaped seat, one Ratna Kiritam, one Naivedya bhojanam or food offering, one Unnatha Keli Mandapam, the lofty porch for the swings, one Sopana Marga or flight of steps on the side of the front facing hill and one Agra or front facing Gopuram to Sri Venkateswara. He installed the image of the Lord on the pathway over the Hill. He also constructed the Sri Pada Mandapam or Padala Mandapam where the sacred feet of Lord Vishnu are engraved on a floor slab and constructed a new Mandapam called Krotta Gopuram along the pathway.

Araviti Aliya Ramanuja who was the Maha Pradhani and the brother-in-law of Sadasivaraya made the largest endowments.

All the sons of Potlapati Thimmaraja namely, Thimmarajayyan, Vittaleswara Raja, Chinna Thimmaraja and Pappu Thimmaraja made endowments. The other royal donors were Matla Varadaraja, Manampoli Sri Rangaraja, Sripathi Obaleswararaja and Thiruvadiraja of Travancore in the present Kerala State, Pendlikoduku Thimmaraja, Nandyala Narapparaja, Tirumalaraja, Aravidu Ramaraja, Konetiraja Kondaraja and Aliya Ramaraja.

The military and other officers made an endowment of 15,000 *panam* each. These included Attilangu Nayakar of Vempattu Palayam, Murthi Nayakar of Kumarapalli, Krishnappa Nayakar, Sevvu Nayakar, Sevvappa Nayakar, Surappa Nayakar, Arani Tirumalai Nayakar, Rayasam Hariappar, Rayasam Venkatadri, Karanika Appalayyar, Karanika Basavarasar and so on.

Aravidu Dynasty

The Aravidu dynasty ruled from 1565 to 1665. Araviti Aliya Ramanuja and Tirumalaraja were the ministers during the reign of Sadasivaraya. With the death of Sadasivaraya, the Thuluva Dynasty rule came to an end. The Aravidu family which hailed from Rayalaseema, came to power. As ministers Aliya Ramanuja and Tirumalaraja had made endowments to the temple. Tirumalayyaraja, son of Aravidu Bukkaraja Ramaraja Rangaraja, constructed the Tirumalaraya Mandapam in 1561. This might be the enlarged structure of Saluva Narasimha Mandapam. He also paid 16,500 *panam* to the temple for meeting the expenses for food offerings and festivals and other services and arranged for offerings to the processional deities in his mandapam during the 10 Brahmotsavams and other festivals and on other specific days. Ramaraja, son of Rangaraja, made many gifts to the Lord.

Tirumalayyadeva or Thirumalendra was Ramaraja's brother and he instituted the Dola Mahotsavam (Swing festival) for the Lord in 1561. He also inaugurated Vasanthotsavam in Tirumala in the same year.

The Temple after the decline of Vijayanagara Empire

The decline of the Vijayanagara Empire started with the battle of Talikota. After this battle, the Aravidu dynasty ruled for 90 years from 1575-1665. Nearly 185 inscriptions out of which 33 are complete, belong to this period.

But even after the decline of the Vijayanagara dynasty, many chieftains and nobles continued to offer gifts to this temple. The Maratha general Raghoji Bhonsle who was a great devotee of the Lord, after visiting this temple, set up a permanent endowment for the conduct of the worship. He also presented valuable jewels to the Lord that included a large emerald that is still preserved in a box named after him. Later, the rulers of Mysore and Gadwal also donated lavishly to this temple.

Raghoji Bhonsale

In 1740, the Marathas invaded the Carnatic under Raghoji Bhonsle and he came to Chittoor district. At this time he visited the Tirumala temple to pay respects to Lord Srinivasa. He presented valuable jewels to the Lord. His offerings included one string of pearls with a pendant containing a ruby inlaid in a flat, etched emerald; one string of pearls with a pendant containing a flat etched emerald, one set of 17 pearl strings with 20 pearls in each string and one Kalikiturayi—a jewel of precious stones to be attached to the crown and one pearl garland of five strings set with a pendant of diamonds and rubies on the reverse. These jewels are still preserved in 'Raghuvari Petti' in the temple. These are taken out to adorn the Lord on festive occasions.

Gifts from English Devotees

It is said that Thomas Monroe who was the governor of Madras (the present Chennai) Presidency was cured of acute stomach ache by the grace of Lord Venkateswara and he became a great devotee. He created an endowment by donating the village of Kotavayulu in Chittoor district of present Andhra Pradesh, for a daily offering of a big vessel (Gangalam) of Pongal to the deity.

It is said Lord Williams who was also cured of a chronic illness by the grace of the Lord, started a drinking water service called 'Lord Williams Chali Pandiri' at Mokala Mettu (Muzhangal Mudichchu in Tamil) that is the most difficult stretch on the pathway to Tirumala.

Contributions Made by the Mahants

The Sri Venkateswara Temple on the Tirumala Hills along with Sri Govindarajaswami temple, Sri Rama Temple, Sri Kapileshwaraswami Temple that are located in Tirupathi and the Sri Padmavathi Temple in Tiruchanoor, were handed over by the East India Company to the-then Mahant Sri Sevadasa of the Sri Hathiramji Mutt in Tirupathi in 1843, to manage the temple through the succession of disciples.

From 1843 till 1933, six generations of Mahants exercised authority over the temple as Vicharanakartas. The Mahants saw to the all-round development of the place, repairs and renovations to the temple and brought about an improvement in the facilities provided to the visiting pilgrims. However, there were several civil as well as criminal cases filed in the court due to the strife between the Mahants and other vested interests. This led to a colosasal waste of temple funds. Charges of misappropriation and misapplication of the funds and breach of trust were the main subjects for these litigations. Only during the period of the first Mahant, Sri Sevadasa, from 1843-1864, did the temple affairs remain free of lawsuits.

In 1849, as per inscriptions and records, Mahant Sevadasa renovated the Swami Pushkarini and enclosed the two major Teerthas, namely the Varaha Teertha and Srinivasa Teertha. These are believed to contain nine holy Teerthas namely, the Markandeya, Agni, Yama, Vasishta, Varuna, Vayu, Kubera, Galva and Saraswathi. He revived the float festival for Lord Sri Venkateswara and Sri Padmavathi. He presented a gold Pithambaram, a gold Yajnopavitham, gold Padmapitam, gem set, ear ornaments, Nagabharanam and a circlet of diamonds for the crown of the Moola Beram or the main deity, a Viramudi or head ornament of pearls for the processional image of the Lord, a pearl-set crown, gilded silver coverings for the deity's hands and legs, Rajamudi or head ornament of pearls that covered the hair of each of the Lord's two consorts, a lattice door overlaid with silver plate at the innermost door sill called the Kulasekhara Padi at the entrance of the sanctum, four silver chains for the cot and silver seats with lion's heads on either side for the processional images. He also renovated the inner or Mukkoti Pradakshinam and arranged for the processional images to be decorated with Vajra Kavacham or gold armour set with diamonds on the Mukkoti Ekadasi day (this was stopped after some time), repaired the Swami Pushkarini, arranged an underground channel for the supply of water to it from the Patha Koneru, that is Achyutharaya Koneri on the west, prepared a silver-plated Thiruchi with Makara Thoranam, gifted a bigger serpent vehicle, the Pedda Sesha Vahnam and gilded it, constructed a new Brahma's chariot or Ratham and a new chariot for the Lord and repaired the fallen southern part of the big Gopuram to the East of Sri Govindarajaswami Temple in Tirupathi. He also built the Mukha Mandapam in Tiruchanoor and gilded the silver covering on the hands of the Goddess.

Mahant Dharmadas, disciple of Mahant Sevadasa assumed charge in 1864. He gifted a gold Kiritam and coverings for the hands, golden foot coverings, two necklaces of gold coins, a big Makara Kanthi of gold embedded with gems, a round tablet set with diamonds and rubies around a palm-sized emerald fixed in the crown and covered the door jambs and the wooden door of Bangaruvakili with the Dasavathara figures on gilded copper plates. For the processional image of Maliappaswamy, he remade the Kalikithurai attached to the coronet that belonged to the jewels gifted by Raghoji Bhosle, remade the strings of pearls with gold wire with the pendant of emeralds and diamonds gifted by Muppanaru Rani, made a new gold-plated Makara Thoranam with Gandharvas on either side, made a Sarva Bhupala Vahana plated with gold, a Surya Prabha Vehicle plated with silver and gifted small and big silver-plated Garuda Vahanas, Hanumantha Vahana, Aswa Vahana and Kalpa Vruksha Vahana. He also repaired the now-demolished 1000-pillared mandapam, the two Gopurams and parts of the Prakaram walls and some mandapams in the Tirumala temple around 1865.

While repairing the Yagnasala at the Kalyana Mandapam, it is understood that five small sealed vessels of gold coins were found relating to the period of King Venkatapathyraya, with the images of Uma Maheshwara and Gandabherunda (eagle coat-of-arms), Ikkeri-Varahalu (gold coins of South Canara) and Sanara-Kasulu worth rupees two lakh at that time. These were seized by the government and kept in the District court as treasure. Later, they were recovered and are now stored in TTD treasury. He also made several repairs and improvements in the temples at Tirupathi and Tiruchanoor. He renovated the steps of Kapila Teertha and mandapams on its east and west banks. In 1865, he also constructed the outer entrance Gopuram of the temple of

Sri Venkateswara, the Padi Kavili Gopuram, together with some mandapams nearby in 1878.

The third Vicharanakartha was Mahant Bhagavandas who took charge in 1880. He set up the Dwajasthambam, repaired some of the mandapams and jewels, laid a telephone line from Tirupathi to Tirumala, repaired the freshwater tank and laid underground pipes for water supply to the town. He built the bungalow to the south of the tank as a guesthouse for the Governor and top officials. He made some improvements in the Tirupathi and Tiruchanoor temples also. He lent money to the Raja of Karvetinagaram.

The fourth Vicharanakartha was Mahant Mahabirudasa. During his period of administration, 1890 to 1894, nothing significant was done.

Mahant Ramkisoradasa was the fifth Vicharanakarta. He took charge in 1895. He made the gem- studded Shankha and Chakra for the processional image of Sri Venkateswara, hand coverings and gem-studded belts for His two consorts and gold coverings with small bells and anklets for Andal in Sri Govindarajaswamy temple in Tirupathi. He adopted three disciples, Prayagadasa, Ramalakshmanadasa and Mularmaniyadasa. Prayagadasa was chosen as his successor.

In the regime of the sixth and the last Vicharanakartha, Mahant Prayagadasa, his brother disciple Rama Lakshmanadasa fixed the golden vase or Kalasam on the Vimana over the temple sanctum in 1908. Prayagadasa constructed a new Nirali Mandapam, reconstructed the dilapilated Sri Varahaswami shrine in the northwest corner of Swami Pushkarini and re-installed the idol in that shrine, moving it from the Aina Mahal in the Sri Venkateswara temple. The idol had been kept there for nearly 12 years. He also prepared a new Ratham or chariot, gilded the Hamsa Vahana and Garuda Vahana and repaired the Gopurams, a few mandapams and the flooring of the Sampangi Pradakshinam. He made a new silver Thiruchi, constructed choultries for pilgrims, established a dispensary, enclosed the Dwarapalakas in the temple with a lattice, covered it with silver plate, cast a tiny gold image of Sri Padmavathi and had it consecrated and suspended on the chest of Lord Srinivasa, gold plated the Shankha and Chakra that are held in the rear hands of the deity and gilded the hands of the idols of Sri Rama, Sita and Lakshmana.

He made several improvements in the Tirupathi and Tiruchanoor temples, too. He invested Rs 5 lakh of the Devasthanams in the Bombay Development Loan and derived an annual interest of Rs 54,500. He purchased a Jadasadu with Kuchchulu (plaited hair with three pendant tufts of silk), covered with gold tablets inlaid with diamonds, rubies and sapphires for the decoration of one of the two Nachimars of the processional deity of the Lord.

In the early 1930's, the dowager Rani Sri Adilakshmi Devammagaru of the Gadwal Samasthanam presented a few old jewels, gold and silver coins with a request to this Mahant to make a Ratnakiritam out of them for the processional deity. The Kiritam contained 681 diamonds, 669 rubies, 125 emeralds, 84 sapphires—in all 1,559 precious stones. The Kiritam measured $7\frac{3}{4}$ inches from top to bottom and $3\frac{1}{4}$ inches in diameter at the base. He also started the work of making a gold Kiritam embedded with four kinds of gems for the Mula Murthy of Sri Venkateswara, but it had to be stopped suddenly.

It can be said that the last Mahant carried out several useful measures of permanent benefit to the temple. He improved the Sopana Marga, the flight of steps to the temple, repaired gopurams, constructed choultries and tanks, improved sanitation, water supply and lighting and repaired the road leading to the temple. He also gilded the Vimana of the Garbha Griha or the sanctum.

Some of the important contributions made by the TTD

1934-35	Balipeetam in Tirumala temple gilded
1939	A gem-studded flower was fixed on the gold Kiritam of the Lord
1940-41	Silver chariot made
1942	Wooden Maharatham made
1944	Opening of the new Ghat Road
1945	Diamond-studded crown for the Lord made
1947	Makara Thoranam refixed
1950	Renovation work started
1953-54	Diamond Vaikunta Hastham made for the Lord
1954	Sri Venkateswara University set up
1966	Diamond Kati Hastham made for the Lord
1969	Tirupathi Airport inaugurated
1974	Second Ghat Road built
1975	TTD transport services were taken over by APSRTC
1975	Vaikuntam Queue Complex built
1981	Dismantling of the 1000-pillared mandapam and widening of the Sannidhi streets
1982	The footpath to Tirumala covered

In addition, the Ananda Nilayam was renovated and gilded, the Golden Chariot for the Lord was made, the inner Gopuram was gilded, Vajra Kiritam was made for the Lord, new Pottu was inaugurated for the preparation of the Laddu Pradasam, new Kalyanakatta was set up, musical fountain was erected, new Asthana Mandapam was constructed, Sarva Darshan duration was extended further, the publication of rare scriptures was undertaken, free bus service was arranged on the Hills, lighting was provided along the footpath to Tirumala, water and first-aid facilities were started, snacks and provisions were sold in the queue complex, and so on.

Thus the TTD's contribution to the temple is seen in almost all the fields including the renovation and extension works of the temples under its control, providing maximum facilities to the visiting pilgrims including boarding and lodging, undertaking medical, educational, social and developmental activities and contributing to the upkeep of Hindu religion and its philosophy.

The Sri Venkateswara temple is one of the richest religious shrines in the world today. Devotees pour into the temple town in huge numbers and the quantum of offerings to the Sri Vari Hundi or donation box is enormous. This is a tribute to the faith that the Lord inspires among devotees.

Renovation of Ananda Nilayam

During the reign of Veera Narasinga Raya (1205-1262), the local king, the Ananda Nilayam was first gilded. Later it was replaced several times by different rulers. Veera Narasingaraya weighed himself in gold and presented it for gilding work. Between 1251-1275 CE, Jatavarman Sundara Pandya I is said to have fixed the golden Kalasa on top of the Vimana. In the year 1359, Saluva Mangi Deva, a general under Kumara Kampanna Udiyar, fixed a golden Kalasa on the Vimana. Amartya Sekhara Mallanna,or Madhava Dasu, a minister under Devaraya II who governed the Chandragiri area, renovated this Vimana in 1417. Krishnadevaraya gilded the Vimana again in 1518. Later in 1630, during the reign of Venkata I, it was gilded again for the fifth time by Koti Kanyadanam Tatacharya of Kanchi. For the sixth time, Adhikari Ramalakshmanadasa, one of the brother disciples of Sri Mahant Prayagadasa, arranged for the fixing of the Kanaka Kalasa over the Vimana in 1908. In 1958, the Vimana or dome was completely renovated and plated with 12000 tolas of gold at a cost of Rs.18 lakh by the TTD and copper plated at the cost of Rs.2.5 lakh. At present, the Vimana is completely gilded. Gilded copper sheets were fixed to the original Vimana and the space between the sheets and the Vimana was filled up with cement concrete.

Contributions Made for Worship and Sevas in the Temple

The festivals celebrated during the temple's early years from the time of Samavai who gifted and installed the silver idol, were according to the solar calendar. In 1491, we find the first mention of Yugadi and Deepavali being celebrated with food offerings and the rulers following the Chandramana Panchanga. These celebrations sidelined the Chitthirai and Thula Vishu celebrations although the Prabandams of the Alwars continued to be sung.

The epigraphs that belong to pre-Vijayanagara times mention offerings for the supply of ghee for the lamps lit before the deities through the day and night or late in the evening or at twilight. The donors either deposited money in the temple treasury or presented milch cows. They also donated for the payment of salaries to those who lighted the lamps. Later, the devotees started arranging for offerings of milk and curd or offering of foods containing milk and curd.

Some devotees gifted lands, jewels and money. Other devotees donated for daily offerings and for several festivals, processions and Asthanams of the deities in the temple. A number of devotees also excavated fresh irrigation channels or deepened the existing channels or brought uncultivated lands in the Devadana villages under cultivation. This generated income that went towards the continuous supply of food offerings to the deity. Gardens were maintained and the flowers handed over to the temple for meeting the requirement for Pujas and for garlands and for decorating the idol and the temple. They set up feeding houses called Ramanujakutams or Chatrams for providing free food to the visiting pilgrims. They also registered the sale of houses or lands and made them over to the temple.

During the Vijayanagara period, donations for daily and occasional special food offerings became more popular than lighting lamps for the deities. The term Sandhi, as seen in the inscriptions, probably indicated the short interval between Pujas. But later this term began to signify the food offerings made during these intervals, Sandhi-Muppadu (30 units of cooked rice), Pongal Sandhi and so on. Some also donated for the purchase of provisions for the food offerings.

In the earlier half of the 15th century, recitation of the Vedas formed an essential part of the Pujas in the temple. This was later discontinued, but revived during the reign of Devaraya II of the first Vijayanagara dynasty. The discontinuation of the *Veda* chanting or Parayanam was brought to the notice of the royal officer Devanna Udaiyar as a defect in the temple procedure by Agappiranar alias Thirukkalikanridasar, with a request that this ancient practice be revived and continued. The king made arrangements to pay the priests who chanted the hymns and effected its revival. The Veda chanting was discontinued and revived a second time during the reign of the second Vijayanagara dynasty. Since then, it has continued uninterrupted.

The earliest mention of the sacred Abhishekam to the Lord in the temple with sandalwood paste, turmeric, musk and refined camphor etc is in the inscription relating to the year 1386 when the daily Thirumanjanam was performed for the Lord. Civet oil or *punugu* was used to anoint the idol (called Punugu Kappu). Then the vertical white namam or mark was drawn with the fine dust of refined camphor. Now the term *punugu* includes not only civet oil and camphor but also musk and saffron. The musk is used for drawing the central line or Kasturi Thilakam as well as for the Abhishekam.

Inscriptions on the Temple Walls Before 1496 CE (Epigraphical Series Volumes 1 and 2)

There are several inscriptions on the temple walls of Tirumala and Tirupathi. The TTD under its Religious Publications series (No 523), has deciphered, classified and transcribed these inscriptions. They were first brought out in print in the 1930's. The reprint of the Epigraphical series in 1998 consisted of six volumes that presented the details of the inscriptions. The 7th volume was an Epigraphical glossary. A report about these inscriptions was also published.

The TTD found a total of 1,167 inscriptions. Besides the Tirumala temple, inscriptions were present in the Sri Govindarajaswami temple, Tirupathi, Sri Kapileshwaraswami temple, Tirupathi and Sri Padmavathi Devi temple, Tiruchanoor.

The first volume contains 236 epigraphs belonging to the Pallava, Chola, Pandya and the first Vijayanagara eras. The second volume has 169 inscriptions of the Saluva Narasimha period. The third volume with 229 inscriptions, belongs to the reign of Krishnadevaraya. The fourth volume has 251 inscriptions relating to Achyutaraya's period. The fifth volume of 147 inscriptions, belongs to the period of Sadasivaraya's rule and the seventh and last volume contains 135 inscriptions belonging to the rule of the Aravidu dynasty. The inscriptions were classified and deciphered by Sadhu Subramanya Sastry and edited by V Vijaya Raghavacharya.

The early inscriptions are recorded in Tamil script whereas the 50 inscriptions dating from the Vijayanagara period are in Telugu and Kannada. Prior to the reign of Krishnadevaraya, there is only one Telugu inscription, that of Saluva Mangi Deva Maharaja and two Kannada inscriptions, one referring to Vira Pratapadevaraya Maharaja and one to Saluva Narasimha. All the gifts made by Krishnadevaraya and his two queens are recorded in Telugu, Tamil and Kannada.

Many inscriptions are either incomplete or fragmentary or even completely damaged because of the renovation of the walls and other structures in the temples carried out during the last 500 or 600 years. The damage was done in spite of the instructions given by the-then feudatory chief Vira Narasinga Yadavaraya to the Sthanathar or the managers of the Tirumala temple. His directions for renovating the central shrine of Lord Venkateswara, were to copy the inscriptions exactly as engraved, before the wall was touched. Later the inscriptions were to be re-engraved when the repair was complete.

Some inscriptions are without the years and dates and in some the donors are not metioned. The dates of the inscriptions range from the 51st year of the reign of Vijayadanthi Vikrama Varman of the Pallava dynasty (about 830 CE) till 1909 CE covering a period of 11 centuries.

The inscriptions detailing the donations include the endowments made exclusively to the temple on Tirumala and also those that were made to other deities and spiritual masters. But it is to be noted that most of the contributions mentioned in the inscriptions were made to Lord Venkateswara at the Tirumala temple. This reveals the temple's prominence even in the early days. The offerings were meant for the worship of the Lord and for the development of the temple.

The first edition of the epigraphical series was published by the TTD in the year 1930. The actual work started in May 1922 and was completed in 1927. Sadhu Subramanya Sastry presented a general survey of the inscriptions during the period of Pallavas, Cholas, and Pandyas and then later of the Vijayanagara Kings. He also incorporated some of the inscriptions belonging to the period of the Mahants.

These inscriptions on the walls of the Tirumala temple and three of the temples below at Tirupathi, help us to understand the history pertaining to the respective periods. We also get a glimpse of the old terms relating to the Temple, the festivals, offerings, the official ranks and so on. They also provide valuable insights into the spiritual and temporal aspects of society and the social and economic life of the people of those times.

As far as the temple is concerned, these inscriptions give us a clear idea about the endowments made by several kings, their chieftains, the Generals, the palace officials, the persons connected to the palace of the king, the spiritual masters, the religious teachers, the Jiyars, the poet-muscians, scholars, Nambimars or Archakas, Vaishnavaites, the Mahants, the temple officials, the merchants, and the devotees. Some donated land, some donated entire villages, some gave money and some gifted gold jewels set with precious gems and pearls. Some donors excavated lands for digging irrigation channels, some gave articles for worship and so on. We also find that the same devotee offered gifts to the Lord in various forms like money, land, construction of mandapams and so on, more than once in the same or at different periods.

Further, the inscriptions throw light on the growth and development of this sacred temple and give a glimpse of the Sevas and festivals conducted for the Lord and the different kinds of food offerings made to the Lord in those days. Some of the inscriptions also state in whose honour the donations were made by the donor and who the recipients of the Prasadams should be. They also provide valuable information about the contribution to the development and growth of the temple as a whole through several centuries.

Finally, these inscriptions reveal not only the names of kings and people connected to the palace but also the contributions made by Bhakthas who were ordinary people without royal connections. However, it is also possible that many more of such contributions made by ordinary people went unnoticed as they might not have been inscribed on the walls of the temples.

VOLUME 1 – Early Inscriptions

This volume contains the inscriptions relating to the period of Pallava kings particularly Koppatra Mahendra Varman and Sarvagna-Khadgamalla and that of Chola kings like Rajendra I, Rajendra Chola II, Kulothunga Chola I, Rajaraja Chola and Pandyan kings like Jatavarman Sundara Pandya I. The inscriptions in this volume also relate to the reign of the Telugu Pallava Kings like Vijaya Ganda Gopala, Raja Ganda Gopala; Yadavarayas like Thirukkalatthi Deva, Vira-Rakshasa, Vira-Narasinga Deva, Thiruvenkatanatha, Sri Ranganatha; the Vijayanagara kings like Bukkaraya I, Hariharaya II, Devaraya II, Mallikarjuna; and many miscellaneous fragments of inscriptions.

A few of the earliest inscriptions do not mention the years in which the gifts were made. Samavai alias Kadavan Perundevi, the queen of Sakthividangan alias Kadapathigal gifted four Tali or plates of cooked rice and a lamp called Nanda Vilakku for the 'Ayana Sankranthi' and the two 'Vishnu Sankranthi' days. She also gifted, installed and consecrated a silver idol of the Lord for the celebration of the Purattasi festival and the nine-day main festival that began two days after that. Along with this, she also donated for the adornment of the idol, a crown containing 23 diamonds, 16 big pearls, two big central rubies, and three cut rubies; two ornaments shaped like a *makara* or goat and a pair of coral *koppu* or earrings; four strings of necklaces with 14 diamonds and rubies, 11 big pearls and many small red pearls, a gold belt, a girdle with four rubies, two circular ornaments for the arms, four bracelets set with two cut rubies, four circular ornaments for the neck, and two solid gold anklets set with precious stones, corals and pearls for the feet. She also offered two anklets with bells and a luminous disc of silver set with a big ruby. The number of pieces totalled 52, made with 47 *kalanju* (a kind of measure used in those days) of gold. She also donated land to the Lord.

As per the inscriptions on the north wall in the first Prakaram of the Tirumala temple, during the reign of Rajaraja III, Paranthakadevi Amma, daughter of a Chera king presented a gold *pattam* (the ornamental band for the forehead), set with diamonds, rubies and pearls. The queen consort of Rajaraja I, Ulagamadevi, gifted a lamp to the temple of Sri Venkatesha. She also presented a gold *pattam* weighing 52 *kalanju* set with six rubies, four diamonds and 28 pearls.

An officer of the King named Arulakki, alias Rajaraja Muvendavelan, gifted 40 *kalanju* of gold to the temple, most likely for Nanda Vilakku. He also gifted some villages on the south bank of river Kaveri. Jatavarman Sundara Pandyan fixed a *kanaka kalasa*, a golden vase, over the *vimana*.

Veera Narasinga Devaraya under Sundara Pandyan, granted several villages to ensure the supply of rice and vegetables to the temple. He also gifted 32 cows for supplying the ghee used in the lamp. His queen Yadavaraya Nachiyar presented 64 cows for supplying ghee for two Nanda Vilakku set up in their presence. Both husband and wife presented three bulls as well. Mahamandaleshwara Misaraganda Mangadeva Maharaja fixed the golden vase and gilded the sanctum of the temple. One of the ministers during the reign of the Rayas donated 28 cows and 16 bulls for Nanda Vilakku. They also gifted several items for the worship of the Lord.

The chief minister Amatya Sekhara Mallanna provided a rich *naivedyam* and a splendid Nitya Deepam (eternally-burning lamp) for the Lord.

Srimallanna alias Sri Madhavadasar dedicated as his *tiruppani* or sacred construction, the front portico (Tirumamani Mandapam) consisting of Tirumutti Nadandal (beautiful flooring), Kal Devaram (the stone entrance), the decorative work extending from the Kuradu or basement up to the Sthapi or roof and the Meyakkal (the sloping terrace) over this.

Mallandiar of Chandragiri constructed a river channel in the Naiaru for irrigating the lands gifted to the temple. These provided grains to the temple for the daily worship.

A devotee Tirukkali Kanridasar of Tirupathi arranged for the resumption of the Veda recital that had been stopped for some time.

Anantasayanar donated 300 *narpanam* (a kind of gold coin used as money) to the Sri Bhandaram or Hundi (treasury) of Sri Venkateswara and Sri Govindaraja.

Anantarayana offered excellent *naivedyam* prepared with jaggery and ghee together with sweet *appam* to the Lord on the first and last days of the grand festivals.

VOLUME 2

Volume 2 contains inscriptions engraved during Saluva Narasimha's reign. From a total of 168 inscriptions, 101 inscriptions are from the Tirumala temple and 67 inscriptions are from the Sri Govindarajaswami temple, Sri Kapileshwara Swami Temple and Sri Padmavathi Devi Temple. Out of the 168 inscriptions only 136 are complete ones while the others are incomplete or damaged.

1504-1542 (Epigraphical Series – Volumes 3 and 4)

VOLUME 3

This volume contains 229 inscriptions relating to the reign of Sri Krishnadevaraya and his elder brother, out of which 165 are complete and the rest damaged or incomplete.

VOLUME 4

This volume contains inscriptions relating to the period of

Important Contributions of Devotees 151

Achyutaraya. There are 251 inscriptions relating to the period of Achyutharaya and out of these 176 are complete, the others being incomplete or damaged.
1543 CE to 1908 CE (Epigraphical series – Volumes 5 and 6)

VOLUMES 5 & 6

These contain inscriptions relating to the reigns of Sadasivaraya and Venkatapathyraya — 176 inscriptions relate to the period of Sadasivaraya, out of which 134 are complete.

 Modern terms and their equivalents in the past as found in the inscriptions

Deities

Sri Venkateswara (Balaji): Srinivasa, Thiruvenkadamudian, Periya Perumal, Mula Murthy

Processional Deities of Lord Venkateswara: Malaikuniyaninra Perumal, Malai Perumal, Malaiappaswami, Utsavamurthy

Ugra Srinivasa: Venkatatthuraivar

Koluvu Srinivasa: Azhagappiranar

Divine consorts of Sri Venkateswara: Alarmelu Mangai Nachiyar, Sri Padmavathi Devi, Lakshmi Devi

Lord Narasimha: Narasimha Perumal, Azhagiya Singer

Divine consorts of processional deity: Nachimar

Sri Varahaswami: Gnana Piran

Vishvaksena: Senai Mudaliar

Garuda Flag, Garudalwar: Thirukkodi Alvan

Sudarsana Chakra: Kaiyar-Chakram

Chakratalwar: Thiruvajialwar

Divine consort of Lord Raghunatha, Andal, Sri Godadevi: Soodikodutha Nachiyar

Festivals and Sevas

Ekantha Seva: Ardha Jama Puja

Brahmotsavam: Thirukkodi Thirunal

Garden festival: Toppu Thirunal, Thotta Thirunal

Hunting festival: Padiya Vettai

Picnic festival: Vana Bhojanam

Float festival: Thiruppali Odam-Jalakrida

Anivara Asthanam (Closing of previous year's accounts and opening of new year's accounts): Adi Ayanam

New harvest festival: Thiruppudiyadu

Tomala Seva or Archana: Tirumala Seva

Civet Oil Abhishekam on Friday: Punugu Kappu

Annual festival: Thirunal Festival

Monthly festival: Thingal Divasam

Special festival days: Visesha Divasam

Sesha Vahana festival: Thiruvanantal

Annual Birth star festival: Attai, Thirunakshathiram

Sowing festival: Anna Unjal Thirunal

Spring channel festival: Navalluru Tirunal

Spring festival: Vasanthotsavam

Summer festival: Kodai Thirunal

Dvadarodhanam festival: Pushpayagnam

Vijaya Dasami festival: Sami, Vannimaram

Dhanurmasa Puja: Thiruppalli Ezuchchi

Makara Sankranthi festival: Sankramam

Kalyana Utsavam: Thirukkalyanam

Mukkoti Dwadasi festival: Thiru Dvadasi

Tamil New Year festival (Now only Kerala New Year): Vishu

Narasimha Jayanthi festival: Vasantha Purnima

Offerings in the past
Food Offerings

Sacred food: Pancha Havis
Sandhi (food offerings)
Thirupponakam, Rajana Thirupponakam, Vellai Thirupponakam (Venpongal Taligai): Cooked rice mixed with green gram, ghee and so on.

Ardha-Nayaka Taligai

Nayaka Taligai

Mattirai Taligai

Thiruppavadai

Thiruvolakkam

Dadhyodanam

Kadugu Ogarai

Ulundu Ogarai

Akkali Mandai

Vadai Padi

Godhi Padi

Idli Padi

Dosai Padi

Pori Padi

Thirukkanamadai

Paruppuavial (Sundal)

Aval Padi

Sweet Preparations

Manoharam

Thiruppaniyaram

Paniyaram

Athirasa Padi

Appa Padi

Sugiyan Padi

Ambili

Rasayanam

Tilannans

Tenkuzhal

Panchahavis

Jamnu Padi

Poruvilangai Padi

General Terms

Interest on money or lands: Poliyuttu

Charity, Service, Donation: Ubhayam

Money: Panam or Narpanam

Incessant Lamps: Nanda Vilakku

Evening Lamps: Thiru Vilakku

Special offering: Sirappu

Sandal paste: Kajakam, Kalabham

Mukkoti Dwadasi: Thiru Dwadasi

Swami Pushkarini, the Temple Tank at Tirumala: Thirukkoneri

Vaishnava Saints: Alwars

Trustees or managers of the Tirumala Temple: Sthanathar

Temple Councillors: Sabhaiyar

Royal Secretary: Rayasam

Temple treasury and stores: Sri Bhandaram, Salai

Room in which the copper plates of Talapakka Sankeerthanas are preserved: Sankeerthana Bhandaram

Gold treasury and jewellery room in Tirumala: Por Bhandaram

Temple Darbar: Asthanam, Thiruvolakkam

Worship: Avasaram

Priests for religious functions: Koyil Kelvi

Temple officers: Vagai

Treasury for public works: Thiruppani Bandaram

Officer in charge of public works: Thiruppani Pillai

Palanquin: Chivikai, Thiruchivikai, Pallayan Tulam

Flour Lamps: Mavilakku

Recitation of portions from the Tamil Prabandam: Sattumurai

Tirumala Temple measure: Malai Kuniya Ninra Kal

Performer of religious duties in the Temple: Jiyar, Ekaki, Sri Vaishnavas

Spiritual leaders: Acharya Purushas

Archakas: Nambimars

Temple accountant: Thiruninraur Udaiyan

Temple servants: Kaikkolar

Temple cooks: Thevai, Thevaiyal

Sculptor: Sippiyar

Temple servants: Uvachchar

Supervisors: Kankanippavar,

Fuel suppliers: Singa Murai

Superior authority: Mel Nayam or Nayakam

Performance of religious duties: Anusandanam

Pilgrim: Desantari

Management: Nirvaham

Flower garden: Nandana Vanam

Works of Alwars: Iyal

Time for distribution of the offered Prasadam and so on: Adaippu

Ablution: Thirumanjanam, Snanapana.

Flowers: Thiruppali Damanam

Vahana Bearer: Thukkan

Note: Panam, narpanam, pon, rekhai pon, varaha are all monetary units (usually gold coins) of those days. The units of measurement used for land, gold and food offerings were kalanju, kulji, uri, padi etc.

6

History of Festivals, Vahanas and Administration

According to the *Varaha Purana* and the *Venkateswara Mahatmyam*, the very first Brahmotsavam, the grand and great festival of the Lord was performed by Lord Brahma. This was continued in Kaliyuga by Thondaiman Chakravarthy belonging to the Chola dynasty.

An inscription from Tiruchanoor dated in the 51st year of the reign of Pallava king Vijayadanti Vikrama Varman mentions that a lamp was placed before the processional image newly installed in the temple of Thiruvenkatattu Emperuman Adigal. This is the earliest mention of the installation of a processional image. We find the record about the consecration of another silver idol of Sri Venkateswara 150 years later, by Samavai the Pallava queen, who was also known as Kadavan Perundevi, wife of Sakthi Vitankan, a Pallava chieftain. She also presented lands and gold for the celebration of a seven-day main festival commencing with Dwajarohanam that is, hoisting of sacred flag of Garuda. The festival was held during the Mukkoti Dwadasi period in Dhanurmasa, in the month of Margazhi.

It is seen that prior to 966 CE, only one Brahmotsavam was conducted in Kanya Masam that is in the Tamil month of Purattasi at Tirumala. The second Brahmotsavam was started by Samavai and she installed the silver idol of Lord Venkateswara, known as 'Bhoga Srinivasa', or 'Manavala Perumal' and consecrated it in the Tirumala temple on a Friday on the day when the Sravana Nakshatram or star was ascendant. She also presented a large number of ornaments including a stone-studded Kiritam and other jewels to decorate the Utsava Murthy from head to foot. She arranged for the conduct of a festival with a procession for two days immediately preceding the main festival, as well during the main festival in the month of Purattasi, commencing on the day of Chittirai star and lasting for nine days. In the same year, she made a further provision for a fresh festival for this silver image with two processions each day for a week prior to Margazhi Thirudwadasi, that is, the Mukkoti Dwadasi. To finance this, she purchased land and granted it tax-free to the temple.

Thus, two Brahmotsavams were celebrated from the 10th century CE. By about 1300, in addition, similar festivals were arranged in the month of Adi by Thiruvenkatanatha Yadavaraya. So there were now three Brahmotsavams or Thirukkodi Thirunal as it was known then, at Tirumala.

Later, after the decline of the Pallava, Chola and Pandya kingdoms, during the time of the chieftains, the Gandagopalas, Yadavarayas, the Kadavarayas and the Sambuvarayas also contributed through gifts and grants, for the continuation of the offerings and festivals.

In 1388, King Harihara of the Vijayanagara Empire instituted a new Brahmotsavam festival in the month of Magamasa or Masi through the agency of Mullai Thiru Venkata Jiyar. For meeting the expenses of this festival, Harihara endowed Pungodu village to the temple. In 1446, Phalguna or Panguni Brahmotsavam was instituted by Veera Narasinga Yadava Raya. In 1516 CE, Krishnadevaraya of the Vijayanagara Empire initiated the Pushya Masa or Thai Brahmotsavam, the temple meeting the expenses from the income of several donated villages. In 1539, the Jyestha Masa or Ani Brahmotsavam that was celebrated for thirteen days, was initiated by Talappaka Pedda Tirumalacharyulu, who was the son of saint-poet Annamacharyulu, through the endowment of 2,000 Varahas to the temple.

An inscription dated 8th July 1551 gives a list of Brahmotsavams that were celebrated in the Tirumala Temple at that time. The inscription also states that Rayasam Venkatadri, a chieftain, arranged for special offerings to the Utsava Murthy in all the ten Brahmotsavams celebrated in the year with the exception of Vaikasi and Ani months. These Brahmotsavams were celebrated for a period of 12 days counted from the day of Ankurarpanam or sowing of nine kinds of grains in the earthern vessels to the day of Vidaiyaru or rest (*vidai* in Tamil means 'farewell' and *aru* means 'rest'). Each day after the procession, the processional deity was lifted from the Vahana and seated in an Asthanam or Assembly inside the temple mandapam. The deity was offered different kinds of food by devotees which was later distributed. Similar Asthanams were arranged by the devotees in the past in the mandapams built by them or in their flower gardens or opposite their houses at Tirumala before the processional deity returned to the temple.

Till a few decades ago, the temple conducted four Brahmotsavams in a year. The first in the month of Purattasi, the second on the Ratha Sapthami day, the third on the Kausika Ekadasi day in the month of Karthika and the fourth on Vaikunta Ekadasi or Mukkoti Ekadasi day. The most important of these was the Purattasi Brahotsavam conducted generally during September-October.

In later years, the number of Brahmotsavams came down to one, celebrated during the Kanya constellation in the Purattasi month, commencing on the day the Shravana star is ascendant, as initiated by Lord Brahma. An additional Navaratri Brahmotsavam is conducted once in three years, when there is an Adhika Masa or intercalary month in the year as per the lunar calendar. In this second Brahmotsavam, there is no Dwajarohanam on the first and last days and the silver chariot is used instead of the wooden chariot for Rathotsavam.

Kalyanotsavam

There are no inscriptions relating to this festival till 1546. It was first introduced by Talapakka Tirumalayyangar. At that time, it was conducted in the Tirumamani Mandapam for five days in the month of Panguni.

Rathasapthami festival

This festival was celebrated at sunrise on the Magha Suddha Sapthami Thithi. It is first mentioned in an inscription dated 1564, when Karanikkar Appalayyar, through the endowment of a village, met the expenses of this festival.

Adyayanotsavam

This festival commences 10 days prior to Mukkoti Ekadasi and continues for a period of about 20 days. During each of these days, the processional deities are taken around the streets amidst chanting of hymns from the *Nalayira Divya Prabandam*. This festival is divided into equal periods. The first 10 days forms the Pagal Pathu (10 days) and the latter, the Ira Pathu (10 nights) that commences with Vaikunta Ekadasi or the Mukkoti Ekadasi. Devotees made their offerings during these days as in the case of Brahmotsavam. The Adyayanotsavam festival in the month of Margazhi was introduced in 1468 through an endowment of Saluva Narasimha Raja. The earliest reference to it occurs around 1467 with Sattumurai and the latest in 1635. It continues to be observed even today.

Pavitrotsavam

This is a purificatory ceremony conducted for the expiation of sins of omission and commission arising in the daily worship and other religious rites performed in the temples. It was originally instituted at Tirumala in 1463 by Saluva Narasimha.

The festival was held during the month of Avani and lasted for six days, including the preliminaries of the seed sowing. The ceremony also consisted of recitation of the *Vedas* and the reading of the *Puranas*. Since inscriptions after the 15th century do not refer to the festival, it is not known exactly when it was discontinued. It was revived in 1962.

Punugu Kappu Murai

This refers to the anointing of the Deity with specially-prepared scented civet oil. This ritual was started in 1434 for the silver idol of Manavala Perumal before the daily Abhishekam. This ritual was maintained by Saluva Narasimha.

Padiya Vettai

The hunting festival was introduced in the year 1456.

Dola Mahotsava Anna Unjal Thirunal

This was a five-day festival introduced by Saluva Narasimha.

Anivara Asthanam or Adi Ayanam

The festival was celebrated on the day when a new account was opened. During earlier times, the opening was called Thiru Andu Ezhuthidal or the writing of the New Year's account. Adi Ayanam is mentioned in the inscription belonging to the year 966 CE, but nowhere is it mentioned in clear terms that the New Year account was opened on that particular day. The first mention of this is seen in the inscription pertaining to the year 1494. It however attained importance during the reign of Saluva Narasimha.

Lakshmidevi Mahotsavam

This festival was introduced by Achyutaraya in 1535 and continued till 1562.

Pallavotsavam

Introduced in 1545 by Mahamandaleshwara Vittaleshwara Maharaja, son of Aravitti Bukkaraja Ramaraja Timmarajayyan, it was celebrated in the month of Vaikasi and continued till 1562.

Phalotsavam

This festival of fruits was conducted in the month of Masi. The total number of fruits offered came to an even 1,200.

Sankranthi and other Visesha Divasangal

The Sankranthis mentioned as Visesha Divasangal (special days) in the inscriptions were celebrated in the temple. These included the Ayana Sankranthi, Makara Sankranthi or Uttarayana Punya Kalam, the Karkataka Sankramam or the Dakshinayana Punya Kala, Vishu Sankranthi or Chitthirai Vishu and Aipasi Vishu and the monthly Sankranthis. On these days, special worship like Tirumanjanam or Abhishekam and Naivedyam or food offerings were provided by the devotees. The earliest reference belongs to the late 1100's. In course of time there was an increase in these special days observed at Tirumala including the Ekadasi days. The full and new moon days, Soma Surya Grahanam, the lunar and solar eclipses, were included in the Visesha Divasangal.

Vasanthotsavam

The spring festival was introduced by Saluva Narasimha. It fell on the sixth day of Brahmotsavam. In the 13th century, there were two spring festivals as there were two Brahmotsavams. In the middle of the 16th century, when two more Brahmotsavams were instituted, there were four Vasanthotsavams altogether. Vasanthotsavam was also arranged on the last two days of the Kodai Thirunal during the reign of Krishnadevaraya. The main Vasanthotsavam festival was celebrated in the month of Chittirai when the star Chitra coincided with the full moon. During the reign of Achyutaraya, another Vasanthotsavam was introduced.

Kodai Thirunal

It was the summer festival conducted for the processional deity Sri Malaiappaswami, His consorts Sri Devi and Bhu Devi and Senai Mudaliar. The festival was introduced by Saluva Narasimha in 1486 and went on for 20 days. The Mahants continued it but it was discontinued when the TTD took over.

Anna Unjal Thirunal (swan swing festival)

The Anna Unjal festival was started by Saluva Narasimha for the processional deities starting on the sixth day of the bright fortnight in the month of Chittirai. It went on for a week including the Ankurarpanam. For meeting the expenses, Saluva Narasimha granted the village of Dommarapatti in Kalavai Parru. The festival was immediately succeeded by the Kodai Thirunal on its 10th day and further continued on to the one-day Makara Sankramam. Thus the Unjal Thirunal lasted for nine days.

Tiruppali Odam Thirunal (Float festival)

The inscription that recorded the Anna Unjal Thirunal by Saluva Narasimha mentions the Thiruppali Odam Thirunal as well. Most probably, the first float festival in the Swami Pushkarini was conducted in 1473. For this occasion, he offered four Appa Padi.

In one of the temple inscriptions it is described as a standalone one-day festival. But according to a couple of other inscriptions, the float festival was celebrated on the tenth day of the Kodai festival. Another inscription states that this Jalakridai-Thiruppali Odam Thirunal was conducted for nine days in the Achyutaraya Koneri.

Jayanthi celebrations of different Avatars and Spiritual Leader

The Jayanthis or birth anniversaries of different Avatars such as Sri Rama Navami, Sri Krishna Jayanthi, Sri Narasimha Jayanthi and those of the Acharyas were observed annually and also on the birth star of the main deity Sri Venkateswara. Besides these, Tai Amavasya, Ani Amavasya, Deepavali, Karthikai, Yugadi, Maha Navami, Ratha Sapthami and so on were also celebrated. Special worship including food offerings and processions were arranged on these occasions.

The festivals and important days in the temple as per the 16th-century inscriptions included seven Brahmotsavams, Adyayanam festivals for 24 days, Kodai Thirunal for 20 days and Unjal Thirunal and Pavitrotsavam for five days each.

In addition, one-day celebrations included Thirukkarthikai, Aipasi Puradam (Senai Mudaliar's birthday), Thiru Dwadasi (Mukkoti Dwadasi) for Venkatatthuraivar, Sri Jayanthi Thirunal for Periya Perumal, Ani Puradam, Ani Pusam, Sri Rama Navami and Vasantha Poornima. Altogether, there were festivals on 153 days during the year.

Important days of worship in the past

Brahmotsavam for 14 days

Anna Unjal Thirunal for five days instituted by Saluva Narasimha in 1473

Pavitrotsavam for five days, that was instituted by Saluva Mallayyadeva Maharaja in 1464

The Archana-Ashtottara Sahasranama for five days

Sahasra Kalasabhishekam for one day

Adyayanotsavam for 25 days in the month of Margazhi

Vasantotsavam for five days instituted by Tirumalaraya

Damana Arohana Vasantotsavam, the covering of the Deities with sweet smelling Damana herbs for five days in the month of Ani

Unjal festival for nine days

Pendli Thirunal or Vaivahikotsavam for five days

Lakshmi festival for five days

Kodai Thirunal for 20 days

Float festival for nine days

Pallavotsavam for five days

Phalotsavam for three days

Adyayanotsavam for Sri Ramanuja for six days

Altogether there were 15 festivals and 10 Brahmotsavams.

In addition to these festivals, special worship was conducted on certain days in every month. They were: 12 days of Masa Sankramas (the first day of each of the 12 Tamil months), 13 Amavasyas, 13 Poornimas, 25 Dasamis, 25 Ekadasis, 25 Dwadasis, 13 days for each of the stars of Rohini, Mrigasirisha, Punarvasu, Pushyami, Uttara-Phalguni, Mula, Purvashada, Uttarashada and Sravanam.

Besides these, certain special days in a year were also celebrated. They were the Sri Jayanthi, Uri-Adi, Uthhana Dwadasi, Aipasi-Purvashada, Deepavali, Karthikai, Makara Sankranthi, Padiyavettai, Tai Pusam, Tannir Amudu, Yugadi, Sri Rama Navami, Vaikasi Visakha and Masi Makha.

Some devotees also offered worship on certain special days marking their own birthdays and so on.

Thus there were 204 Visesha Thirunal or festivals, 217 Thingal Divasams and 12 Annual Vishu Divasams. The total came to 433 festivals in a year.

Vahanas

The inscriptions also tell us about the various Vahanas or vehicles on which the deity was taken in procession during different festivals like Brahmotsavams. The inscriptions belonging to the period of Achyutaraya's and Sadasivaraya's reigns mention the names of about six Vahanas. From the inscriptions it is also seen that the same Vahana was used for processions on different days since there were many festivals and a limited number of vehicles.

Nandanavanams or Flower Gardens

The flowers required for the Temple were grown in the gardens maintained by the devotees themselves. They also built mandapams in their flower gardens. In some cases, they transferred the possession of the garden together with the

History of Festivals, Vahanams and Administration

mandapam to the temple treasury and the garden was maintained by the temple.

The inscriptions reveal details of the horticulture from about 1300 CE. But the inscriptions of the latter part of the 14th and the earlier part of the 15th centuries indicate that there was a shortfall because of the tremendous number of festive days.

One of the inscriptions points out that the Thiruppani Pillai, that is, the officer in charge of public works took the responsibility of supplying flower garlands to the deity on behalf of Mukhappalam Nagama Nayakar, a general under Saluva Narasimha Maharaya Udiyar. Nagama Nayakar instituted the service and gifted the village of Tiradampadi. Of the different kinds of flowers and aromatic herbs like Maruvam, Damanam and Tulasi that were offered, the red lotus is specially mentioned.

Devadana Villages and Lands

Land and more than 150 villages were endowed to the temple. The majority of them were situated in Chandragiri region in the Tirukkadavur Nadu and Vaikuntavala Nadu, the two sub-districts of Thiruvenkata Kottam. It is also to be noted that a majority of these gifts were made during the Vijayanagara era.

The earliest gift of land as per the inscriptions was 7000 *kulji* in Tiruchchokkanur, the present Tiruchanoor, made by the Kadava queen Samavai.

The next gift of land in the form of villages was made by Rajendra Chola I (1016 CE), then Rajaraja III.

Later the powerful local chiefs of the 13th and 14th centuries, the Gandagopalas and the Yadavarayas, made several gifts of lands to the temple.

During the Vijayanagara period also, there were several gifts of villages by the rulers. Among the Vijayanagara rulers, Saluva Narasimha and Krishnadevaraya seem to have been the greatest benefactors. The latter in particular, regarded Lord Venkateswara as his patron god. He followed the example of his great predecessor Saluva Narasimha. This tradition was followed by the later Vijayanagara kings like Achyutaraya, Sadasivaraya and so on.

Sopana Marga or Flight of Steps to Tirumala

It is said that in earlier times, the pathway from Tirupathi to Tirumala ran beside the Kapila Teertha. It is seen from the inscription engraved in the small temple of Sri Venkateswara at the foot of the Hills, built in the year 1550, that it was Matla Anantaraja who laid the flight of steps or Sopana Marga. It began at the foot of the Hills at Alipiri and continued up to Gali Gopuram or Agra Gopuram that stands at the summit of the foremost Hill.

However, a staircase may have already existed before this, as an inscription of 1387 mentions another flight of steps called Muzhangal Murippan Padi or Mokala Metlu. Matla Ananta may have merely laid a new road made of sandstone over the old one.

Thanneer Pandal

There is a reference to a water tank installed by a devotee in an inscription beloging to 14th century. Later Saluva Parvataraja, son of Saluva Raja provided for a water tank at the Muzhangal Murippan mandapam built by him on the pathway to Tirumala. He also made repairs to the mandapam. In the later inscriptions, there are references to other permanent and temporary water tanks set up along the pathway to the Hills.

Feeding Houses or Ramanuja Kutams

The earliest reference to feeding houses (places where free food was given to pilgrims) can be seen from the inscriptions belonging to the earlier part of the 10th century. Later, a record of the 14th century and other later inscriptions also contain references to such Ramanuja Kutams. The first was set up by Saluva Narasimha Deva Maharaja. He established a separate Ramanuja Kutam with an independent administration that was unconnected to the temple.

Extensions and Repairs

There is clear evidence of the extension and repair of the temple in an inscription beloging to the 40th year of the reign of Sri Vira Narasimha Yadavaraya. The order for repairing the central shrine is also found on the walls.

In 1339, the Mukha Mandapam was added to the central shrine at Tirumala as a gift of the minister Mallanna also known as Madhava Dasar of Chandragiri and it was designated as the Tirumamani mandapam. Saluva Mallayya Deva, in 1385, arranged Pavitrotsavam for five days in the Avani month for this mandapam. He constructed another mandapam in front of the temple where he made provision for an Asthanam of the processional deity with food offerings during the Brahmotsavams and on Thirukarthikai.

In 1404, the Sthanathar undertook the construction of a mandapam along with gopurams for the merit of Saluva Narasimha. He also constructed another mandapam on the bank of Thirukkoneri and one in the midst of it, the Nirali Mandapam or Vasantha Mandapam. The other two mandapams that are referred to are the Periya Tirumamani Mandapam and Thiruvenkatanathan Mandapam where the processional Deity was propitiated with food offerings during the Brahmotsavams.

Saluva Narasimha also built a gopuram in 1389 in the spot where the feeding house established by him was located. Prior to 1404, there is a reference to the construction of another gopuram by the Sthanathar for the merit of Saluva Narasimha who confirmed in that year his previous grant of

Durgasamudram village. The income from the village was dedicated to the repairs and construction of gopurams at Tirumala and Tirupathi and the Narasimharaya Mandapam.

Other kings and chiefs also built several extensions or made renovations to the temple at Tirumala. Some others decorated the shrine.

Administration of the Temple from the Past till 1933

It is believed that traditionally the Kurumbas built temples on top of the Hills and worshipped their gods.

However, we have no recorded information about the administration of this temple, the rituals, worship or festivals before the time of Pallavas. The first administrative set-up might have been the one constituted by Samavai, a Pallava princess, with those who had the Matathipathyam over the temple. However, the officers of the kings had their say in the administration of the temple.

Later the Sthanathars began to administer the temple. They also received the money for the expenses. From an inscription of 966 CE, it is understood that there was some administrative machinery operating in the temple on Tirumala. It reveals that the Matathipathis or managers and Sabhaiyars who were the members of the assembly or village council of Thiruchokkanur, controlled the affairs of the temple. It can be inferred from the inscriptions that the Sabha or temple committee of Tiruchanoor at that time, transacted all business relating to the Sri Venkateswara temple at Tirumala because it was at a convenient place. The village Thiruchchokkanur, the present Tiruchanoor, was a Devadanam to the Sri Venkateswara temple. By the second quarter of the 13th century, the Sthanathar and the Sri Bhandaram or treasury of the temple might have become independent of supervision by the Sabhaiyar of Tiruchanoor.

With the defeat of the Pallavas, Thondaimandalam, the area

around Vengadam, passed into the hands of the Chola kings. The temple administration during the Chola reign was controlled the managers as before. However their work was supervised by the king's local officers. One of the inscriptions reveals that the provincial governor or Adhikari who was called Korramangalamudian sat in judgement over the affairs of the Tirumala temple. The temple was administered and managed by the Sabhaiyar or village councillors of Thirumundiyam village. They were appointed Trustees to light the temple lamps.

During the time of the Telugu Pallavas, one of the inscriptions belonging to the period of Vijaya Gandagopala of Nellore (1250-1282 CE) mentions the Kaikkolai, the temple servants, receiving gold for the Sri Bhandaram and undertaking to provide certain services to the Lord. In the 12th century, it is presumed that when Sri Ramanuja visited the temple, he appointed Ekakis or bachelors to look after the temple administration. The Ekakis were given the yellow robes of Sanyasis along with the image of Sri Rama, a seal with a mark of Anjaneya for sealing the Lord's treasury and a lock and key to lock the temple at night.

The Sthanathars had to give up their rights to the Yadavarayas, who were the local chieftains of the Chola kings and who subsequently became the rulers of Thondaimandalam. Although the Sthanathars were the trustees, the Dharmasasanas or the orders of the rulers of this area, were issued without any specific mention of Sthanathars. During the period of the Vijayanagara kings, around 1380 CE, the office of the Thuruninraur Udaiyar, or accountant came into being. Till 1387 CE, the Sthanathar was not a regulatory body. From then onwards, the Sthanathar became the trustees of the temple for executing the works and for accepting endowments and gifts. The inscriptions also mention that there were 10 or 12 members in the assembly of the Sthanathars.

The temple also had Ekakis who were Sri Vaishnavaites, Nambimars the temple priests, Koil Kalkum Jiyars and two temple accountants. As per the Tirumala temple inscriptions dated 1495, an agreement was entered into between Kandadai Ramanujayyangar, the manager of the Ramanujakutams at Tirumala and at Tirupathi and the Sthanthars, that is, the managers or trustees of the Tirumala temple, for the necessary repairs, renewal and making of new jewels, gold and silver vessels for Sri Venkatesha and Sri Govindaraja that were in a damaged condition.

The problem of finance was solved by Kandadai Ramanujayyangar who ensured that an annual sum of 3,000 *panam* would be available for the work. Saluva Narasimha conferred upon him, the hereditary right to become the custodian of the key to the temple treasury. Ramanujayyangar agreed to undertake the repairs in the presence of the Sthanathar council.

He issued an order to the Sthanathar for an annual salary to the temple servants namely, the temple manager, gold treasurer, public works officers, Vahana bearers, distributors, lamp lighters, temple cooks, supplier of firewood, drummer and pipers, craftsmen, watchmen and so on. Kandadai Ramanuja became so powerful that 'Ula' or singing of his praises was arranged during the summer festivals conducted for Sri Venkateswara and Sri Govindaraja.

After 1600, the number of Sthanathars was reduced to six. The last that we hear of the existence of the Sthanathars is from an inscription dated 1684 in Telugu script (after 1638, there are no Tamil inscriptions), when Sri Sivaraja Ramachandra Yadadamatara Dabirsa and Thimmanayyangar made an endowment for the temple. When the temple passed into the hands of the Golconda Muslims around 1656, an inscription from 1684 mentions a new body of Telugu Sthanalavaru of four members who did not possess the power to receive any endowments.

After the fall of the Vijayanagara Empire, the Nawab of

Golconda and Bijapur succeeded in acquiring the territories of the Vijayanagara Empire. Thondaimandalam came under the rule of Mir Jumla, the prime minister of Aurangazeb. Later the temple along with its subsidiary temples, came under the Nawab of Arcot. He assigned the temple's revenues to the English East India Company around 1753-58. The French occupied Tirupathi in 1758, but they were routed by the English. Then the Marathas invaded Tirupathi. With the advent of the British Raj, in 1801, when Lord Wellesley was the Governor, the Tirumala temple passed into the direct management of the EEIC. The Company appropriated the entire revenue of the temple. They paid the salaries of the temple staff. The management of the temple was then in accordance with the Madras Regulation No.7 of 1817. As per this, the Board of Revenue was empowered to supervise the endowments and look after their proper use. The District Collector working under the Board of Revenue became the administrative head. During the rule of the EEIC, the temple was administered according to a set of rules called Bruce's Code.

In 1841, the Board of Directors of the EEIC decided that the company should not interfere in the affairs of the temples in India. Thus in 1843, the administration of the temple and a number of estates was entrusted to Sri Seva Dossji of Hathiramji Mutt at Tirumala on the basis of an 1841 court order directing the British officers not to interfere in the routine matters of the temple.

The temple was under the administration of the Mahants for nearly a century till 1933. During the period of the Mahants, several improvements were made in the temple and the Teerthas were renovated. However, during this period, several suits were filed against the Mahants.

The Madras Hindu Religious Endowment Act was passed in 1927, but it did not improve matters. It was replaced by the TTD Act of 1932.

Administration for the Temple Since 1933

Special Act of 1932

In 1932, the Madras Government in the composite state of Madras that included all the four states i.e. the present Tamil Nadu, Andhra Pradesh, Karnataka and Kerala, promulgated a special Act bringing the temple under the direct administration of a Board of Trustees.

The Tirumala-Tirupathi Devasthanams, the TTD, was formed to administer a fixed number of temples through a commissioner appointed by the Government of Madras. Before the formation of Andhra Pradesh, Tirupathi was a part of the composite state of Madras. A committee of seven members led by a commissioner was appointed. Two Advisory Councils were formed to advise the Committee. These were: the Religious Advisory Council consisting of priests and the temple administrators to advise the committee on matters relating to temple administration and the Ryots Advisory Council consisting of farmers for advising the committee about Tirumala land and transactions concerned with the temple estates.

Hindu Religious and Charitable Endowment Act

In 1951, the Act of 1933 was replaced by an enactment, known as the Hindu Religious and Charitable Endowment Act. According to Section 80 of the Act, the temple administration was entrusted to a five-member Board of Trustees headed by an Executive Officer appointed by the State Government. Each member had a tenure of five years. The officer was to implement the policies laid down by the Board, subject to the control of the Commissioner of Endowments and the State Government.

The Executive Officer was made responsible for the properties and operations of the TTD, safekeeping of records, jewels, finances, accounting of income and expenditure and execution of activities sanctioned by the Board of Trustees.

These included maintenance and operation of temples, educational institutions, hospitals, choultries, paid cottages and rooms, the veterinary hospital, water and electricity, sanitary facilities, roads, communications, lighting, training of priests and acquiring of land and immovable property with the permission of the State Government.

The Executive Officer was given the power to spend beyond the budget sanctioned by the Board, provided the expenses involved pilgrim safety or services, and later obtain the approval or sanction of the Board of Trustees. As per this Act, the Commissoner had certain powers such as deciding disputes, appropriation of endowments and so on.

Section 85 laid down the purposes for which the temple funds could be used.

Administration of the Temple after the Formation of Andhra Pradesh

In 1956, Andhra Pradesh was formed and Tirupathi and the TTD came under the jurisdiction of the Andhra Pradesh government.

Charitable and Religious Endowment Act of 1966

The provisions of the 1951 Act were retained by the Charitable and Religious Endowment Act of 1966 following the report of the HR and CE Commission and the Report of the Estimates Committee of 1963-64. Act no.17 of 1966 was called the Andhra Pradesh Charitable and Hindu Religious Institutions and Endowment Act. Chapter 14 of this Act made provision for the administration of the TTD.

Section 85 to 91 laid down the provisions governing the TTD. Section 86 laid down that the temple should be administered by a Board of Trutees consisting of 11 persons to be appointed by the State Government with compulsory representation from certain communities for looking after minority interests. Three members were chosen from the State Legislative Assembly. It was made mandatory to have one member belonging to the Scheduled Caste and one woman member. Their term was fixed at three years.

Section 87 directed the government to appoint an Executive Officer (EO) and if necessary a Deputy Executive Officer. Under section 87(2), the EO was empowered to delegate statutory duties to the deputy EO.

Sections 88 and 89 laid down the division of powers between the EO and the Board of Trustees.

Section 91 laid down the purposes for which the TTD funds were to be utilised.

Thus the temple was completely brought under the control of the Endowment Department of the State Government.

The Tirumala-Tirupathi Devashanams Act of 1979

The Act of 1979 superseded the earlier Act of 1966. However, Sections 47 and 48 of the new Act repeated sections of the old Act and certain other Acts. Under it, the real administration of the temple rests in the hands of a small committee consisting of a Chairman and two other members nominated by the Government. The Commissioner of Endowments Department and the EO of TTD were made ex-officio members. The EO was an officer who held a post not inferior to the rank of a District Collector.

The new Act, for the first time, provided for a Financial Advisor and Chief Accounts Officer to advise the Temple about financial matters. It provided for the continuation of the Hindu Dharma Prathishtanam under a new name and established the Sri Venkateswara Sistachara Vidya Samastha, to be in complete charge of Vedic learning, Vedic schools, Vedic research and so on.

The Act also defined for the first time, the methods by which the temple funds were to be utilised for promoting Hindu religion and culture. These included promotion and study of Indian languages and operation of SV University, establishment and operation of Hindu Dharma Prathishtanam for propagating Hindu Dharma through research, teaching and training and creation of literature and reading material.

The AP Charitable and Hindu Religious Institutions and Endowments Act of 1987

At present, the TTD is a conglomeration of temples brought under the Act 30 Schedule 2 of the AP Charitable and Hindu Religious Institutions and Endowments Act of 1987 enacted by AP Government. It came into force on the 28th May, 1987. This Act superseded the 1979 Act. However, in many respects the provisions in the new Act are the same as those of the Act of 1979.

Section 96 of this Act provides for the formation of a Board of Trustees. Section 106 provides for the appointment of Executive Officer and other officials. Section 107 lays down the qualifications for the Executive Officer and for the trustees. Section 109 and 110 describe the powers and extraordinary powers of the Executive Officer. Section 111 lays down the guidelines for the utilisation of the TTD funds. Section 112 provides for the establishment of the Dharma Prachara Parishad by abolishing the Hindu Dharma Rakshana Samastha that was established under the Act of 1979. Section 114 provides for the civic administration of the Tirumala Hills, Section 116 for the budget of the TTD, Section 119 for enquiries and Section 120 for appeals to the Executive Officer and the Board of Trustees. Under section 121 and 122, the government has review powers that has increased its hold on the temple.

The 11-member Board of Trustees was expanded to include 15 members. The Chairman and the members other than than the ex-officio members, hold office for a period of three years. No salary or remuneration is paid to the Chairman or the members of the Board other than the honorarium or compensatory allowance for travelling and conveyance as prescribed. This Act retained the minority and legislative representation as per the previous Act, that included one person belonging to the Scheduled Caste and one lady member to represent women.

It also details the procedure to be instituted following the resignation of the Chairman or any other member of the Board, the circumstances under which the members cease to hold office and the suspension or removal of Chairman or any member of the Board. The issues of vacancies in the Board, dissolution and reconstitution of the Board, the appointment and qualifications required for the Executive Officer, Joint Executive Officer, special grade Deputy Executive Officer, Financial Advisor, Chief Accounts Officer and so on, are discussed in various sections of the Act.

The Act spells out the tenure of the Executive Officer and Joint Executive Officer, the powers and functions of officers appointed under section 106, the extraordinary powers of the Executive Officer, the funds of the TTD, establishment of Dharma Prachara Parishad, establishment of S V Sistacharya Vidya Samastha and the civic administration of Tirumala Hills area.

It also talks of the EO presenting the budget before the Board of Trustees, showing estimated receipts and expenditures for the new financial year. The EO is also responsible for getting the government to sanction the budget with any necessary modifications.

The Act details the keeping of accounts and their audit, encroachments, enquiries and appeals, the administration report, oath of office, suits and other legal proceedings by or against the TTD, annual inspection of the statutory returns, approved budget, audit report and all other correspondence with the Government, for information of the Annual Inspection Commission.

The administration as per this Act is vested with the Board of Trustees. This Board is to manage the properties, funds and affairs of the TTD and arrange for the conduct of the daily worship and ceremonies and of the festivals in the temples. The members of the Board have the powers to fix fees for the performance of Archanas and any of the services or rituals or festivals connected to the TTD. The members can ask for any information that is necessary for satisfying themselves about the proper maintenance and administration of the TTD as also the proper utilisation of the TTD funds. The Executive Officer and the other officers under him are to furnish such information as required by the Board. The Board shall exercise the overall supervision and control over the administration of the TTD. The Board has the powers to determine the procedures in the temple and the amounts to be expended on carrying them out.

The Executive Officer who heads the TTD and the Commissioner of Endowments are its ex-officio members. The Executive Officer is its member-secretary as well. The EO and the JEOs usually belong to the IAS. They are assisted by the officers in charge of accounts, vigilance, security, forests, engineering, education, law, public relations and project execution. In addition, there are departmental heads to look after the different branches of administration.

As per the first Schedule II of this Act, the TTD maintains and administers 12 temples and their subsidiary shrines.

Two controversial clauses in the Act were the abolition of the hereditary rights of temple priests as well as a limitation imposed on their right to a share in the Hundi proceeds. But bowing to pressure from the priests, the AP Government in its amendment to the Act in 2006, struck these clauses down.

7

The Structure of the Temple

The present structure of the shrine at Tirumala is comparatively modern and dates approximately from the 13th century CE.

The Temple Complex

The temple of Lord Venkateswara faces east. It is an enclosed structure with big stone walls on all the four sides. The main entrance is on the eastern side. The temple is rectangular in shape and is 109 m wide and 124 m long. It covers an area of 2.2 acres. To its left is the temple tank, the sacred Swami Pushkarini. The temple is surrounded on three sides by compound walls or *Avaranams* with *Prakarams* or enclosures. The space enclosed between each Prakaram is called a Pradakshinam or Antarmandalam. There are two Gopurams or towers besides the Ananda Nilayam. The three Avaranams are the incomplete Mukkoti Pradakshinam that is close to the sanctum, the Vimana Pradakshinam surrounding the sanctum that lies in-between the inner Gopuram and the main shrine and the Sampangi Pradakshinam that is between the outer and inner Gopurams. The Maha Pradakshinam is outside the temple along the Mada streets.

The entry into the Temple is through the Mahadwaram, the main entrance, on the East Mada Street. Walking up to the sanctum, one passes through the Prathima Mandapam. Here one can see the statues of Krishnadevaraya and his two queens, the Thulabharam scales to the left and the shrine of Sri Ranganatha in the Ranganayakula Mandapam where the temple Vahanas are kept. The Tirumalanayaka Mandapam with its beautiful carvings is next. One can find the statues of Raja Todarmal, a general of the Karnataka nawab and of his mother and wife in a corner of this mandapam. Further ahead is the Dwajasthambam Mandapam that is also beautifully carved. Then one enters the inner Prakaram. To the left of this Prakaram is the shrine of Varadarajaswami and the Pottu or kitchen in which the shrine of Vakula Devi is located. Near the Pottu is located the gilded well, the Bangaru Bavi. Then one reaches the Bangaru Vakali, the golden threshold. Guarding the entrance to the sanctum sanctorum are the two Dwarapalakas, Jaya and Vijaya.

The Padi Kavali Mahadwara (Mukkhia dwaram, Periya Gopura Vasal or Thiru Vasal)

This is the outer Gopuram of the temple and it is 3.3 m wide. It stands on a quadrangular base in the centre of the structure. The base measures 11 m south to north and 9.6 m east to west. The distance between this Gopuram and the inner Gopuram is 36 m. The compound walls are 10 cm thick. There are two symmetrically-placed cut stone door frames. The folding doors are hung on pivots. There is also a trapdoor entrance into the temple on the left side of the main door.

The architectural style of the Gopuram belongs to the later Chola period and the inscriptions belong to the 13th century. Several figures of the Vaishnava gods like Narasimha and Anjaneya can be seen on the Gopuram. The outer Gopuram has an inscription on the right side belonging to 1217, that describes the donations made by Yadavaraya Vira Narasinga Deva. This shows its antiquity. It also leads to the conclusion that although the outer Gopuram was constructed before 1217 CE, it might have had only a bald entrance until about 1260 when the Gopuram was raised by one more level. The superstructure is made of brick and mortar and has a height of 15 m. It has been renovated with white cement.

Sampangi Pradakshinam

From the Mahadwara, one enters the courtyard of the temple. Cheek by jowl with the Gopuram, there is a small mandapam with two wings on either side and a pathway in the middle. This is the Sampangi Pradakshinam that forms the outer Prakaram inside the temple complex. The Mandapam measures 11 m square. It stands on 16 pillars. The open space here is about 3.6 m wide but on the other three sides it is hardly 1.5 m wide. There are several structures in this Mandapam. The Bali peetam and *dwajasthambam* are located here. The Sampangi Pradakshinam has a small mandapam in each of its four corners. These were constructed by Saluva Narasimha around 1470. The mandapams have four pillars measuring about 3 m sq. During Vasantotsavam, the processional deity is seated here.

The Sampangi Prakaram, that is the pathway for circumambulating the temple, lies between the first and the third *Prakarams*. The Sampangi Prakaram contains Prathima Mandapam, Ranga Mandapam, Tirumalaraya Mandapam, Saluva Narasimha Mandapam, Aina Mahal and the Dwajasthamba Mandapam. Previously, the south, west and north facing *Prakarams* of the Sampangi Pradakshinam were mere open spaces. In due course, corridors of the mandapam type were constructed touching the walls on one side and with pillars at the other end. On the south side the corridor is about 6 m wide, leaving an open space 9 m wide for Pradakshinam.

In recent times, a number of storerooms or Ugrams have come up in the corridor. On the west the corridor is about 9 m wide with three rows of pillars. A large part of this space has been converted into rooms for storing provisions like jaggery required for the food offerings. The pounding and cleaning of these provisions also take place here.

The rooms for keeping the long and heavy dresses of the Lord, His bed rolls, Padi Pottu where the sweet and fried preparations are made, Yamuna Thurai where flower garlands are strung, the room where the soiled clothes of the Lord are kept, are all located here. The Vijaya Nadi, i.e. the divine spring, is also located nearby. Currently this pathway is closed to the public.

In the Ramanuja Kutam here, provisions for pilgrims' Annadanam are kept. The open space or Pradakshinam on the western side is 6 m wide and that on the eastern end is 7.5 m wide.

Legend has it that it is called Sampangi Pradakshinam because there were Champaka trees here at one time.

Pratima Mandapam or Krishnadevaraya Mandapam

This is a small Mandapam adjoining the outer gopuram walls. It is adjacent to the big Ranganayakula Mandapam. It is an open Mandapam and comes after the Padi Kavali Maha Dwara. It is believed to have been built during the later Vijayanagara period, around the early half of the 16th century. This Mandapam has exquisite carvings from the Vijayanagara period that include the carvings of Sri Rama breaking the bow, Sri Rama Pattabhishekam, Sri Krishna Leela and so on. The tall pillars of this Mandapam depict a variety of designs. On the top of two pillars, one can find the carvings of the Vaishnava symbols, the Urdhvapundras flanked by Shankha and Chakra. There are a number of statues here on either side of the passage with their backs towards the west wall of the Gopuram. All the statues of the emperors are bare except for the loincloth that was customarily worn during worship.

As one enters, to the left, there are three statues. One is a copper statue of King Venkatapathi Raya that is 1.5 m high, standing on a copper pedestal about 60 cm high. The crown is about 30 cm high. The statue wears large pearls in the ears. Around the neck is a Rudrakshamala in two strings. The king wears an embroidered loincloth. Around his waist is a beautiful Kati Bandham. He was known as Venkata I and belonged to the Aravidu dynasty. For some time he governed Chandragiri as viceroy.

Next to this statue there are two beautiful statues of Vijayanagara king Achyutaraya and his queen Varadaji Amman both in an attitude of prayer, with folded hands. Achyutaraya was the half-brother of Krishnadevaraya and his successor. The king's statue is about 1.54 m high and he wears the Vaishnavite 'Vadagalai' mark. He has three necklaces, one of which is made of pearls. A loincloth is tied around his waist and hangs down to his knees. There are ornaments on his hands, shoulders and feet. The delicately-carved queen's statue is about 1.35 m high and rests on a platform. She wears circular earrings, three necklaces and other ornaments around her neck, shoulders and waist.

On the northern side of the Prathima Mandapam, there are three bronze statues of Krishnadevaraya and his queens, Tirumala Devi on the left and Chinnamma Devi on his right. The statue of the emperor is about 1.68 m high and he stands on a lotus pedestal. He wears a crown that is said to be of his own design. There are two rings on his fingers. Several ornaments cover his hands, shoulders and legs. Chinnamma Devi wears necklaces in addition to the Mangala Sutram and other ornaments.

All three statues are in a prayerful attitude with folded hands.

Ranga Mandapam or Ranganayakula Mandapam

A big Mandapam that is located on the southeast corner of the Sampangi Pradakshinam and to the left of the Pratima Mandapam, it houses several statues of royal devotees. It measures 32 m north to south and 18 m east to west. At its southern end, there is a small granite shrine about 3.6 m sq built with cut stones. It is surrounded by a Vimana that has been kept closed. This shrine might have been the abode of the Utsavamurthy of Sri Ranganatha of Srirangam during His stay in Tirumala between 1320 and 1360. This was to safeguard the idol from destruction when Srirangam was invaded by Mallik Khafur in 1320. The deity was worshipped here till 1360 when it was sent back to Srirangam. The shrine might have been closed after the idol was returned. Now the processional deities of Malaiappa and His consorts are housed in this small shrine. The Mandapam is decorated during Brahmotsavam and other festival days. The Asthanam is held here for the Dwajorahanam during Brahmotsavam, on Deepavali and for 23 days in December in connection with the Adyayanotsavam and some other festivals.

The space for Pradakshinam here is only about 3 m wide. This Mandapam is supposed to have been constructed between 1320 and 1360 by the Yadava ruler Sri Ranganada Yadavaraya. The top portion of the pillars in this Mandapam is carved with panels depicting scenes from the *Ramayana*. The style and architecture belong to the Vijayanagara period. On the pillars, there is a sculpture of a boar holding a sword that resembles the Vijayanagara royal crest of Varaha holding a long sword.

On the southern side of this shrine there is a Yagnasala where Homas are performed. It has an inner mandapam with four beautiful polished stone pillars. This mandapam is full of sculptures carved in the Vijayanagara style. A portion of it is now used as the office of the Peshkar and TTD Publications' sales counter. Kalyanotsavams are also performed here.

Tirumalaraya Mandapam/Tirumalanayaka Mandapam/Anna Unjal Mandapam

The spacious Tirumalaraya Mandapam is located towards the west of Ranganayaka Mandapam. He was the first king of the Aravidu dynasty. It faces the Dwajasthamba Mandapam. It is 32 m long and 12 m wide. It has a spacious complex of pavilions and there are two parts, constructed at different periods. Its front portion is at a lower level and the rear portion is at a higher level.

Saluva Narasimha constructed the elevated southern or inner portion of this Mandapam in the middle of the 15th century to celebrate the Anna Unjal or Dolotsavam that he instituted in 1473. There are four smaller mandapams in the four corners of the Pradakshinam. The pillars here are constructed in the Vijayanagara style. The major pillar is about 1.8 m square while the three other minor pillars are almost circular in shape and have 16 facets. They emit musical notes when struck.

This structure was renovated and further extended to its present size by Ariviti Bukkaraya Ramaraja, Ranga Raja and Tirumala Raja who gave his name to this mandapam in the last quarter of the 16th century. There are carvings on the pillars of warriors astride horses rearing over lions. The riders have umbrellas that show their royal status. There are also bas-reliefs from the Vaishnavite pantheon of Sri Narasimha killing Hiranyakashipu, Sri Lakshmi Narayana in the *abhayahastha* pose in front of Prahalada, Srinivasa, Sri Krishna dancing on the snake Kaliya, Lord Vishnu with His consort Lakshmi seated on His lap, Lord Vishnu riding on Garuda, and Sri Rama holding the Gandiva. The pillars of the main Mandapam are carved with riders on lions that stand on elephants. There are also bas-reliefs depicting a man consoling a woman, the Gopis bathing and Sri Krishna sitting on a tree, the Gopis praying to Sri Krishna, Lord Krishna playing the flute, holding Shankha and Chakra and so on.

The Vasanthotsavam was held here during the time of Tirumalaraya. The Utsava Murthy, Malaiappar holds His annual Darbar or Asthanam during the hoisting of the Garudadwaja on Dwajasthambam to mark the commencement of Brahmotsavam. In the middle of the older structure stands the cut stone carved pavilion where the deity is seated. The Prasadam for this event is Tirumalarayan Pongal.

The Aina Mahal or the Hall of Mirrors

The Aina Mahal is an enclosed room and is located on the northern side of the Tirumalaraya Mandapam. It measures 11 m x 13 m. It has an open Mukha Mandapam in the front that has six rows of six pillars each and a shrine behind it with an Antarala and Garbhagriha. It has big mirrors that reflect the images infinitely. In the middle of the room there is an unjal or swing hung on silver chains for the Lord to be seated during certain Sevas. This is of recent origin.

Phoola Bavi

To the south of the Aina Mahal there is a stepwell called Phoola Bavi. The used flowers and garlands of the Lord are thrown into this well. It is said that this practice was introduced by Sri Ramanuja in the 12th century.

The Dwajasthamba Mandapam

It is a small Mandapam with a roof located in the outermost Prakaram or enclosure and has the Dwajasthambam and the Balipitam. It has on the north and south, two rows of five pillars each. On each of these pillars there are lovely bas-reliefs of Yoga Narasimha, Matsya and so on. The Trimurthi figure has four arms in which the two upper hands hold Shankha and Chakra, the lower right hand is in Abhayahastha pose and the lower left hand is in the Katyavalambitha pose. The deity is seated on a bird that is either a swan or a peacock, in Sukhasana with the right leg folded in and the left leg hanging down gracefully in a posture that resembles Lord Subramanya's. There are also the carvings of Srinivasa and Anjaneya carrying Sanjeevani Mountain in his hand. There are several erotic figures including that of a woman holding a parrot in her right hand while a maid disrobes her.

Dwajasthambam and Bali Pitam

Dwajasthambam is the tall, circular wooden flagstaff carved with small sculptures including that of Lord Krishna in the Kaliya Mardhana posture. The Bali Pitam and the Dwajasthambam put together measure about 4.5 m east to west and stand at the centre of the Mandapam in front of the inner Gopuram. The Dwajasthambam stands on a cube-shaped cut stone structure that is covered with gilded copper sheets.

The Bali Pitam is square in shape and built of cut stone. It is also gilded. It is broader at the base and narrows to about 30 cm wide towards the top. It stands around 1.5 m tall. In the Bali Pitam, cooked food is offered as per the Agama Sastras.

Nadimi Padi Vakili or Vendi Vakili (silver door)

It is the inner Gopuram that leads to the temple proper. The base of the inner Gopuram is rectangular in shape and east to west it is about 7 m wide and 11 m long from north to south. The width of the gateway is 2.7 m. In design it is similar to the outer Gopuram or Mukha Dwaram. The wooden doors here are covered with silver carvings. So it is also referred to as Vendi Vakili. The compound wall or the Prakaram of this Gopuram measures 70.5 m east to west and 48 m north to south. The thickness of the walls is 90 cm.

There are numerous inscriptions on the outer as well as inner face of these walls and also on the base and walls of the Gopuram. The older inscriptions can be seen on the basement and walls of the Gopuram while the inner face of the Prakaram walls depict the inscriptions belonging to a later period of time. The outer face of these walls contains inscriptions belonging to the 15th and 16th centuries. From the earliest inscriptions belonging to the year 1209, it is assumed that the inner Gopuram has been in existence at least since then. It is also assumed that the base portion of this Gopuram might have been constructed sometime between 1160–1170. These inscriptions are found on the north base of the Gopuram that are partially hidden by the Prakaram wall.

There are two bas-reliefs on the walls at the entrance of this inner Gopuram. One is Hathiramji playing dice with Lord Venkateswara and the other is the scene of Sri Rama Pattabhishekam. Sri Rama is seated on a platform in Sukhasana and His right hand is in Abhayahastha Chinmudra pose. His consort Sita is also seated in Sukhasana like Her Lord; Her right hand holds a Lotus while the left hand is in the Parasarita Vamahastha pose. Lakshmana and Bharata are shown with folded hands in Anjali posture. Shatrughna standing to the right of Sri Rama holds the royal umbrella. The carvings of Anjaneya and the two Paricharakas are also seen.

On the inside walls there are several inscriptions, the earliest one related to Pandya king Jata Varma Sundara Pandya who came to the throne in 1251.

Vimana Pradakshinam

After crossing the inner Gopuram, one enters the open space that is known as the Vimana Pradakshinam. This is the second Pradakshinam path circumambulating the inner shrine. This space is in-between the walls of the 2nd Prakaram of the inner Gopuram and the walls of the 1st Prakaram that surround the sanctum. The open space combined with the Tirumamani Mandapam measure hardly 5 m. The Vimana or Gopuram can be seen from here.

The devotees who have taken a vow for Anga Pradakshinam or circumambulation by rolling on the ground, perform it here. There are many cut stone structures, shrines and Mandapams inside in addition to the Garbhagriham. The corridor has pillars built in typical Vijayanagara style. They are carved with sculptures of a monkey and snake, lady with a bow, Kamsa, Puthana, Krishna tied to a stone, Ranganatha etc.

On the western verandah, Veda Parayanam takes place every day. This verandah leads off into a number of rooms like the Kaikolas, Sangeetha Bhandaram and so on.

Sri Varadarajaswami Shrine

On the eastern side of the Vimana Pradakshinam, to the left, is located the small shrine of Sri Varadarajaswami. It is about 6 m long and 4.5 m wide. This shrine is about 2 m distant from the inner Gopuram and 60 cm away from the east Prakaram wall. It is crowned with a small Vimana. The idol faces west and is about 25 cm high and stands on a platform that is about 10 cm high. It has four arms. The upper right and left arms hold the Shankha and Chakra respectively. The lower right hand is in Abhayahastha pose and the lower left is in the Katyavalambitha pose. Varadaraja or 'the king who bestows boons' is a form of Vishnu. There is also an inscription on the temple wall from the 16th year of Ranganatha Yadavaraya's reign (1354–55). This means that the temple dates from an older era.

It is said that this shrine was built to house the Utsavamurthy idol of Kanchi Sri Varadaraja, during Malik Khafur's invasion of the south. The outer walls are built in the architectural style of the later Chola period.

Pottu

Pottu is the main kitchen where the food offerings of the temple are prepared. It is located south of Sri Varadarajaswami shrine in the Vimana Pradakshinam. It is about 18 m x 9 m and stands on a 2-m-high base. The food is cooked in new earthen pots everyday. Once used, the pots are destroyed.

Vakula Devi Shrine

Inside the Pottu, there is a small shrine for Goddess Lakshmi called 'Pottu Amma', or 'Madapulli Nachiar' which means 'the lady of the kitchen'. She is identified with Vakula Malika, the foster-mother of Lord Venkateswara. She is believed to have nurtured the Lord and arranged for his wedding with Sri Padmavathi.

She is worshipped on the day of Varalakshmi Vrutham that falls in the month of Shravana. The idol here is seated in Padmasana. The two upper hands hold lotuses and the two lower hands are in Abhaya and Varadahastha.

In the Sampangi Pradakshinam, there is a 'Padi Pottu', another kitchen where an idol of Goddess Lakshmi is kept. Usually rice Prasadam is prepared in the inner Pottu while the other Prasadams like Appam are prepared in the Padi Pottu. Laddu is prepared in another Pottu.

Bangaru Bavi

This is a well located in front of the Pottu and adjoining the corridor running towards the west. It is constructed in the Vijayanagara style of architecture. The water runs through stone pipes. It is said that Sri Ramanuja permitted the use of the water of this well for the temple along with the water from Akasha Ganga and Papavinasam waterfalls.

The Corridor

There is a corridor that starts from the kitchen. Its roof is supported by the 2nd Prakaram wall on one side while the other end has cut stone pillars supporting it. There is also an intermediate row of pillars 2 m distant from the last row. The Kalyana Mandapam is located in the western end of the corridor. The corridor branches into a number of rooms for storing Vahanas and other objects.

Previously, the Kalyana Mandapam, where the celestial wedding of the Lord was performed, was located in the western end of the corridor in the Vimana Pradakshinam. It measures 24 m x 11 m. It has 29 pillars. It might have been constructed around the 16th century. The mandapam contains beautiful sculptures belonging to the Vijayanagara period. They include Lord Narasimha with His consort in a meditative pose, holding a lily bud in Her right hand and another damsel in a different pose. There is the figure of a hunter with his consort, a bas-relief of wrestling between Vali and Sugriva, a beautiful Vimana reaching the skies, and so on. Architecturally it is similar to the Tirumalaraya Mandapam. The pillars are exquisitely carved and the ceiling of the central portion is breathtaking.

At its western end, is a small shrine of black granite with four slender pillars of polished cut stone where the processional deity of Lord Ranganatha is presumed to have been kept for its safety. The granite pillars have carved figures, one of Thrivikrama with four hands: the upper right hand is stretched into space with the index finger pointing upwards; the lower right hand holds the Shankha; the upper left arm holds the Chakra, while the lower left hand is in the Katyavilambitha pose. The right leg shoots straight up while the left foot is placed on the head of Mahabali.

In another carving, the Lord is shown with six arms and riding on Garuda.

There is also the sculpture of a hunter and a woman. The lady's left hand holds a bow while her right hand embraces her husband. The hunter's left hand is around the waist of his consort and the other rests on his hip. He holds two arrows in his right hand.

There is also a carving of Lord Narasimha destroying the demon Hiranyakashipu. This figure is in Sukhasana. The figure has 16 arms out of which 14 hands hold various weapons of Lord Vishnu like the Shankha, Chakra, Khadga, Khetaka, Parasu etc. Two arms are seen killing the demon.

There is a carving of Lord Vishnu in a dancing pose. His right hand is in Abhayahastha and the left hand is flung into the air in a graceful mudra.

There is a depiction of the Sudarsana Chakra with 16 arms and figures of Lord Krishna dancing as Kaliya Mardhana, a woman dancer, two monkeys fighting with each other, and Garuda.

Behind the shrine in the Kalyana Mandapam is the Yagnasala where Homas are performed. From the day of Dwajarohanam up to Deepavali, Lord Malaiappaswami resides here and not in the sanctum. In December, for a period of 23 days in connection with Adyayanotsavam, the Asthanam takes place in this Mandapam.

Vahana Store Room

The Vahanas or the vehicles of the Lord, the silver chariot and the Rathams used for the Lord during festivals are stored in a room located in the Vimana Pradakshinam. It is located on the western side of Sampangi Pradakshinam.

Sankeertana Bhandara or Talapakamara

Near the porch on the western side of Bhashyakara Sannidhi is a small room. It is called Talapakamara or Sankeerthana Bhandara.

This room was once used to store the copper plate collection of Annamayya *keerthanas*, songs composed by Talapakka Annamacharya, his son Pedda Tirumalacharya and grandson Chinna Tirumalacharya. There is a bas-relief of Talapakka Annamayya and his son on the storage rack here. It is stated that Annamacharya visited the main shrine in 1424 and composed songs on Lord Venkateswara. He was a contemporary of Purandaradasa. His songs were preserved in this room for more than 400 years and then transferred to the TTD Administrative Office in Tirupathi for the preparation of transcripts for publication.

Kaikola Room and Gammikars Room

This is also located in the Vimana Mandapam area. Once it was used as a duty room by the cooks and the employees working in the processions.

Other Rooms in the Vimana Pradakshinam

There are also rooms along the corridor of the mandapam surrounding the Vimana Pradakshina to house the Lord's palanquin, the Lord's bed rolls (Sabha Arai) and the Vagapadi (Prasadams to pilgrims). The Chandanam or sandal paste and the Parimalam, the perfumes, turmeric paste, saffron paste etc required for the Friday Abhisheka of the Lord were stored previously in a room here near the Narasimhaswami shrine.

Ananda Nilayam

The dome-like canopy, the Vimana or roof over the most sacred area, the Sanctum, of the temple of Lord Venkateswara is called Ananda Nilayam meaning 'the abode of joy.' It is plated with gold. It is said that the first Vimana was constructed by Thondaiman Chakravarthy.

It is a three-storeyed structure with a base measuring 8 m sq and a height of 11 m that includes the Kalasas on top of the Vimana. The first, second and the third storeys measure 3 m, 3.3 m, and 4.9 m respectively. The first two tiers are rectangular in shape while the third is circular in shape. The Vimana shows traces of the Pallava style of architecture with a circular Shikharam or top and a single Stupa that reminds one of the Mahabalipuram shore temples. The styles of architecture used for the pillars resemble the Chola and the Vijayanagara although the basic structure is Pallava.

A few bas-reliefs are seen on the first tier of the Ananda Nilaya Vimana. There are about 40 such figures on the second tier and these are the figures of Anjaneya, Garuda in Anjali Hastha pose, Lord Vishnu with four arms in sitting posture, Thrivikrama, Lakshmi, Kodandapani Rama, Kaliya Mardhana Krishna and so on. The third tier has about 20 bas-reliefs. It has a carving of a Lotus. There are also the figures of lions that are standing, Lord Vishnu in Sukhasana, Garuda and so on.

Vimana Venkateswara

There is an icon called 'Vimana Venkateswara' in the second tier of the Vimana of the Ananda Nilayam. It is a small-scale replica of the Moola Vigraha carved on the northwestern corner of the Vimana. Devotees who visit this temple make it a point to worship this idol with the belief that they would attain salvation. There is a silver 'Thiruchi' to the icon to distinguish it from the other idols and there is also a name board.

According to one story, when the outer *Prakarams* and the Sanctum were built, a worried Kubera from whom the Lord had taken a huge loan for His marriage, expressed his anxiety that the Lord might not repay his debt and might indeed vanish from his sight! The Lord assured Kubera that he would get His prototype installed on the Vimana so that Kubera would know that the

Lord was ever-present. Tradition also says that Vyasa Teertha, also known as Vyasa Raja, a great saint of the Dwaitha cult, ate only after worshipping this Vimana Venkateswara and thereby obtained the Lord's grace.

Sri Ramanuja Shrine

In the northern corridor of the Vimana Pradakshinam, is the shrine of Saint Ramanuja. It is also called Bhashyakara Sannidhi. It is 4.5 m x 3.6 m with a Mukha Mandapam that is 6 m long. It was Ramanuja who designed the temple garden. He also formulated the procedures of worship in this temple. It overlooks the western end of the Tirumamani Mandapam. Next to the entrance, on the wall, the Pandyan emblem of two fishes and a hook is carved. The right hand of the statue of Sri Ramanuja is in the Vyakhyana Mudra the gesture of exposition and the left hand is in Pusthaka Hastha that is, holding a book. Pujas are not performed here but the Lord's prasadams are offered to this statue. It is supposed to be a later addition in the Vijayanagara style of architecture.

Sri Yoga Narasimhaswami Shrine

This small shrine is located in the northeast corner of the courtyard touching the eastern wall of the Prakaram, in the Vimana Pradakshinam. It is built on a raised verandah to the northeast of the central shrine, opposite the Ramanuja Shrine, on its left. It was probably built between 1330 and 1360. The shrine is surrounded by a polished Mandapam. There are artistic carvings of dancers here.

The Sri Yoga Narasimhaswami or Girija Narasimhaswami idol faces west. He is also known as Azhagiya Singer. He is seated with His two hands on His knees in a yogasana. The two rear hands hold Shankha and Chakra. On Saturdays, the idol is given

Abhishekam in the Sanctum. On Narasimha Jayanthi that falls on the 14th day of the bright half of the month of Vaisakha on the day of Swathi Nakshathram, there is a special worship. It is believed that this shrine was constructed to house either Sholingapuram or Ahobilam Utsava Murthis.

The Srivari Hundi

This is located in the Vimana Pradakshinam on the northern side of the Tirumamani Mandapam where a big Gangalam is kept. This vessel is called Koppara. It is the Srivari Hundi, into which pilgrims drop their offerings. The devotees offer cash, coins, ornaments and other valuables. These are sorted inside a room with glass walls in the temple complex. The Hundi collection is one of the main sources of income for the temple.

Tirumamani Mandapam/Asthana Mandapam/Mukha Mandapam

The Mandapam was built by Mallanna alias Madhavadasa who was the chief of Chandragiri near Tirupathi, in 1417. The Mandapam is supported on 16 carved stone pillars which have lions as their bases. Bas-reliefs are carved on all pillars. The figures depicted include Lord Vishnu with four arms seated in Sukhasana on an elephant, Sita Devi giving Her Chudamani to Hanuman to be delivered to Sri Rama, and that of Prasanna Varaha Murthi with His consort Sri Lakshmi. There is also a 67.5-cm-tall bas-relief of Ugra Narasimha appearing from the pillar, Sri Rama sitting on a throne with Lakshmana standing by His side, and Anjaneya standing on the other side with His tail directed towards the sky, that of Kali Purusha on a flying horse, a warrior with a long sword and shield, Thara requesting Vali not to enter into a fight with Sri Rama, Gopala Krishna, Srinivasa and so on belonging to the early period of Vijayanagara architecture.

The Mandapam measures about 12.9 m x 12 m. It serves as the

Asthana Mandapam. The Koluvu Srinivasa holds His Darbar here after Tomala Seva, listens to the reading of Panchangam and presides over the apportioning of the daily rations of rice. The report of the daily collections is given to the deity. It is known as Parakkamani. Priests chant hymns and sing during the early Suprabhatham or awakening of the Lord from His celestial sleep. On the afternoon of the commencement of the annual Brahmotsavam, the Utsava Murthy with His two consorts are decorated and seated here in a Thiruchi. This Mandapam is also used to keep the cooked rice. The Sahasra Kalasabhishekam and the Anivara Asthanam are held here. Previously Kalyanotsavam was conducted here. There are two bells here—the 'Tirumani' and 'Thirumahamani'. These bells are used during Naivedyam in the inner shrine. This mandapam was open to the public till the 1950s, but later enclosed with grilles and mesh for security purposes. The Hundi collection of the Lord is sieved and separated and then counted here during the morning Darbar.

Sri Garuda Shrine

The small shrine to Garuda, the vehicle of Lord Vishnu is directly opposite the Sanctum. It has a small roof or Vimana over it. It was probably built around 1417 after the construction of the Tirumamani Mandapam, where it is located.

The 150-m-tall statue is in a standing pose with folded hands and with outstretched wings. He wears huge earrings and is adorned with several other ornaments. The idol is visible from every corner of the Prakaram, mandapams and the Vimana.

On the outer wall there is a figure of Lord Vishnu in Sayana.

At the commencement of the annual Brahmotsavam, the Garuda flag is hoisted on the Dwajasthambam. It is believed that one who eats the Prasadam offered to Garuda here would be blessed with children. Every day after the early morning Puja, the Bali Bera offering to the Lord is taken on a palanquin called

Sibhika, considered to be Garuda Himself, to be offered to His Parivara Devatas. It is believed that the Lord personally supervises the food arrangements for his subordinates and devotees.

The Utsava Murthy of Garuda is kept in the Ramar Medai along with the other bronze idols.

Bangaru Vakili (The golden door)

The inner Shrine is entered through Bangaru Vakili. It is located towards the western end of the Tirumamani Mandapam. The copper images of the Dwarapalakas, Jaya and Vijaya stand on either side of the door. The thick wooden doors are plated with gold and depict the 'Dasavatharam', that is, the ten Avatars or incarnations of Lord Vishnu. Every day Suprabhatham for the Lord is sung in front of this door.

Tiruvilan Koil or Snanapana Mandapam

The inner shrine includes the Sanctum and three Mandapams or halls in front leading up to the Bangaru Vakili, the golden door. After Bangaru Vakili one enters the Tiruvilan Koil or the Snanapana Mandapam that is dimly lit. It is a square Mandapam with four central pillars bearing bas-reliefs of Bala Krishna in the Kaliya Mardana posture, Yoga Narasimha in Yoga pose, a woman chastising her son under a tree, monkeys playing and fighting among themselves, Kali Purusha riding on a horse, and Lord Vishnu in the sitting posture with His two consorts on either side. There are etchings of serpent Sesha, that of Garuda and bearded figures playing on drums.

It is now used as a safe room. Originally, the Snanapana Mandapam was used for the performance of special Abhishekam on certain prescribed days. The four cut stone pillars standing in the centre of the room are the only reminders to show that it was a Mandapam once. The silver idol of Bhoga Srinivasa was consecrated and anointed in 966 CE in the Thiruvilan koil. The Snanapana Mandapam was a strong-room in the early years of the 15th century CE for keeping costly articles and jewels.

Ramar Medai

The Ramar Medai is a passage connecting the Tiruvilan Koil and Sayana Mandapam. It is a rectangular elevated platform where the idols of Sri Rama, Sita and Lakshmana were once kept but have now been shifted to the sanctum. There is also a bronze Deepam that is 60 cm high. It has a small platform on which are carved the figures of Angada, Hanuman and probably that of Sugriva. The Medai measures 3.6 m x 3 m.

Soon after the repair and reconstruction of the Sanctum and the Vimana by Vira Narasingaraya, the first Prakaram was closed for the pilgrims who came to worship the Lord. The front or the eastern wing was covered on the northern and southern side coverting the enclosed space into a small room called the Ramar Medai.

The two inscriptions on the south wall lead one to conclude that this enclosure might have been constructed between 1265 and 1285. It might have formed part of the interior Mukkoti Pradakshinam once.

Mukkoti Pradakshinam

This is the first Pradakshinam path of the shrine that is close to the sanctum. It is a pillared verandah, that is enclosed on its eastern side. The southern section has a row of six pillars, the western section has four pillars and the northern section has two rows of seven pillars each. All the pillars are circular in shape.

There is a shrine of Vishvaksena also called as Senai Mudaliar on the northern side. The pillars here are 4.5 m tall and are built in the Chola and Vijayanagara styles of architecture.

The three sides of the first Prakaram except for the enclosed space of Ramar Medai, became the Mukkoti Pradakshinam around the sanctum. It is an incomplete circumambulation through the Vaikunta Dwaram. This pathway has walls on three sides. It is closed to the public with locked doors on either end. The width of this Pradakshinam is not the same on all the three sides. The north wing is more than double in width.

There are many Poorna Kumbha sculptures in the Mukkoti Pradakshinam. At the exit point of the Vaikunta Dwaram one can see Dasavataram in the lower portion and a bas-relief of a four-armed Lakshmi with a long sword in Her hand.

On the northern side, there is a cement tank in which the water used in the Abhishekam collects and flows out. This pathway is opened to pilgrims only twice a year once on Mukkoti Ekadasi during Dhanur Masa and then on Mukkoti Dwadasi on the following day. The doors are opened after 'Tiruppavai' during the early hours of Mukkoti Ekadasi and closed on the night of Mukkoti Dwadasi.

Sri Vishvaksena Shrine

This shrine is located on the northern side of the main shrine in the Mukkoti Pradakshinam. His image is in Sukhasana. His two upper arms hold Shankha and Chakra. The lower right hand is in Abhayahastha posture while the lower left hand rests on his knee.

In the Vaishnavite tradition, Vishvaksena, the chief of the Lord's army is worshipped first for protection from evil. The idol is adorned with the Nirmalyam, that is the garlands that are removed from the idol of Lord Venkateswara after the daily worship. Before the commencement of Brahmotsavam, as the Senadhipathi, or the commander-in-chief of the army, Vishvaksena Utsavam is celebrated and followed by

Ankurarpana. It is believed that Vishvaksena looks after the arrangements for this grand festival and then gives his consent to start the Utsavam or festival.

Sayana Mandapam

The Ramar Medai leads to a rectangular Sayana Mandapam or Antarala Mandapam or Ardha Mandapam in front of the Sanctum. It measures 5.5 m square. A swing with a bed is hung from the ceiling for the last Seva of the day, the 'Ekanta Seva' for putting Bhoga Srinivasa to sleep in the night. There are no sculptures or structures here.

Kulashekharapadi

It is a threshold to the Sanctum. It is the stone step between the Sayana Mandapam and the Garbhagriha. It is given this name because Kulashekhara Alwar, one of the great Vaishnavite saints, wished to be reborn as the threshold to the Lord's shrine. Rituals that cannot be accommodated in the Sanctum are performed here.

The Garbha Griha

The Sanctum or Garbha Griha was called Koyil Alwar in olden days. The Sanctum and the Mukha Mandapam attached to it is a double structure. The Garbha Griha is located to the west of the Sayana Mandapam. The Garbha Griha, the sanctum sanctorum, is the innermost and most important spot in the temple as it houses the idol of Lord Venkateswara. It is closed on all three sides with granite blocks that cover the ancient inscriptions and bas-reliefs on the walls. The thickness of the walls here is about 2.2 m. The Sanctum is 3.6 m sq. This is the largest size mentioned in the Agamas. The walls seen here are made of cut stones and probably belong to the 8ᵗʰ or 9ᵗʰ century CE. They are bare of inscriptions. Actually there are two sets of walls here, one old and the other new, with a space in-between.

The outer face of the old wall had a few inscriptions on it belonging to the period from 966 CE to 1013 CE. From the inscriptions that have survived, it is assumed that the old walls were demolished before the construction of the new walls. In the process of demolition, the inscriptions were lost due to negligence. A few stones with the inscriptions on them were salvaged and used to build the inner faces of the new walls. A few ancient inscriptions that were copied from the old walls of the Sanctum were reproduced on the outer faces of the new walls.

8

The Deity, Sevas, Festivals and Darshan of the Lord

The Deity

The Temple houses the Pancha Berams mentioned in the Vaishnava Agamas. The five representations of the Lord or the Pancha Berams include the Moola Vigraham or Dhruva Beram, Bhoga Srinivasa or Manavala Perumal, the processional Deities or Utsavamurthis of Malaiappaswami and His consorts Sri Devi and Bhu Devi, Ugra Srinivasa or Snanapanamurthi and Koluvu Srinivasa or Bali Beram. It is believed that the Lord Himself self-created four images when Lord Brahma inaugurated the Brahmotsavam festival. The fifth one, the Malaikuniya Ninra Perumal or Malaiappaswamy with His consorts might have made His appearance in the 14th century equipped with the Shankha and Chakra. There are also idols of Sri Krishna along with Rukmini Devi and Satyabhama, idols of Sri Rama, Sita, Lakshmana, Sugriva and so on.

Bhoga Srinivasa/Manavala Perumal/Kouthuka Beram

This gilded silver idol is similar to the Moola Vigraham. It is in a standing pose with four arms. It has a permanent Shankha and Chakra held in the upper right and left hands. The lower arms are in the Varada and Katyavalambitha poses. The idol has a *yantram* installed on it and was donated by Princess Samavai or Kadavan Perundevi of the Pallava kingdom in 966 CE. All the rituals like Abhishekam, Ekanta Seva and so on, are performed for this idol which is regarded as a representative of the main idol. The exception is during Dhanurmasa when this idol is repaced by Lord Krishna's idol.

He is the one who distributes food to the heavenly beings at Bali Pitam, the stone structure near Dwajasthambam, at the four corners of the temple and in the four streets surrounding the temple.

Apart from the Moola Vigraham that is older, the idol of Bhoga Srinivasa seems to be the earliest one, belonging to the Pallava period along with the Ugra Srinivasa idol.

The idol is connected to the main idol by means of a silk cord and a gold link. He is supposed to represent the Dhruva Beram.

Malaiappaswami/Utsavamurthy/Malaiappar/Malaikuniya Ninra Perumal

This idol is a replica of the main idol but on a smaller scale. It is 90 cm tall and stands on a lotus pedestal that is about 38 cm high. The Shankha and the Chakra are held in the right and left hands respectively, the lower right hand is in the Varadahastha pose and the lower left hand is in the Katihastha pose. It is decorated with gold and platinum jewellery set with precious gems.

His consorts Sri Devi and Bhu Devi are about 72 cm tall and stand on a platform that is 10 cm high. They have one hand in the Kataka or lotus bearing pose and the other hand is in the graceful downward-drooping Prasiratha Hastha.

According to a widely-held belief, the idol was found in the valley of the Tirumala mountain range and hence He came to be known as 'Malaikuniya Ninra Perumal', that is, 'the Lord who stood in the valley of the Hills'. The place where the idol was found is known as Malaiappa Konai. Only on rare occasions does He go on procession without His consorts, for example, on the Garuda Vahana on Garudotsavam day during the Brahmotsavam.

However, during the reign of Ranganatha Yadavaraya (1355-1356 CE) an inscription mentions Malaikuniya Ninra Perumal as the name of the processional deity of Lord Srinivasa with his two consorts.

It can be inferred that these new images of Malaikuniya Ninra Perumal and His consorts Sridevi and Bhudevi were cast and brought into use in the middle of the second quarter of the 14th century CE. Since the silver image of Manavala Perumal installed by Samavai was too small and also without His consorts, three new images were made for the processions.

Ugra Srinivasa/Snanapanamurthy/Venkatatthuraivar

The idol is supposed to be older than the Bhoga Srinivasa idol and was known as Venkatatthuraivar. The 36-cm-tall idol stands on a 17.5-cm-high platform and represents the destructive aspect of the Lord. The idol has a furious mien and is in the constant company of the Moola Vigraham in the Sanctum. It holds a discus in the Prayoga Chakra Mudra that is tilted to one side and looks as though it is ready to be used.

The idols of His consorts Sridevi and Bhudevi are smaller with two arms each, one in Katakahastha pose and the other hanging gracefully. These images are about the same height as their Lord.

Ugra Srinivasa depicts the fierce aspect of the Lord. Till 1330 CE, this idol was the processional deity or Utsavamurthy. Later, this idol was replaced by Maliappaswamy. The Ugra Srinivasa idol is brought out in procession only on Kaisika Dwadasi day (which falls in mid-October) before sunrise. It is said that the Ugramurthy should not be seen in a blaze of sunlight, because its sudden direct gaze would have dire consequences.

It is likely that the Thirumantrasalai Perumanadigal mentioned in the inscriptions had been made the Snanapanaberam or Murthy to hear the chanting of Vedic hymns and invocations during religious rituals and sacrificial obligations and to give constant company to the Dhruva Beram.

Koluvu Srinivasa/Bali Beram/Darbar Srinivasa

This idol holds court, called the Darbar or Asthanam, every morning in the temple, in the Tirumamani Mandapam and the total amount offered in the Hundi the previous day is announced before the deity. He is like the supervising guardian of the temple.

The Darbar is held after Tomala Seva. The idol is seated in a silver chair under a gold umbrella and is adorned with a Simha Thoranam. The Panchangam for the day is also read out, followed by a report of the Hundi (Kopparai) collections of the previous day. The daily rations are given here.

Most probably, the Thiruvilan Koil Perumanadigal mentioned in the inscriptions, must have become the Bali Beram.

Moola Beram

In the centre, below the dome, stands the Moola Vigraham, the firmly-fixed idol of Sri Venkateswara, the main deity of this temple. The idol is called 'Moolabera' and is believed to be Swayambhu, that is self-manifested. There is no record of a human hand in its creation. The stone idol stands on a Lotus base directly beneath the Ananda Nilayam or Ananda Divya Nilaya Vimana, or the sacred dome of the Abode of Bliss.

The idol is a majestic 2.4 m tall and has four arms. On its head is a carved crown that is more than 50 cm high. A shape which may be a crescent moon can be seen on the forehead just below the crown.

Originally the Lord's head was adorned with a crown gifted by Akasha Raju. Now it wears a gold Kiritam embedded with precious gems. What may well be the largest emerald in the word, the 7.5 cm 'Meru Pachchai' forms the centrepiece. The fabulous diamond crown, the 'Vajra Kiritam', that is worth more than Rs. 30 crore, is worn on special occasions like Brahmotsavam. It has 27 diamonds and 9 other gems from Antwerp and one diamond from the TTD. His long, curly tresses hang loose over the shoulders.

On His forehead, the idol sports the thick double lines of the upright 'Namam' drawn with refined camphor that completely covers the eyes. In-between the white lines is the golden 'Kasthuri Thilakam'.

The ears are adorned with Makara Kundalams or gold earrings shaped like crocodiles. The gilded Shankha and Chakra are studded with precious stones.

The chest of the idol spans a broad 100 cm and the waist measures between 60 and 64 cm. The idol glitters with gold ornaments, costly gems and pearls even on ordinary days. His neck is hung with several gold chains and necklaces of varied attractive designs. A 'cobra jewel' or Nagamani gleams just above the abdomen, there is a necklace with a pair of tiger claws, a Lakshmi Haram with 108 images of Goddess Lakshmi, a gold Salagrama Haram that hangs on both sides of the weapons, on which the 'Sahasranama' or the 1000 names of the Lord are carved, a Makara Kanthi jewel, a Thulasi Necklace, two Nagabharanam or circlets for the arms, Vankis on the upper portions of the arms, a Vanki-like gold ornament around the knees, a pair of gold anklets and so on. The arms are covered till the elbow with gold bracelets studded with precious stones.

On Fridays, one can have a glimpse of the Lord without ornaments called 'Nijapada Darshanam'. The Lord is always decorated with roses and other flower garlands. The image of His consort Sri Devi is etched on the right side of His chest while the other consort, Bhu Devi is etched on the left side of His chest. The Nagabharanam ornaments embellish His shoulders. The gold 'Yajnopavitham', the sacred thread, crosses the chest over His left shoulder. A cobra-like mark is seen around his right hand. The four arms are adorned with ornaments that resemble Naga jewels. The slightly outstretched diamond-encrusted lower right hand, is in the boon-granting or Varadahastha pose, pointing symbolically towards His lotus feet, the only refuge of His devotees in their quest to overcome the cycle of birth and death. His lower left hand is in the Katihastha or Katiyavalambita pose in which the thumb is placed on the thigh and the other fingers are almost parallel to the waist. It symbolically indicates that the troubles of life are only knee-deep once the devotees seek His refuge and assures His devotees of His protection.

His dark body is clothed with a Pithambaram fastened with a golden string and encircled with a Dasavatharam gold belt to which are attached tiny, jingling gold bells. The 'Surya Katari' or the Sword of the Sun hangs from the Dasavatharam belt. It is believed that the Sun God presented this belt to Lord Venkateswara.

His legs and Lotus feet are covered in gold and sport golden anklets with tiny bells. Since the idol of Lord Venkateswara has not been sculpted according to the specifications given in the Agama Sastras for idols, it is presumed to belong to an older era when the Sastras had not yet been formulated.

Other Idols

Sri Krishna

The idol of Sri Krishna is a dancing child holding a ball of butter in one of His hands. He is balanced on a lotus pedestal. This idol is taken in procession during Brahmotsavam and is worshipped in Ekanta Seva during Dhanur Masa.

Sri Rama, Sita, Lakshmana and Sugriva

These are copper idols said to be installed by Sri Ramanuja around the 12th century. The raised left hand of Sri Rama is holding the bow and the right arm holds an arrow. The idol of Sita is towards His right. Sita's left hand is in the Katakahastha pose holding a lotus bud and Her right hand falls gracefully by her side. The idol of Lakshmana is smaller than the one of Sri Rama, but similar in other aspects. The idol of Sugriva has folded hands in Anjali pose in reverence to Sri Rama.

Angada and Hanuman

These images are installed on the Ramar Medai in the Antarala Mandapam.

Chakratalwar (Sudarsana Chakra)

This is a copper representation of the Chakra of Lord Vishnu. In all Utsavams, it leads the procession. The last day of Brahmotsavam is celebrated as Chakra Snanam when the celestial bath or Abhishekam on the banks of the Swami Pushkarini is celebrated with all pomp and glory.

Worship of the Deity

In the 12th century, Sri Ramanuja, with the support of the Yadavarayas who were reigning then, introduced the Vishnu form of worship and fixed the Shankha and Chakra onto the till-then empty palms of the Idol. He also introduced the Vaikhanasa form of worship and installed the images of Sri Rama, Sita and Lakshmana. He initiated the singing of the *Nalayira Divya Prabandam*.

From an inscription, we understand that the Andal Thiruppavai recital was introduced in the temple in the second half of the 13th century CE. Another inscription also mentions the provision for the recital of Thiruvaimozhi during the second or third quarter of the 14th century.

Sevas to the main Deity

The daily programme starts with Suprabhatham at 3 am and ends with Ekantha Seva at 1 am the next day. Several Sevas and Utsavams are performed for the Lord on a daily, weekly and periodical basis.

Suprabhatham

Suprabhatham is the first Seva of the day. The half-hour ritual awakens the Lord from His celestial sleep with hymns that include 'Kausalya Supraja Rama' Stotra, Sri Venkatesha Prapthi and Sri Venkatesha Mangalam, and other hymns. During this worship, Navanitha Harathi is done to the Lord and a mixture of cow's milk, butter and sugar is offered. It is performed in the 'Sayana Mandapam' of the Lord. Children below ten years are not allowed for this Seva.

After this ritual the 'Bangaru Vakili' is opened. During Dhanurmasa, instead of Suprabhatham, 'Andal Thiruppavai' is recited to awaken the Lord. The Teertha that is stored in the vessels at night is distributed to the devotees. It is believed that Brahma and the other celestials worship the Lord at night and this Teertha belongs to that worship.

Suddhi

In this ritual, all the flowers adorning the main idol are removed and the vessels are cleaned. It is also called Nirmalya Sodhana.

Tomala Seva

This Seva is performed after Suddhi and when the Deity is decorated after Abhishekam. During this Seva, the main deity as well as the Utsavamurthys are decorated with Tulasi leaves and flower garlands. The origin of the term 'Tomala Seva' is presumed to derive from the Tamil word 'Thodutha Malai' that means 'strung flower garlands'. It is also known as Bhagavathi Aradhana and lasts for 30 minutes. It is conducted as paid or Arjitha Seva on Tuesdays, Wednesdays and Thursdays. During the rest of the week, it is conducted in Ekantam in the presence of only the priests who perform the Seva. During this time Archana and Abhishekam of Bhoga Srinivasa are also conducted.

Koluvu

Koluvu Srinivasa is brought and seated in a silver-plated chair with a golden umbrella in the Tirumamani Mandapam. He is offered a mixture of fried ginger seeds and jaggery and the income of the previous day is announced followed by the reading of the daily Panchangam.

Sahasranama Archanantara Seva

This Seva is performed on all days except Fridays. The 1,000 names of the Lord are chanted by the priests, while the idol is worshipped with Tulasi leaves. After this, the Tulasi leaves collected at the Lord's feet are placed at the feet of Mahalakshmi amidst the chanting of Mahalakshmi Chaturvimsati, the 24 names of the Goddess. This ritual lasts for 30 minutes. Devotees are allowed to be present only on Tuesdays, Wednesdays and Thursdays. On Fridays, Saturdays, Sundays and Mondays, this ritual is performed in Ekantam, that is, only the priests are allowed and not the devotees.

Naivedyam or the first Bell

Food is offered to the Lord amidst the ringing of the two big bells kept in the Tirumamani Mandapam. It is followed by Sattumurai through the recitation of the *Nalayira Divya Prabandam*. This is done in Ekantam where only the Archakas are present and the Bangaru Vakili is closed during this time. This is usually called the first bell in the temple.

Yatrasana

The Archakas go round the Vimana Pradakshinam and offer Bali to Vishvaksena, Garuda, and so on and deposit the balance of the Bali in the stones between the Balipitam and Dwajasthambam.

Sattumurai

It is the recitation of the Tamil *Prabandam* of the Alwars in the traditional manner in Ekantam.

Aparanhapuja or second bell

Naivedyam is offered for the second time in Ekantam. During this time Ashtottaranama or the 108 names of Lord Vishnu from the *Varaha Purana* are recited. With this, the first half of the day's ritual worship comes to an end.

Sevas for the Processional Deities (Utsavamurthis)

Kalyanotsavam

Kalyanotsavam marks the hour-long celestial wedding ritual performed according to the Sastras for the Utsavamurthis of the Lord along with His consorts Sri Devi and Bhu Devi in the Kalyana Mandapam. This Seva is not performed on important festival days like Brahmotsavam, Pavitrotsavam and Pushpayagnam and also on the days of Solar and Lunar eclipses.

Pratyeka Kalyanotsavam

In this, the same rituals as in Kalyanotsavam are followed.

Arjitha Brahmotsavam

In Arjitha Brahmotsavam, the rituals of Brahmotsavam are performed daily in an abridged manner in the Vaibhavotsava Mandapam that is opposite the main temple. This ritual is performed after Kalyanotsavam. The Utsavamurthi, Malaiappa Swamy, is seated on the Pedda Sesha Vahana, Garuda Vahana and Hanumantha Vahana and is worshipped along with His two consorts.

Dolotsavam (Unjal seva)

In this ritual, the idols of the Lord and His consorts are seated on the Unjal or Swing in the Aina Mahal or Addala Mandapam, that is the Mirror Hall, opposite the Ranganayaka Mandapam. The entire area is lit with lamps. During this ritual, the priests chant *Vedas* to the accompaniment of the Mangala Vadyam or the sacred musical instruments.

Arjitha Vasanthotsavam

This hour-long Seva is performed in the Vaibhava Mandapam. During this Seva, the idols of the Lord and His consorts are given Abhishekam or the sacred bath with water, milk and honey. A paste of turmeric and then sandalwood is finally applied. Purusha Suktham, Sri Suktham and Vedic hymns are chanted during the Seva.

Sahasra Deepalankara Seva

This Seva is performed at 5:30 pm in the Unjal Mandapam located in the eastern corner of the main temple. The idols of the Lord and His consorts are taken in procession and seated on the swing in the Mandapam which is lit with a thousand lamps. The Lord and His consorts are rocked gently amidst the Vedic chanting by the priests and the singing of Annamayya songs.

Ratri Puja

The Ratri Puja is the night worship.

Pavalimpu Seva and Ardhajama or Midnight Puja

Before the Lord is put to bed, He is offered sweets and so on in this ritual.

Ekantha Seva/Panuppu Seva/Pavalimpu Seva

This is the final ritual in the daily Sevas. In this ritual, the silver idol of the main deity, the Bhoga Srinivasa, is seated on the velvet bed in the swinging golden cot suspended by silver chains in the Sayana Mandapam. A descendant of Annamacharya the poet devotee of the Lord, sings Annamayya *keerthanas* to put the Lord to sleep. Tarigonda Vengamamba's Harathi is performed in a plate inlaid with the pearl-studded image of one of the Dasavatharas, a different plate and different Avathara for each day. Perfumed sandalwood paste biscuits are placed at the feet of the Lord and on the chest of Bhoga Srinivasa and Alarmelumanga. During this Seva, the Lord is offered sweets, milk, fruits etc.

During Dhanurmasa, Lord Krishna is put to sleep in this cot instead of Lord Venkateswara.

Weekly Sevas

Visesha Puja on Mondays

In this ritual, that starts around 5:30 am, the Utsava murthy is brought to the Mandapam for 'Chaturdasa Kalasa' (14 Kalasas) Visesha Puja. In the midst of chanting of Pancha Sukthas, Thirumanjanam is performed starting with milk, then water, curds, sandalwood powder and finally with water. After the sacred bath, Harathi and Purnahuthi, Naivedyam is offered to the Lord.

Astadala Pada Padmaradhana on Tuesdays

This ritual was introduced in 1984 when a Muslim devotee offered 108 gold lotuses to the Lord. It starts around 6 am. After offering Dhoopa and Deepa to the main deity, the priests recite the Dwadasa names of the Lord, and with the utterance of each name, one gold lotus is offered at His feet. After this is over, Archana is performed to the consorts of the Lord, Sri Devi and Bhu Devi. In conclusion of this ritual, Harathi is offered to the Lord.

Sahasra Kalasabhishekam on Wednesdays

In this ritual starting around 6 am, 1,000 silver vessels filled with sacred water, sandalwood paste and so on are placed on a bed of paddy. Abishekam is performed for Bhoga Srinivasa, Malaiappa Swamy, His consorts and Vishvaksena. Later, in the sanctum, Ekantha Ashtottara Archana is offered to the main deity in front of the temple officers.

Thiruppavada Seva on Thursdays

This ritual takes place at 6 am, in Tirumamani Mandapam. A large quantity of Puliyohara (tamarind rice) is cooked and offered to the Lord along with several sweet preparations. They are placed along with coconuts, flowers, sandalwood paste and vermillion and deepam is offered to the Lord amidst the chanting of *mantras* by the priests.

Pulangi Seva on Thursdays

This ritual takes place every Thursday after the midday Puja. All the ornaments, flower garlands and decorations are removed from the Dhruva Beram and the idol is given a light dressing of Dhoti and Uttiriyam. Only a slight trace of Tiruman Kappu, the Namam and the Kasthuri mark are visible. Then in the evening Suddhi is performed. This process is called Sadalimpu or Sallimpu. After evening Puja and Naivedyam and offering of Panakam and split green gram, a lacy velvet gown is put on the Lord and the idol is decorated from top to toe with garlands of flowers brought from Yamuna Thurai. This decoration is Pulangi Seva.

The reference in the early Tamil classics to the 'Poovadiyil Polinduthondriya', that is, 'the one who shines in the garland of flowers' probably indicates that this particular Seva was in vogue even in the 8th century.

Abhisekam on Friday or Punugu Kappu

Punugu Kappu means anointment with civet oil or scented oil, called Meditta Punugu. In the Friday Abhishekam, conducted around 3:30 am, the deity is anointed with a mixture of Pachcha Karpuram, saffron paste and musk mixed with a few drops of civet oil. This is collected in silver cups and taken around the Sanctum on the Vimana Pradakshinam in procession accompanied by music. A ball of civet oil mixed with refined camphor is placed at the feet of the Lord. Then Thirumanjanam or the sacred bath is given to the deity first with water brought from Akasha Ganga which is poured through a conch covered with gold. Then the Lord is bathed with milk and then with water. Sri Ramanuja is supposed to have initiated this weekly Tirumanjanam. This became a weekly Seva during the time of Krishnadevaraya. After this Abhishekam, a mixture of sandalwood paste, saffron and refined camphor is applied on the idol. Again Abhishekam is performed with water amidst the chanting of Purusha Suktha, Narayana Suktha, Sri Suktha, Nila Suktha and the *Prabandam*. It is followed by Vastralankara Seva and Nija Pada Darshanam at 5:30 am Pachcha Karpuram (Gambura) and Kasturi (musk) are used after Abhishekam and Punugu Kappu is used for putting on the Urdhava Pundram for the idol.

This Thirumanjana Teertha is collected in silver cups. This is the Abhishekam Teertha from the body of the Lord with a little refined camphor and saffron that is distributed to the devotees. Then the deity is dried and receives a light smearing of civet oil from head to foot. The face is lightly powdered and the usual Namam of camphor and musk is drawn on the forehead.

Abhishekam is performed to the Goddess Lakshmi resident in the pendant of the gold chain resting on the chest of the Lord amidst chanting of Sri Suktham. Finally Harathi is performed. Then the white Namam is made thicker and broader. The Lord is dressed in Pitambaram and adorned with valuable jewels and ornaments.

The Sri Padarenu that is the Gambura or Pachcha Karpuram and Kasturi removed from the face of the Dhruva Murthy are mixed with civet oil collected from the feet of the Murthi and kneaded by hand. A portion is distributed to the devotees in packets. This practice perhaps is related to the legendary tale in which Anandalwar pressed camphor to the chin of the deity to stop the oozing of blood from the wound on his chin.

According to an inscription, the hour-long ritual or 'Punugu Kappu' for the main idol was introduced by Krishnadevaraya in 1429.

Utsavams or Festivals

Vasanthotsavam

It is an annual spring festival conducted around 2 pm, for three days, on Trayodasi, Chathurdasi and Pournami in the month of Chitra (March/April). During this period, the Lord and His consorts are taken round in procession and brought to the Vasantha Mandapam. Then Abhishekam is performed. On the third day, the idols of Sri Rama along with Sita, Lakshmana and Anjaneya and Sri Krishna with Rukmini and Satyabhama are brought to this Mandapam in procession. This festival was started by Vilambi, son of a temple accountant.

Koil Alwar Thirumanjanam

This festival is conducted around 11 am, four times in a year in accordance with Agama Sastra. It is held before Ugadi (the Telugu New Year day), before Anivara Asthanam, before Vaikunta Ekadasi, and before the annual Brahmotsavam. This ritual relates to the purification of the sanctum sanctorum and the premises of the temple. All the idols and other articles within the sanctum are removed and the main deity, the Mula Murthi is covered with waterproof cloth. The sanctum including the floors, ceilings and walls are cleaned and brushed. The entire area is then cleaned thoroughly with water and smeared with vermillion, camphor, sandalwood paste, saffron, turmeric etc. Then the covering is removed and all the articles and the other idols are replaced. After this, the purificatory worship is carried out and Naivedyam is offered to the deity.

Pavitrotsavam

This is an annual purificatory ceremony seeking expiation for any sins which may have been committed during the performance of the daily rituals and worship of the Lord in the temple. This ritual is performed around 8 am for four days along with the chanting of *Vedas*, recitation of Prabandam and performance of Homas. It starts from the Dasami (10th day) of Sukla Paksha (bright half of the moon) in the month of Sravana (August). After the rituals, the deity is decorated with Pavithrotsavam garlands of five colours that look like a garland of beads. This festival was initiated during the rule of Saluva Narasimha.

Pushpa Yagnam

It is a festival held after the annual Brahmotsavam around 6 am, on the day of Sravana Nakshathram, the birth star of Lord Venkateswara. Ankurarpanam is done before Pushpa Yagnam. After the daily Pujas, the Utsavamurthi, Malaiappa Swami, along with His consorts Sri Devi and Bhu Devi, are worshipped with a large variety of flowers and sweets. In the evening these deities are taken out in procession.

Teppotsavam (Float festival)

This annual festival is celebrated on Phalguna Pournami (full moon) in the Swami Pushkarini (the sacred temple tank) for five days. It starts at 6 pm on the first day, Lord Rama along with Sita and Lakshmana are worshipped. On the second day, Sri Krishna and Rukmini are offered worship. During the remaining three days, from Trayodasi till Pournami, Malaiappa Swami, that is the processional deity of Lord Venkateswara and His consorts are worshipped. The deities are worshipped in a decorated float erected in the Swami Pushkarini.

Abhideyaka Abhishekam or Jyestabhishekam

This three-day festival starts around 8 am and is meant to protect the processional deities from damage while conducting processions and during Abhishekams or Thirumanjanam (the sacred bath). The festival is held in July, when the star Jyeshta is in ascendance. So it is also called Jyeshtabhishekam. On the first day after Abhishekam, the Utsavamurthi, Malaiappa Swamy is brought to the Kalyanotsava Mandapam in the Sampangi Pradakshinam along with His consorts. After Snanapana Thirumanjanam, the deities are decorated with Vajra Kavacham, that is, armour studded with diamonds and taken along the Mada Veethis, the temple streets, in procession. On the second day, after Abhishekam, the deities are decorated in Muthyala (pearls) Kavacham and taken out in procession. On the third day, they are adorned with Swarna (gold) Kavacham that remains on the deities throughout the year.

Padmavathi Parinayam

It is an annual celestial wedding festival celebrated in the month of May in the specially-arranged Kalyana Mandapam (marriage hall) in the Narayana Gardens on Tirumala. It commences around 3 pm. It is a three-day celebration that is performed in the evening and is conducted on Navami, Dasami and Ekadasi in the month of Vaisakha. The processional deity arrives on Gaja (elephant), Ashwa (horse), and Garuda (Eagle) Vahanas and His consorts arrive on separate palanquins. After the wedding ceremony is performed each day, the deities sit in Koluvu (Darbar) in the Kalyana Mandapam. During this time, cultural programmes like Harikatha, dance and music are held. The Utsavamurthis are returned to the sanctum each day.

Pushpa Palki

As per the tradition, the temple accounts begin from Dakshinayana, in July. Anivara Asthanam, the grand Darbar festival of the Lord is celebrated on that day, usually on the 16th of July. On this day, the accounts of the previous year are submitted to the Lord and a new account is started with the opening of a new book.

It starts around 5:30 pm. All the main officers of the TTD keep their insignia of office at the feet of the Lord and take them back. A new account book is opened to mark the new financial year. It symbolises the Lord's approval and His finding them fit to hold their posts.

In the evening, the Utsavamurthi along with His consorts, are taken out in procession along the main street in a lavishly-decorated floral palanquin.

Adyayanotsavam

It is an annual Vedic festival when the *Vedas*, Tamil Prabandams and Nammalwar's Thiruvaimozhi are recited in the temple. This festival is conducted on the Mukkoti Ekadasi day and is held for 20 days. During this festival, the Utsavamurthis are taken round the temple amidst the chanting of *Nalayira Divya Prabandam* of the Alwars. The last day is Sattumurai day.

Ratha Sapthami

On Ratha Sapthami day, the Utsavamurthi is taken around on the Surya Prabha Vahana. Three more processions then take place with the deity seated on the Sesha Vahana, Ganesha Vahana and Hanumantha Vahana. After Teerthavari and second Archana to the idol, the Utsavamurthi again goes on procession on Sarva Bhupala Vahana, Kalpa Vriksha Vahana and Chandra Prabha Vahana. Thus seven processions on seven Vahanas take place before sunset.

Brahmotsavam

The Brahmotsavam is the most important and glittering festival in Tirumala. This is the biggest festival and attracts a large number of devotees from far and near, especially on the days of

Garudotsavam and Rathotsavam when the abode of the Lord transforms into a Kaliyuga Vaikunta. One can witness a sea of humanity enjoying the grand events on all the days of the festival. The entire area, the temple and the chariot are magnificently decorated.

According to the *Varaha Purana*, Lord Brahma performed this festival for the first time in the month of Asvayuja as per Salivahana calendar (September-October) when the Sun is in the Kanya Rasi. The present Brahmotsavam is celebrated for nine days continuously. It is believed that the festival originally commemorated the day Lord Venkateswara took on this avatar.

According to 'Venkatachala Mahatyam', in the twenty-eighth Yuga before the present Kaliyuga, Sri Venkateswara appeared before Brahma and other gods and rishis, kings and devotees on a Monday when the Sravana Nakshatram was ascendant. It was the Sukla Paksha Dwadasi of Kanya Masa as per solar calendar (Bhadrapada Asvayuja months according to the lunar calendar). It is also said that Lord Brahma worshipped Lord Venkateswara on the banks of Swami Pushkarini. Hence this festival is called Brahmotsavam.

In preparation for this festival, the sanctum and the other places in the temple are cleaned and smeared with a rich paste of sandalwood, refined camphor, saffron and other fragrant materials in a ritual known as the 'Koil Alwar Thirumanjanam'. During this period, Homas are performed and the Utsavamurthi or the processional deity is beautifully dressed up and specially decorated with several costly ornaments. He is taken around the four main streets of the temple in procession on all days of this festival on different Vahanas or vehicles accompanied with Mangala Vadyas, Bhajans and so on, both in the morning and night. The deity is accorded all the traditional royal paraphernalia during the processions along the temple streets on some days with consorts and other days without them. The chariot believed to represent Lord Brahma's chariot, leads the procession.

On the ninth and last day of the festival, on the day of Sravana Nakshathram, Chakra Snanam is held in the Swami Pushkarini. It is believed that Lord Brahma and the other Devas and all the devotees present there take a dip simultaneously in the sacred waters.

A second Brahmotsavam takes place whenever there is Adhika Masam and that happens every third year. The second Brahmotsavam is called Navaratri Brahmotsavam.

The 'Sri Venkateswara Mahatyam' states that the ancient Brahmotsavam was continued in Kaliyuga by Thondaiman Chakravarthy, a great devotee of the Lord.

The present-day Brahmotsavam is in accordance with the procedure described in the Bhavishyottara Purana, with the exception of a few items. As per the Purana, the Dhwaja Arohana takes place in the early morning. The Vahanas used on the different days of this festival remain the same as in olden days, but the Purana mentions 'Udyana Viharotsavam' or pastime in the garden, a procession on the seventh evening on the Mangalagiri Vahana, that is no longer held. Similarly, the 'Pushpa Yagnam' as per the Purana, is to be performed on the tenth day that is the day after the 'Chakra Snanam'. Although this was renewed in the year 1980, it is not conducted on the specified day.

The programmes and Vahanas of the Deities during Brahmotsavam

DAYS	MORNING	NIGHT
First day	Dwajorahanam	Pedda Sesha Vahana
Second day	Chinna Sesha Vahana	Hamsa Vahana
Third day	Simha Vahana	Mutyala Pandiri Vahana

Fourth day	Kalpa Vruksha Vahana	Sarva Bhupala Vahana
Fifth day	Mohini Avataram Palanquin	Garuda Vahana
Sixth day	Hanumantha Vahana	Gaja Vahana
Seventh day	Surya Prabha Vahana	Chandra Prabha Vahana
Eighth day	Rathotsavam	Aswa Vahana
Ninth day	Pallaki Utsavam	Golden Tiruchi Utsavam/Chakra Snanam

Ankurarpana

The ritual namely, 'Mritsangrahanam', that is the process of collecting earth, is performed on the day prior to the first day of Brahmotsavam. This ritual is a prayer by the officials of the temple to deities like Garuda, Sudarsana, Anantha and Vishvaksena for seeking their help and blessings for the smooth and successful conduct of the nine-day festival.

Mother Earth or Bhumi Devi is also worshipped. A small quantity of earth is collected in specially-decorated Palikas or earthen plates. Ankurarpana is done by sowing Nava Dhanya, i.e. nine kinds of grains in the soil for germination. It signifies fertility, prosperity and abundance. This is held on the evening prior to the first day's celebration.

Vishvaksena, the leader of the retinue of Lord Vishnu, is worshipped for removing obstacles. He, along with Ananta, Garuda and Sudarsana are taken to the Vasantha Mandapam where the Ankurarpana rite is in progress. Vishvaksena inspects the arrangements that are made for Brahmotsavam. After the procession, he is honoured by an Asthanam in Tirumalaraya Mandapam and then he goes to the Ankurarpana Mandapam with Anantha, Garuda and Sudarsana and they stay till the Brahmotsavam festival is concluded. A 'Poorna Kumbham' is also installed in the Yagnasala.

First Day

On the first day, the chief priest of the temple hoists the Garudadhwaja on the Dhwajasthambam or flagpost. It is believed that Garuda goes to the abode of the Devas, the Devaloka, to invite them to the function. For this event, Sri Malaiappa Swami, the Utsavamurthi of the Lord who is decorated with very costly ornaments including Vajra Kavacham, the diamond armour and flower garlands, accompanied by His two consorts Sri Devi and Bhu Devi are brought in a golden palanquin called 'Tiruchi' to the Tirumalaraya Mandapam. At the appointed Muhurtha, the Garuda flag is hoisted on the Dhwajasthambam located opposite the sanctum, amidst the chanting of Mantras and Mangala Vadyas.

The Ashta Dik Palakas, the deities of the eight cardinal points are invoked and enjoined to see that the festival is conducted properly and smoothly. On the first night, the deity goes around the temple in Pedda Seshavahana, that is the big seven-hooded serpent vehicle. From 10 pm till midnight, the deities are taken around the four streets (four Mada Veedis) of the main temple. Tirumala Hills is believed to be the manifestation of Adi Sesha.

Second day

On the second day, the Lord is taken round the temple on Chinna Sesha Vahana. The deities are taken for Unjal Seva in the night to the Uyala Mandapam and then they are taken in procession around the temple on Hamsa Vahana.

Third day

On the third day, the processional deity goes round in Simha (lion) Vahana in the morning and after the Unjal Seva in the night, He is taken round on the Muthyala Pandiri Vahana, that is the vehicle strung with pearls.

Fourth day

On the fourth day, the deities are taken in procession in Kalpa Vriksha (the celesal wish-fulfilling tree) Vahana in the morning and after the Unjal Seva in the night, in Sarva Bhoopala Vahana (gilded vehicle).

Fifth day

On the fifth day, to commemorate His Mohini Avatara, Lord Vishnu is dressed up as Mohini who offered Amrutham to the Devas. The decorated Utsavamurthi is adorned with the costly jewels and ornaments of a woman and is taken in procession around the temple accompanied by the idol of Lord Krishna, on a Palki that is Palanquin Vahana. In the night after the Unjal Seva, the Lord adorned with rare and special jewels like Lakshmi Haram and Makara Kundalam that belong to the Moola Vigraham, is taken in procession on the Garuda Vahana, his favourite and most popular Vahana. A large number of pilgrims throng the temple.

The Lord is given 'Uyyala Seva' in the evening in the open area near the Dhwajasthambam. During the Asthanam, songs are sung and Vedic hymns are chanted. Then the deity is taken in procession on Garuda Vahana. On this occasion, on behalf of the Government of Andhra Pradesh, the Chief Minister carries special silk garments on his head to present to Lord Venkateswara.

Sixth day

On this day, the deities are taken on Hanumantha Vahana in the morning. In the evening, instead of Unjal Seva, Vasanthotsavam is performed. Sri Malaiappa Swami and His consorts proceed to the Vasantha Mandapam. After He enjoys the Vasantham that is, spring festival there, the Lord returns to the temple. In the night, the deities are taken in procession on the Gaja Vahana that symbolises Airavatha, the elephant vehicle of Devendra as well as the elephant that Lord Vishnu liberated.

Seventh day

On the seventh day, the deities are taken round the main streets of the temple on Surya Prabha Vahana. In the night, after the Unjal Seva, the Lord, along with His consorts, is taken in procession in Chandra Prabha Vahana.

Eighth day

On the eighth day Rathotsavam is celebrated. The Lord and His consorts are taken out in procession around the temple on a richly-decorated and exquisitely-carved huge wooden chariot or Ratham that is strung with floral wreaths, flags and festoons. It is believed that there is no rebirth for those who witness the chariot scene. The Rathotsavam attracts a large number of devotees. In front of the deities, the idols of the Charioteer of Lord Krishna, Daruka, and the four horses Saibyam, Sugreevam, Megha Pushpam and Valahakam are kept. Devotees pull the chariot all along the temple streets. After the Unjal Seva in the night the deities are taken in procession on the Aswa (horse) Vahana.

Ninth day

On the final day of Brahmotsavam, that coincides with Sravana Nakshatram, the birth star of the Lord, Pallaki (Tiruchi) Seva and

Chakra Snana Mahotsavam are held in the morning and in the evening.

After the Dhwajarohanam in the morning, the processional deities are anointed with oil, turmeric and other sacred and scented ingredients and after a prolonged ritual that lasts for an hour, Choornabhishekam is performed.

In Swami Pushkarini, the Sudarsana Chakra of the Lord is immersed by the priests and the devotees who throng the area at that time, take a dip in the Swami Pushkarini simultaneously. This is called 'Avabratham' or 'Chakra Snanam'. The deities are also given the holy bath after the ritual. This is called Choornabhishekam. The devotees then circumambulate the Sudarsana Chakra that is placed on a high platform. The Lord is taken in a procession and the sandalwood powder that is used for the ritual is distributed to the devotees all along the route. Then the deities return to the temple.

The Brahmotsavam celebrations conclude with Dhwaja-varohanam in the evening, that is the lowering of the Garuda flag after worship and offering of Naivedyam amidst Vedic chanting. The mantras pay obeisance to the gods, sages and other celestial beings who attended the festival and are a kind of farewell or seeing off to their abodes. This ritual is known as Devatodwasanam. In this ritual, Lord Brahma is particularly propitiated for having come down to Earth to conduct the proceedings.

The daily schedule – approximate timings

Note: Sarva Darshan on all days may continue beyond the fixed timings depending on the number of pilgrims. The timings are subject to change as per the decision of the TTD Committee.

Saturdays/Sundays

2.30-3.00	Suprabhatham
3.30-4.00	Tomala Seva
4.00-4.15	Koluvu, Panchanga Sravanam
4.00-4.30	First Archana-Sahasranama Archana
5.00-5.30	Archananthara Darshan
6.30-7.00	Bali and Sethumara
7.00-7.30	Suddhi, Second Archana (Ekantham)
7.30-19.00	Sarva Darshan
12.00-17.00	Kalyanotsavam, Brahmotsavam, Vasanthotsavam, and Unjal Seva
17.30-18.30	Sahasra Deepalankara Seva
19.00-20.00	Suddhi, Night worship (Ekantham)
20.00-01.00	Sarva Darshan
1.00-1.30	Suddhi, preparation for Ekantha Seva
1.30 hours	Ekantha Seva

Mondays

5.30-7.00	*Special Seva*–Visesha Puja
2.30-3.00	Suprabhatham

3.30-4.00	Tomala Seva
4.00-4.15	Koluvu and Panchanga Sravanam
4.15-5.00	Archana-Sahasranama Archana
5.00-5.30	Archananantara Darshanam
5.30-7.00	Visesha Puja
7.00-7.30	Suddhi-Second Archana (Ekantham)
7.30-19.00	Sarva Darshanam
12.00-17.00	Kalyanotsavam, Brahmotsavam, Vasanthotsavam and Unjal Seva
17.30-18.30	Sahasra Deepalankara Seva
19.00-20.00	Suddhi, Night worship (Ekantham)
20.00-1.00	Sarva Darshanam
1.00-1.30	Suddhi, Preparation for Ekantha Seva
1.30	Ekantha Seva

Tuesdays

6.00-7.00	*Special Seva*–Ashtadala Pada Padmaradhana
2.30-3.00	Suprabhatham
3.30-4.00	Tomala Seva
4.00-4.15	Koluvu, Panchanga Sravanam
4.15-5.00	Sahasranama Archana
5.00-5.30	Archananthara Darshanam
6.00-7.00	Suddhi, Ashtadala pada Padmaradhana
7.00-19.00	Sarva Darshanam
12.00-17.00	Kalyanotsavam, Brahmotsavam, Vasanthotsavam, and Unjal Seva

17.30-18.30	Sahasra Deepalankara Seva
19.00-20.00	Suddhi, night worship (Ekantham)
20.00-1.00	Sarva Darshanam
1.00-1.30	Suddhi and preparation for Ekantha Seva
1.30	Ekantha Seva.

Wednesdays

6.00-8.00	*Special Seva* –Sahasra Kalasabhishekam
2.30-3.00	Suprabhatham
3.30-4.00	Tomala Seva
4.00-4.15	Koluvu, Panchanga Sravanam
4.15-5.00	Sahasranama Archana
5.00-5.30	Archanananthara Darshanam
6.00-8.00	Sahasra Kalasabhishekam
8.30-9.30	Second Archana (Ekantham)
9.30-19.00	Sarva Darshanam
12.00-17.00	Kalyanotsavam, Brahmotsavam, Vasanthotsavam and Unjal Seva
17.30-18.30	Sahasra Deepalankara Seva
19.00-20.00	Suddhi, Night worship
20.00-1.00	Sarva Darshanam
1.00-1.30	Suddhi, preparation for Ekantha Seva
1.30	Ekantha Seva

Thursdays

6.00-8.00	*Special Seva* –Thiruppavada
21.00-22.00	Poolangi Alankaram
2.30-3.00	Suprabhatham
3.30-4.00	Tomala Seva
4.00-4.15	Koluvu, Panchanga Sravanam
4.15-5.00	Sahasranama Archana
5.00-5.30	Archananantara Darshanam
6.00-8.00	Sallimpu-second Archana, Thiruppavada
8.00-19.00	Sarva Darshanam
12.00-17.00	Kalyanotsavam, Brahmotsavam, Vasanthotsavam and Unjal Seva
17.30-18.30	Sahasra Deepalankara Seva
19.00-21.00	Pedda Suddhi, Night worship, Poolangi Alankaram
21.00-1.00	Poolangi Alankaram, Sarva Darshanam
1.00-1.30	Suddhi and Preparation for Ekantha Seva
1.30	Ekantha Seva

Fridays

4.30-6.00	*Special Seva* –Abhishekam
2.30-3.00	Suprabhatham
3.00-4.30	Sallimpu, Suddhi, Nitya Kala Worship and preparation for Abhishekam
4.30-6.00	Abhishekam and Nijapada Seva
6.00-7.00	Samarpana
7.00-8.00	Thomala Seva and Archana

9.00-20.00	Sarva Darshanam	
12.00-17.00	Kalyanotsavam, Brahmotsavam, Vasanthotsavam and Unjal Seva	
18.00-20.00	Sahasra Deepalankara Seva at Kolini Mandapam and procession along the Mada Streets	
20.00-21.00	Suddhi, Night worship.	
21.00-22.00	Sarva Darshanam	
22.00-22.30	Suddhi and preparation for Ekantha Seva	
22.30	Ekantha Seva	

Darshan of the Lord

There is free Darshan that is Sarva Darshan, as well as special paid Darshan that is called Arjitha Seva. The fee for the Arjitha Sevas is as per the decision of the TTD Committee and is subject to change.

Senior citizens and the disabled are permitted go through the Mahadwaram, the main entrance for Darshan.

(a) *Sarva Darshan* is the free daily Darshan for all. The timings are as per the daily schedule of the temple programmes. Usually on normal days, 18 hours are allotted for Sarva Darshan and on peak days it is extended up to 20 hours.

(b) *Special Darshan for the Disabled and Aged*

Special Darshan for the physically disabled and aged along with one attendant is provided through a separate gate near the main entrance, that is, Mahadwaram.

(c) *Seegra Darshan (quick Darshan)*

This facility of quick Darshan is on payment.

(d) *Divya Darshan*

This facility is meant for those pilgrims who walk up the Hill through Gali Gopuram or 'Srivari Mettu'. Biometric counters are set up on the pathway for free Darshan, free accommodation and free food on the Hill.

e-Darshan

The TTD has introduced e-Darshan facilities to enable the pilgrims who visit Tirumala to enter the Queue complex as per their timings. These counters are established in most of the TTD Kalyana Mandapams and Information centres of the TTD. In the e-Darshan facility the pilgrims are provided the time slot for Darshan online to avoid inconvenience.

Vaikuntam Queue Complex

The Darshan of the Lord is through the Vaikuntam Queue complex. It consists of spacious, airy and clean interconnected halls where the pilgrims wait for the Darshan of the Lord. This facility makes the long wait less tedious and tiresome. There are closed-circuit TVs that display devotional programmes of the TTD, restaurants, toilets with clean water facility, medical aid, and so on, here. The Lord's pictures, photographs of the temple, calendars and other TTD publications, food packets, snacks, coffee and fresh milk are sold inside the queue complex at subsidised rates. Cloakroom facility and a centre to keep the footwear free of cost are also provided near the Vaikuntam entrance.

9

The Tirumala Tirupathi Devasthanams (TTD)

The TTD has around 14,000 employees and there are 12 temples and their subsidiary shrines under its control. The primary task of the TTD is to be the custodian of the Tirumala temple and the other temples that are under its control and their properties, offer services to the devotees who visit the shrines, and propagate Hindu religion and culture and to safeguard the serenity and sanctity of the Tirumala and Tirupathi area. The other activities of the TTD include the preservation and protection of the religious, educational, social, economic, environmental and developmental needs of the pilgrims and the people who live in and around the shrines.

To fulfil these aims, several schemes and projects are undertaken by the TTD in the areas of education, medical treatment, rehabilitation of the physically challenged and economically backward to mention a few. TTD also provides financial assistance to authors of books on Hindu religion and culture and provides equipment, idols etc to many other temples at subsidised rates. TTD's role in the development of education through the establishment of schools and colleges at various levels, in infrastructure development like roads and drinking water supply in Tirupathi, in the financial assistance that is provided to the government-run Sri Ram Narayan Ruia General

Hospital and to the S V University and S P Mahila University, are noteworthy. In order to develop the schemes and also to encourage devotees to participate in them, donations are accepted by the TTD.

Usually the donations are exempt from income-tax. In most cases, only the interest on the capital amount of the donation is utilised by the TTD under a particular scheme. The TTD also in many cases provides a matching grant that is equivalent to the donation amount extended by the devotees. All the donations are deposited in nationalised banks only. The donors are extended certain privileges by the TTD depending upon the amount of their donation to any particular scheme.

1. FACILITIES OFFERED TO PILGRIMS

The TTD has established nearly 125 Kalyana Mandapams in major towns and cities of Andhra Pradesh and some outside the state in Puducheri, Guruvayoor and Rishikesh and in cities like New Delhi, Chennai, Bengaluru, Mumbai and Kolkata as also in foreign countries. Audio and video cassettes are available here.

Sri Venkateswara temples are built in foreign countries for the benefit of the NRI devotees.

Free bus facility is provided to pilgrims from East railway station to RTC Bus Stand and to Alipiri via RTC Central Bus Stand, Kapila Teertham and so on from 4 am to 11 pm.

APSRTC runs bus services from TTD Airport to Tirumala and back. Pilgrims can contact the 'Information Centres' located at the Railway Station, Airport, RTC Bus Stand, 1st and 3rd Choultries, Alipiri Toll Gate and Renigunta Railway Station for all required information.

Paid package tours are arranged daily by the TTD to nearby holy places, temples, religious sites and a few other places that are worth seeing. The temples covered are: Sri Venugopala Swamy temple, Karvetinagaram, Sri Veda Narayana Swami Temple,

Nagalapuram, Sri Kalyana Venkateswara Swamy temple, Narayanavanam, and Sri Padmavathi Temple, Tiruchanoor. The pilgrims who avail the package tour are given Anna Prasadm. The bus starts from the Central Reception Office, Tirumala at 6 am everyday and returns on the same day.

Daily local temple visits by bus are also provided to the pilgrims on payment. The buses start at 6 am, 10 am, and 2 pm from the choultry behind the East Railway Station. The bus that starts at 2 pm halts at the Regional Science Centre. The temples that are covered are: Sri Padmavathi Temple, Tiruchanoor, Sri Rama Temple, Tirupathi, Sri Govindaraja Swamy Temple, Tirupathi, Sri Kapileshwara Swamy Temple, Tirupathi, Hare Rama Hare Krishna Mandir (ISKCON), Tirupathi, Sri Kalyana Venkateswara Swami Temple, Srinivasa Mangapuram, Sri Agastheeswara Swami Temple, Thondavada and the Regional Science Centre, Tirupathi.

Free bus service on fixed routes is provided to pilgrims to go round Tirumala covering cottages, choultries and temples.

Free meals are provided to the pilgrims in the TTD Canteen in the Nitya Annadanam Hall at Tirumala from 10 am till 11 pm on production of Free Meal Coupons by the pilgrims. Meals at moderate prices are also given.

Free medical aid is given to pilgrims in the Aswini Hospital near Seshadri Nagar on Tirumala, at VQC and New Vaikuntam Queue Complex. The luggage of the pilgrims who walk up to Tirumala are transported from the foot of the Hills, that is from Alipiri to Tirumala and back round-the-clock free of charge. Pilgrims can give their luggage properly locked at a counter in Alipiri and this will be handed over to them when they reach the top of the Hill at a Mandapam near the Central Reception Office, Tirumala.

The pathway to Tirumala that is nearly 11 km long, and has cement steps with railings on the sides for supporting the pilgrims who climb the Hill. All along the route, pilgrims can listen to the religious programmes relayed through the local broadcasting system of the TTD. Drinking water and toilet facilities are also provided. The pathway has electric lights and security guards patrol it round the clock. Small restaurants keep refreshments and snacks. To enable the pilgrims to rest at certain points which are very steep (called 'Muzangal Mudichu' in Tamil and 'Mokala Parvatham' in Telugu), small Mandapams are provided. There are sunshades built at certain points.

There is an automobile clinic that provides services for a fee to vehicles which break down on the way. The pilgrims can contact the toll gate either at Tirupathi or at Tirumala for repairing their vehicles.

The TTD also provides free cloakroom facility near the Central Reception office and at Vaikuntam 'Q' Complex on Tirumala and in the Sri Venkateswara Choultry opposite the Railway Station at Tirupathi. There is also a Posts and Telegraph office near the Central Reception office.

The large airy halls of the Vaikuntam Queue Complex enable the pilgrims to rest while they are waiting. It also helps in the smooth flow of pilgrims into the temple. Refreshments available on sale include coffee by the Coffee Board, milk by the AP Dairy Development Corporation and food packets at reasonable prices. First aid facilities, ceiling fans in the waiting halls, catering by the TTD Canteen, toilet and bathroom facilities can also be found in the Queue Complex. There is relay of religious programmes through the Broadcasting system of TTD to the Vaikuntam Queue Complex. Close circuit television sets are installed here as well.

Kalyana Katta or the Tonsuring Centre of the TTD enables the devotees to fulfil the vow of tonsuring their hair as a mark of giving up one's ego, and as an offering to the Lord free of cost. It is one of the main offerings in this temple. The Kalyanakatta is a four-storeyed building that functions round the clock. The hair offered to the Lord by the devotees is sold by the TTD to international buyers.

TTD ensures that pilgrims can fulfil their vows of Thulabharam, Anga Pradakshinam and Niluvudopidi, that is, offering of ornaments, money, jewels and other valuables to the Srivari Hundi.

Devotees who perform Anga Pradakshinam are allowed entrance through Special Darshan sheds at 2:30 am.

All the publications of the TTD are made available at the TTD Publication stalls, in the waiting halls in the Queue Complex and at Asthana Mandapam on Tirumala.

There are facilities to conduct rituals like Namakaranam, Upanayanam, marriage and so on by purohits from the Purohit Sangam on charges fixed by the TTD. Some TTD Cottages like the Alwar Tank cottage no. 99, 10 cottages in the Sankar Mitta Cottages, S R M Kalyana Mandapam and 5 Traveller's Bungalow cottages are exclusively allotted for the performance of marriages. (Some religious Mutts on Tirumala also provide marriage halls.)

A free public address system that is located opposite the temple makes announcements about missing persons and other announcements to help the pilgrims.

Free counters are set up to leave footwear near Varahaswami temple, queue complex and near Kalyana Katta.

There are special queues in front of the main entrance of the temple for disabled people and senior citizens (75 years and above) along with one attendant each for Darshan.

There are free and unfurnished choultries at Tirumala to meet the need for accommodation of the pilgrims both in Tirupathi as well as at Tirumala. Paid accommodation is also provided in guest houses, rooms and so on.

The pilgrims may buy Srivari Seva Tickets one day in advance from the Vijaya Bank located opposite the Vaikuntam Queue Complex on a first-come-first-served basis. The tickets are limited to a certain number for the different Sevas. Those who wish to perform paid Sevas are to draw DD for the amount prescribed by the TTD from time to time, in favour of EO-TTD and send it to the Peshkar, Sri Tirumala Temple, Tirumala at least three months in advance. The Seva tickets will be sent to the devotees by post.

However during festivals and certain important days, certain Arjitha Sevas as notified by the TTD are not performed and hence the tickets for such Sevas are not sold for those days. Usually, these days are: Anivara Asthanam for one day in July, Pushpa Yagnam for one day during October/November, Vasantotsavam for three days annually, Brahmotsavam for 10 days during September-October annually, December 31st to 2nd January, Pavitrotsavam for three days in August, Ugadi Asthanam on Ugadi Day in March for one day and one day on Makara Sankranthi in January. There is no sale of tickets for Archana and Tomala Sevas performed on Fridays, Saturdays and Sundays.

Under the e-Hundi service, the devotees can donate amounts to the temple online and this will be acknowledged over the net with a receipt. Sevas and cottages can be booked, subject to the availability online under e-seva and e-accommodation. For these a devotee has to declare his identity by means of driving license or passport or voter's identity card or PAN card. Those who seek e-accommodation are to approach Sri Padmavathi Guest House Reception Office on the specified date with his identity and surrender the internet receipt. This facility can be obtained through e-booking logo on the Home page of the TTD's website—www.tirumala.org. Once the needed information is provided by the devotee, the link will lead to the Citibank Payment gateway for processing the payment and then the request is processed. Once the procedure is completed successfully, it will lead to the TTD site again in which the official receipt will be available on the net, the printout of which may be taken by the devotee. For security purposes the entire transaction is made through 128 bit SSL. In e-accommodation the categories available are: Rs. 100 for a two-bedded room with attached toilet and Rs. 750 for a two-bedded A/C room with attached toilet. On arrival, higher rental accommodation, if required by the devotee and if available can be got on payment of the difference in cash or through credit card.

Under the supervision of the TTD, ATM and Credit Card facilities are available on Tirumala.

There is a Bus and Railway booking office at the TTD Central Reception office on Tirumala.

The biometric system has been adopted by the TTD to curb black-marketing and other malpractices in the sale of paid or Arjitha Seva tickets. Under this scheme the thumb impression of the pilgrim who buys the tickets for any particular Arjitha Seva is taken at the counters and they are digitally transmitted to the entry point into the temple, the Vaikuntam Queue Complex. At the time of entry the ticket is produced and the thumb impression is verified by the officials on duty.

There are two big marriage halls of the TTD in Tirupathi with all modern catering facilities. They are, Sri Srinivasa Kalyana Mandapam and Sri Padmavathi Kalyana Mandapam.

Wheelchair facility is available for the disabled and very old people.

TTD sells gold and silver dollars with the image of Lord Venkateswara on the obverse and that of Goddess Padmavathi Devi on the reverse at counters inside the temple near Vimana Venkateswara, at TTD Srinivasam Complex, Govindaraja Swamy Temple, Tirupathi and at Sri Padmavathi Temple, Tiruchanoor.

There is provision for making complaints to the Chief Vigilance Officer, TTD at Tirumala or the PRO, TTD at Tirupathi. Boxes are also kept in the Sub-enquiry Office for people who want to drop in written complaints.

2. ACTIVITIES RELATING TO RELIGION AND FOR PRESERVATION OF INDIAN CULTURE

Supply of Idols and Equipment to other Temples

The TTD supplies stone and panchaloha idols, Sesha Vasthram for the idol, microphone sets including an amplifier, two speakers, a tape recorder and a cable with a few audio cassettes and temple umbrellas at subsidised rates to other temples.

Kalyana Mandapams and information centres

The TTD has established several Kalyana Mandapams and Information centres in many towns including Tirupathi and cities in Andhra Pradesh and in a few places outside AP Audio and video cassettes of the TTD are available here.

Hindu Dharma Prachara Parishad

This was established to propagate Hinduism by conducting Hindu religious programmes. It has 20 centres in AP and three centres in other states of India. It maintains two Veda Patasalas, one at Dharmagiri at Tirumala and the other at Keesaragutta in Ranga Reddi District. The students of these Patasalas under the Kumara Adhyapaka Scheme are encouraged to learn *Vedas* and are given a stipend and free boarding and lodging for the entire duration of the course. The DPP also gives Sambhavana to nearly 500 Veda Pandits who render Veda Parayanam in the temples, as per their qualifications, under the Veda Parayana Scheme. Financial assistance is also given for developing Veda Patasalas, for conducting Veda Sammelans, Yagnas and so on.

A Pouranika Training Centre was established at Tirupathi for explaining ancient traditions and sayings and for preserving the tradition of Purana Pravachanam. Harikathas, musical concerts and discourses are also conducted on a regular basis in the Asthana Mandapam at Tirumala, Annamacharya Kala Mandiram at Tirupathi and in the nearby places like Narayanavanam and Nagalapuram. Yagnas, Bhajan Melas and Geetha Yagnams are also organised in towns and cities like Mumbai, Kolkata, Kolhapur, Bengaluru, Vizag and Guntur with the help of local organisations. In remote rural areas, Hindu religious programmes are also conducted by the field staff. Selected reading materials are distributed and Epic Study examinations and competitions for schoolgoing children of Andhra Pradesh are also conducted. More than two lakh children are being trained as part of this scheme. During fairs and festivals, the centre conducts religious programmes. It also distributes Hindu religious materials to devotees.

S V Bhakthi Channel (SVBC)

The Sri Venkateswara Bhakthi Channel is a 24-hour channel that telecasts various devotional, religious and spiritual programmes mainly in Telugu. There are also live programmes relating to Srivari Sevas and other programmes not only relating to Sri Venkateswara Temple but also those of other temples. The telecast also includes music concerts, dance programmes, discourses and religious news, serials connected to Ethihasas and *Puranas* and so on. The TTD intends to start SVB Channel in Tamil shortly.

Sri Venkateswara Veda Patasala

The Veda Patasala in Tirupathi is located a few miles from Tirumala in a place called Dharmagiri Hill. The Gurukul covers an area of 50 acres on the Hills and is covered by forests. This Patasala is very old. It imparts training to temple priests and teaches *Vedas*. It has more than 400 students and has 14 branches of study. The training for priests lasts 12 years. It is called Veda Dhyanam course. The course starts when the pupil is 8 years old.

There are three other short-term courses that involve 8 years of study from 12 years of age.

S V Institute of Traditional Sculpture and Architecture (SVITSA)

This institute was started in 1960 to preserve and promote the age-old cultural heritage of India in traditional sculpture and architecture. The institute offers two courses, each lasting four years. It is affiliated to the State Board of Technical Education and Training (SBTET). The outstation students are provided with free boarding and lodging facilities and the local students are given a monthly stipend. The students here are also taken on educational tours every year to various temples and places of historical significance in India. The deities carved by the students in practical sessions and the teachers during demonstrations are sold to the public at low prices.

Projects

Annamacharya Project

This was established in 1978 to train musicians for research, publication and recording and sale of Annamacharya songs for spreading the glory of the Lord. Sri Talapakka Annamacharya of Talapakka village in Cuddapah district was a saint-composer of the 15th century. He was the first composer in Telugu who composed nearly 32,000 Keerthanas on Lord Venkateswara. The objective of this Project is to inculcate Bhakthi among the general public through the Keerthanas of the poet-saint. In the Music Wing the music troupes perform concerts in temples, educational institutions, pilgrim centres, villages and in other cultural organisations. The Annamacharya Vardhanthi, Annamacharya Jayanthi and Annamacharya Aradhana festivals are conducted every year in Tirumala, Tirupathi and at

Talapakka. During Unjal Seva at Tirumala and other TTD managed temples, the Annamacharya Keerthanas are sung daily. Harikathas and folk programmes are also conducted regularly by this troupe. Research fellowships are granted for pursuing doctoral programmes on Annamacharya's life and works. The compositions of Annamacharya and works of other Talapakka poets are printed and published and the audio cassettes of their songs are marketed to popularise the songs. The Annamacharya Project has direct control over the Alwar Divya Prabanda Project, Dasa Sahitya Project, Bhagavatha Project and Veda Recording Project.

Dasa Sahitya Project

This was intended to popularise the saint-composers of Karnataka known as Haridasas and their compositions. They had composed innumerable songs on Lord Venkateswara. This project undertakes publication, conducts exhibitions, releases audio cassettes and conducts religious programmes at various places to acquaint people with the life and teachings of the Karnataka Haridasas.

Alwar Divya Prabanda Project

This was started in 1991 for popularising the life and works of the 12 Alwars and other Acharyas belonging to the Sri Vaishnava cult. It conducts programmes periodically about the Alwars, publishes booklets mainly in Tamil language and releases audio cassettes of the *Nalayira Divya Prabandam* of the Alwars.

S V Veda Recording Project

This project is meant to record and thereby popularise the *Vedas*.

S V Video Audio Recording Project

This was established in 1990 for producing, distributing and marketing TTD pre-recorded video and audio cassettes of *Vedas*, *Puranas*, Sankeerthanas, Pravachanams, temple chanting, Srivari Brahmotsavam and other temple rituals at subsidised rates.

Tarigonda Vengamamba Project

Under this project, literary sammelans are held. Books and CDs containing the songs of Vengamamba are released and programmes on the literature of Vengamamba are conducted.

Temple Renovation and Reconstruction Project

This project is meant for restoring Hindu sculpture and architecture as per Shilpa Agama Sastra and also to safeguard and promote ancient Hindu architecture.

Sriman Veturi Prabhakara Sastri Vangmaya Peetam

This was set up to publish all works of Veturi Prabhakara Sastri.

Schemes

Sri Venkateswara Nitya Annadana Scheme

This scheme started on a small scale in 1984, provides free meals to the pilgrims on Tirumala. In the beginning, food was served to around 2,000 persons daily. Today the number has increased to 15,000 people. The number increases to about 25,000 to 30,000 a day during festivals and other important occasions. Further food packets numbering around 10,000 to 15,000 are distributed to the pilgrims who are waiting in the Queue Complex for the Sarva Darshan of the Lord. During festivals and important occasions, the number increases to 20,000 per day. Free food is also served to nearly 2,000 patients a day in the SVIMS, BIRRD, Ruia and

Maternity Hospitals. Certain facilities are given to the donors to this Scheme.

Sri Padmavathi Ammavari Nitya Annaprasada Scheme

Under this scheme, free Annaprasadam is given to pilgrims everyday at the temple of Sri Padmavathi Devi, Tiruchanoor. Donations are also received for free distribution of Anna Prasadam to pilgrims on Panchami Teertham celebrated during the annual Brahmotsavam here. TTD gives certain priviliges to the donors.

Sri Venkateswara Nitya Laddu Danam Scheme

This scheme was started in 1981. According to this scheme, Laddu Prasadam is distributed to all pilgrims free of cost at the end of distribution of Anna Prasadam. 25,000 Laddus of 25 gms each are prepared and distributed with the interest earned on deposits in the donor's name on the day of his choice. These donors are given certain privileges by the TTD.

Kalyanamastu Trust

This was introduced in 2007 for the performance of marriages on a mass scale in the traditional way.

Srivari Pushpa Kainkaryam Scheme

It is a scheme in which the devotees, who are usually wholesale flower merchants or who own big gardens, make their offerings to the Lord in the form of huge quantities of flowers.

Online Schemes

The online schemes under this category include e-Seva Booking and e-Accommodation that help the devotees to book their tickets for the Sevas and accommodation well in advance online and the e-Hundi and e-Donation, for making offerings to the Hundi and donations to the schemes of the TTD. The e-Sales and e-Procurement display the tender notifications of the TTD for procuring the provisions required.

Srivari Seva

This voluntary scheme was launched for providing opportunity to the devotees to serve the Lord by serving fellow pilgrims. Under this scheme, the devotees can offer their free service in the areas of Annadanam, maintaining queues at Kalyanakatta, gardens and Laddu centres, Vaikuntam queue complex, free bus, pilgrims, amenities complex, information centres, vigilance, health, Central Reception office, Srivari Thirunamam, bus stops, Pushkarini, Pusthaka Prasadams, helping the pedestrians on Tirumala, cloakrooms, for parking vehicles and so on. Professionals are also invited to participate in this programme. The service can be chosen by the devotee. Bhajan troupes can also participate in this service. Groups of 10 people or more who are willing to serve at least a week continuously can inform the TTD well in advance. They will be provided with free accommodation in addition to free food at Tirumala. The devotees who are willing to offer their services may enrol their names in the 'Seva Sadan', Tirumala.

S V Veda Parirakshana Trust

This scheme is meant to preserve and protect traditional and ancient sources of knowledge and also give financial grant-in-aid for carrying out such activities. Donations are invited for this scheme and the donors are extended certain privileges by the TTD.

Sri Venkateswara Heritage Preservation Trust

This scheme is meant for renovating dilapilated temples and temple-like edifices in every village and in every town. TTD extends certain privileges to the donors to this scheme.

Sri Venkateswara Information Technology Seva Trust

This scheme is meant for implementing modern technology in all the schemes of the TTD and to extend modern technology to the public. Under this scheme, the public has access to IT-enabled services for food, accommodation, medical facilities to pilgrims and so on. The activities under this scheme include e-seva, e-darshan, e-accommodation facilities to pilgrims, converting books on Indian philosophy, Indian literatrure and ancient Indian scriptures to digital form and making them available to all. It is also meant to support the facilities provided by the TTD for the general convenience of the pilgrims like people's rest room, special escorts for the aged and disabled pilgrims, locker and cloakroom facilities, first aid centre, shopping complex, ticket counters, parking space, restaurant, multimedia projects, lounge and so on. Some special privileges are extended to the donors to this scheme.

Sri Venkateswara Go Samrakshana Trust

This scheme is meant to protect and emphasise the spiritual importance of cows that are considered divine by the Hindus by creating a modern Goshala with all facilities for maintaining cows. The Trust also aims at improving the living conditions of cows outside the Goshala by providing technical inputs to the general public. The schemes under this are, Kama Dhenu and Ksheera Sagaram. Donors are extended certain privileges by the TTD.

Publication of Books

The TTD has a Publication Division that publishes books in different languages. The books published by the TTD are sold at subsidised prices and these are available in the book stalls located in the railway station, Car street, and RTC Bus Stand. The projects undertaken by this division include printing and publication of *Rig Veda* in Telugu running to 5 volumes, *Krishna Yajur Veda* and *Atharva Veda*, the encyclopaedia of ancient Hindu religious literature in 10 volumes, *Srimad Bhagavatham* in Sanskrit with Advaitha, Dwaitha and Visishtadvaitha commentaries, the *'Bhagavatha Suddha Lahari'* the translation of *Srimad Bhagavatham* in Telugu, *Srinivasa Bala Bharathi* for children, *Kavithraya Bharatham* in 15 volumes with word-to-word meaning and special notes on the works of Nannayya Thikkanna and Erranna in Telugu, publication and reprinting of Agama books like *Vaikhanasa* and *Pancharatna Agamas*.

Besides these projects, the TTD has also published works like *Bharatha Kosa, Bhagavad Githa, Maharshula Charithalu, Sangeetha Sourabhams* and *Bharathiya Tatva Saramu* written by well-known authors. The TTD has also published several other books in Sanskrit, Telugu, Tamil, Kannada, Hindi, Urdu and English. The authors who write original books are paid Rs 20/- per printed page and translated versions are paid Rs 15 per page. The authors are also given 50 complimentary copies of their books. If the authors do not want to receive any remuneration, then one-tenth of the number of printed copies in the first edition, not exceeding the value of remuneration, is given to the authors. A Publication Committee constituted by the Board of Trustees selects the books for publication.

Audio/Video Cassettes and CDs

In the temple complex, audio and video cassettes pertaining to Hindu religion are available for sale. It also releases several video and audio cassettes, compact discs and publications periodically.

Temple Calendar

TTD prints calendars of two types, big and small, every year with the pictures of Lord Srinivasa and His consort Goddess Padmavathi.

Sapthagiri Magazine

The *Sapthagiri* magazine was started as '*Sapthagiri* Bulletin' in 1949. It is a monthly published in five languages, namely, Telugu, Tamil, Kannada, Hindi and English, for propagating Hindu religion and philosophy and to develop Bhakthi and positive thinking among the public through articles on Hindu philosophy and culture. It provides information of the departmental activities of the TTD.

'AID to Authors' Scheme

Under this scheme, the TTD encourages authors of spiritual and religious literature. This scheme was introduced in the year 1978. The authors if they so desire, would be given financial assistance not exceeding Rs 15,000. The author is required to mention TTD's financial assistance prominently in the book. He will also have to submit 50 complimentary copies to TTD. The eligibility for the financial assistance is decided by a committee constituted by the Board of Trustees, consisting of experts in various languages.

3. ACCOMMODATION FOR PILGRIMS

TTD provides free accommodation to those who cannot afford it and paid accommodation to those who can, both in Tirupathi and at Tirumala. The pilgrims can contact the Central Reception

Office for free accommodation. There are also sheds and dormitories. There are Public Amenities Complexes with dormitory system of accommodation with locker facilities, bathroom and toilet facilities that are free for the pilgrims who visit Tirumala.

The TTD offers accommodation at moderate rates for those pilgrims who can afford to pay. Information about paid accommodation at Tirumala can be obtained from the CRO, Tirumala. Pilgrims may also write to Assistant Executive Officer (Reception-1), TTD, Tirumala well in advance by making the necessary payment. Advance reservation at Tirumala can also be made at all Information centres and Kalyana Mandapams well in advance by making the necessary payment of the amount fixed by the TTD. The accommodation on Tirumala can be booked in advance online also during the off-season. An Advance Reservation Daily Chart is displayed on the Notice Board outside the ARP counter in the Central Reception Office at Tirumala containing the names of pilgrims who are given accommodation as per advance reservation made by them.

The accommodation in Tirumala on payment includes different types of accommodation in the Sri Padmavathi Guest House area that has the Ampro Guest House AC with 2+1 suites, Bela Kuteeram AC with 6 suites, Gayatri Sadan AC suites 2+3+1, Godavari Sadan AC with 3 suites, Gumble Guest House AC with 4 suites, Gokulam Guest House AC with four suites, Hari Sadan Guest House AC with 7 suites, Hill View Deluxe Cottages with big and small suites, Indira Guest House AC with 4 suites, Jagannada Bhavan with 4 suites, Karam Nivas with 1+3 AC suites and 2 non-AC suites, Lakshmi Nilayam AC with 3 suites, Modi Bhavan with 8 suites, Rajya Lakshmi Guest House with 4+1 AC suites and one non-AC suite, S P Guest House (Main) with 2+9 AC suites and 1 non-AC suite, Sri Niketan with 3 AC suites, Srinivasa Nilayam with 4 non-AC and 1 AC suites, Venkata

Vijayam Guest House with AC 3+6 suites, and Vidya Sadan with 1+4 suites.

In the Sri Venkateswara Guest House area, are the Sri Venkateswara Guest House with corner suites, five special cottages with A/C, 12 with AC, 13 with AC and HRG 'A' wing and 'B' wing, MBC Cottages 20+22, TBC (Traveller's Bungalow Cottages) with A/C 13 numbers, Narayanagiri Guest House I with corner suite, Narayanagiri Guest House II with corner suites, Narayanagiri Guest House III with corner suite, Srivari Kuteer Guest House suite numbers 1 to 4 and Surapuram Thota Cottages.

In the Varahaswami Guest House area are the Alwar Tank Cottages with single rooms, Anjanadri Nagar Cottages, Garudari Nagar Cottages, Hill View Cottages, Mangala Bavi Cottages, with 2 suites and 4 cottages, Ram Bagicha Guest House I, II and III, Sankhu Mitta Cottages, Seshadri Nagar Cottages, T B Cottages with 2 suites, single room and separate cottages and Valley View Cottages with 6 suites. (A few religious mutts also provide accommodation subject to their own terms and conditions).

Moderately-priced accommodation at Tirupathi includes Srinivasam Complex opposite RTC Bus Station where there are both AC and non-AC, ordinary and deluxe rooms, Madhavam Guest House adjacent to Srinivasam Complex with AC and non-AC deluxe suites, Sri Venkateswara Dharmasala opposite Tirupathi East Railway Station, Sri Venkateswara Guest House to the north of Tirupathi East Railway Station, Sri Padmavathi Guest House in the west of Tirupathi on Chittoor road with AC suites and conference hall, TTD Alipiri Guest House at the foot of the Seven Hills and Sri Kodanda Rama Choultry to the south of Tirupathi Railway Station. However, there is no advance booking facility in Tirupathi in the accommodation provided by the TTD. (There are numerous private hotels offering rooms at different tariffs in Tirupathi which can be booked in advance).

The free accommodation in Tirupathi are: Sri Govindaraja Dharmasala, on the south of Tirupathi East Railway Station with 233 rooms, Sri Kodanda Ramaswami Dharmasala to the south of Tirupathi East Railway Station with 127 rooms and Sri Venkateswara Dharmasala (1st New Choultry) opposite the East Railway Station with 94 rooms. There is also a Pilgrim Amenities Complex at Alipiri bus station at Tirupathi for pilgrims to take rest with cloakroom, toilet and bathroom facilities.

Srinivasam complex Donation Scheme

This scheme is meant for the construction of accommodation consisting of different categories of rooms, cottages and guest houses in Tirumala. A few privileges are extended to donors.

4. EDUCATIONAL INSITUTIONS AND ACTIVITIES

The TTD runs several educational institutions. There are four elementary schools. They are the SV Elementary School at Tirupathi, SKS Elementary School at Thatithopu and SV Elementary School at Tirumala.

There are five high schools in Tirupathi and one each at Vellore and at Tirumala. They are, SV Higher Secondary School, Vellore, SV High School, SV Girls' High School, SGS High School, SV Oriental High School, SKRS High School, all in Tirupathi and SV High School in Tirumala. The first educational institution was the Hindu High School in Vellore established in the year 1876 and the Hindu school established in Tirupathi in the year 1886 by the Hathiramji Mutt which administered the Tirumala temple of Lord Venkateswara till 1933. After TTD came into being, the names of both these schools were changed to SV High School.

The TTD also runs two junior colleges in Tirupathi, one for men and one for women. There are four degree colleges with postgraduate courses in Tirupathi out of which one is a women's college and one a degree college in Delhi. These are, SV College, New Delhi, SV Arts College, SGS College and SPW College, all in Tirupathi.

There are two Oriental Colleges, one at Tirupathi and another in Secunderabad. These are, SV Oriental College, Tirupathi and SVVVS College, Secunderabad.

Four professional colleges are run by the TTD out of which one is a women's college. They are, SV Ayurvedic College with attached hospital, SV Yoga Institute, SV College of Music and Dance and SPW Polytechnic.

In addition the TTD also has a school for the deaf-mute, one institute of traditional sculpture and architecture and two Veda Pathashalas, one at Dharmagiri and the other at Keesaragutta in Ranga Reddi district.

Oriental Research Institute

This institute was established by the TTD in 1939 to promote Indology.

SV Central Library and Research Centre (SVCLRC)

The SVCLRC was established by the TTD in 1993 in a spacious building. It has around 40,000 rare and valuable books mainly on religion and philosophy. It also publishes Hindu religious and philosophical materials and papers on original Sanskrit texts with translations in regional languages, Hindi and English. The research wing is concerned with research and publication of material related to Hindu religion.

SV Digital Library

This library was established in 2001 in association with Universal Digital Library and Carnegie Mellon University, Pittsburgh, USA, for converting rare and valuable books, scriptures and palm leaves to digital form.

SV Vidyadana Trust

Under this scheme, scholarships worth Rs. 300 a month are awarded yearly by the TTD to 1,000 meritorious students who have passed Std. X with more than 500 marks and are below poverty line as per AP State Government. Donations are welcomed under this scheme.

Training Academy (SVETA)

The TTD established the Sri Venkateswara Employees Training Academy (SVETA) in the year 2001 for providing refresher training courses to all sections of TTD employees. The duration of the training period is from three days to two weeks. Based on a specific theme, there are one-day programmes, theme-based conferences once or twice in a year relating to specific aspects of temple administration and so on. Follow-up training programmes are also conducted in this Academy.

5. SOCIAL SERVICE ACTIVITIES SRIVARI POOR HOME

This caters to the needs of leprosy patients. There are 20 in-patient wards in the hospital. The outpatient block has a physiotherapy section and an operation theatre. Patients are given intensive multi-drug therapy and physiotherapy. In addition to treatment, the patients are also educated about the prevention and cure of leprosy. During the period of treatment, the patients are given free food as well as accommodation. The duration of treatment is roughly 6 to 18 months. The patients are also trained in various skills like carpentry, shoe-making, weaving, agriculture and so on. The produce from agriculture is used in the hospital itself and the excess produce is sent to other TTD Institutions. Under the National Leprosy Eradication Programme of the Government of India, the TTD set up the Leprosy Rehabilitation Promotional Unit (LRPU) in 1988.

Sri Venkateswara Bala Mandir

The Sri Venkateswara Bala Mandir (SVBM) is the TTD Orphanage established in 1943. There are 500 orphans. Those ranging in age from five to ten at the time of admission and with no record of crime are admitted here. They are given free education, free boarding and lodging facilities up to graduate level in TTD-run educational institutions. Separate accommodation is provided to boys and girls. Along with formal education, vocational courses like tailoring and typing are also taught here. The SVBM organizes special feeding for destitutes during festivals and other important national holidays.

Sri Venkateswara Bala Mandir Trust Scheme

This scheme is meant for the Bala Mandir. The donors are extended some privileges by the TTD.

SV School for the Deaf

This was established in 1974. It imparts free general education and vocational training to deaf children. It also provides placement. The TTD has three such schools in three different places, one in Tirupathi, the second at Bhimavarani and the third at Warangal. Free boarding and lodging facilities are provided to resident students and free midday meals are given to the day scholars. Yoga is also taught here. Sports and games form part of the curriculum. The teacher pupil ratio here is 1:10.

Srivari Training Centre for the Handicapped

It is meant for the orthopaedically and visually handicapped and the hearing impaired. It provides aids to the handicapped and imparts vocational training in three areas. These are: cane weaving, electronic assembling and packaging, rope-making for home-bound individuals and thirdly, typewriting, vulcanizing, rubber stamp making and training for shorthand to those wanting to work in cities. This centre also provides consultancy services to help its handicapped students get employment.

6. MEDICAL ACTIVITES

Sri Venkateswara Institute of Medical Sciences (SVIMS)

This caters to the medical needs of the poor and needy, particularly of the Rayalseema region in Andhra Pradesh. It also undertakes teaching and research. In 1995, SVIMS was upgraded to a medical university. Ten postgraduate courses are offered here in various specialties. Besides this, the SVIMS University offers undergraduate courses in physiotherapy and nursing, P G Diploma in various paramedical courses and postdoctoral certificate courses in different branches. There are 18 Departments here. The SVIMS has a modern medical library. It also runs outpatient clinics in eight different areas. It has introduced Sri Balaji Arogya Vara Prasadini scheme for providing sophisticated medical facilities at an affordable cost for needy patients.

Balaji Institute of Surgery, Research and Rehabilitation for the Disabled (BIRRD)

The Balaji Institute of Surgery, Research and Rehabilitation for the Disabled (BIRRD), started in 1985 with 50 beds and a handful of doctors, now provides free medical treatment and facilities to those who suffer from polio, cerebral palsy, congenital anomalies, spinal injuries and orthopaedically handicapped poor people irrespective of the religion they follow. The TTD provides free food daily to all the patients. In 1994 the BIRRD was converted into a Trust. TTD provides a matching grant to the trust equal to the donation that it receives. Now, it has a capacity of 250 beds, five operation theatres and a modern artificial limb fitting centre that supplies the aids free of cost to physically handicapped people. It has a state-of-the-art physiotherapy department. This institute conducts research as well. It also proposes to start a total spinal trauma care centre and introduce graduate and postgraduate courses in physiotherapy.

BIRRD Scheme

This is meant for the development of BIRRD. The donors are extended certain privileges by the TTD.

Ayurveda Hospital

It is run by the TTD and is attached to the S V Ayurveda College.

Help to SVRR Hospital

The Government-run Sri Ram Narayan Ruia Hospital is given financial help by the TTD.

Sri Venkateswara Pranadana Trust

This is meant to provide free medical facilities to poor patients afflicted with life-threatening diseases related to heart, kidneys and brain and also to encourage R & D in the treatment of major diseases. This scheme is in operation in all the TTD-run Hospitals that includes the SVIMS, BIRRD, SVRR and the Maternity and Ayurveda Hospitals. The interest from the deposits of the donors is utilised for the scheme. The TTD invests an amount equal to each donation made by the devotees. The donors are extended certain privileges by the TTD for the Srivari Darshan, Prasadam of the Lord and so on.

Sri Venkateswara Arogya Varaprasadini Scheme

This scheme is meant to provide free modern medical assistance to the patients who are economically poor. Donors can also offer vehicles, equipment and so on to SVIMS or may sponsor Health Camps in rural areas. The donors are given certain privileges.

7. DEVELOPMENTAL ACTIVITIES

Haritha Project

This was started for the conservation of groundwater resources and forests on the Tirumala Hills. The activities are taken up by the TTD Forest Department based on the satellite images of the areas provided by the State Forest Department. Its objectives are to conserve rainwater and improve groundwater levels by constructing check dams, to plant about a crore of saplings to green 29,500 acres of forest area of the TTD and State government in three years, to protect forests from fire and to develop areas adjacent to important Teerthas.

Sri Venkateswara Jalanidhi Scheme

This scheme aims at evolving a comprehensive programme to provide adequate water for meeting the needs of pilgrims in Tirumala, Tirupathi and surrounding villages.

SV Jalanidhi Trust

The funds raised under the SV Jalanidhi Trust are used for

maintenance and payment of the electrical charges for supplying 20 lakh gallons of water per day. It is also spent for improving water resources at Tirumala by constructing dams, check dams, storage tanks and percolation tanks, and for the improvement of available water resources and for undertaking new massive projects.

Sri Venkateswara Vanabhivriddhi Scheme

This scheme is meant to protect and maintain the ecological balance in this area. It includes Vriksha Sowbhagya, Vriksha Vardhini, Vriksha Pravardhini, Vriksha Samvardhini, Vriksha Prasadam, Smaraka Vanalu, Vana Samrakshana and Bhagyaswamyam schemes. Certain privileges are extended by the TTD to the donors. The TTD maintains 15 sq km of the forests via satellite.

Do's and dont's prescribed by the TTD to preserve the Sanctity of Tirumala

- Cigarettes, alcohol and non-vegetarian foods are prohibited.
- Wearing of flowers banned.
- The devotees who perform Utsavams must wear dhoti and angavastram.
- All pilgrims except senior citizens and the disabled along with one attendant, must enter the temple through the Queue Complex only.
- The use of plastic bottles is banned on Tirumala.
- No cell phones or cameras are allowed inside the temple complex.
- All vehicles have to follow the procedure at the security check point near Alipiri.

|| OM NAMO VENKATESHAYA ||

www.ingramcontent.com/pod-product-compliance
Lightning Source LLC
Chambersburg PA
CBHW070638160426
43194CB00009B/1498